BUCKY

A Guided Tour of Buckminster Fuller

Buckminster Fuller, Santa Barbara, California, December 1967

BUCKY

A Guided Tour of Buckminster Fuller

Hugh Kenner

William Morrow & Company, Inc.
New York   1973

Kenner, Hugh.
    Bucky.

    Bibliography: p.
    1. Fuller, Richard Buckminster, 1895-   I. Title.
TA140.F9K46   620 [B]   79-182966
ISBN 0-688-00141-6
ISBN 0-688-05141-3 (pbk.)

For John and Michael

CONTENTS

ONE | What Am I Doing Here? | 1

TWO | The Star-Spinner | 13

THREE | The Outlaw Area | 52

FOUR | Modeling the Universe | 86

FIVE | Bubbles and Destiny | 129

SIX | Dymaxion Messiah | 163

SEVEN | Stillbirth of an Industry | 200

EIGHT | Domes | 229

NINE | Dialogue with a Skeptic | 263

TEN | Incoming | 290

Appendix I: Glossary | 317

Appendix II: Model Making | 321

Acknowledgments | 325

Reading List | 327

Index | 333

BUCKY

A Guided Tour of Buckminster Fuller

ONE

What Am I Doing Here?

Thirty years ago I used to breakfast at a drugstore called Mac's, where the toast was fresher than in campus dining halls and moreover you had your pick of magazines from the newsstand by the door. Magazines were in their golden age: cornucopias of novelty. You leafed one while you ate, put it back if you didn't want to buy it. Most got put back. Mac made his money from the lunch counter, and wrote off the dog-earing of his newsstand stock as goodwill. So you could monitor the abundance, and paying for the odd item you really wanted didn't strain an undergraduate budget.

In the first week of March, 1943, I spent ten cents for the current *Life,* and back in my room cut out the pieces of the Dymaxion World Map. There were tabs to fold and glue, and you ended up with a sort-of-spherical shape, made of squares and triangles on which colorful continents were printed. The colors demarked not countries but mean low temperatures, which were alleged to make more sense in an airpower world. The sort-of-sphere was attributed to Archimedes, and if I'd taken it around to the math department they could have told me it was a cuboctahe-

1

dron. Being an English Lang. & Lit. major I didn't, and so missed meeting Professor H. S. M. Coxeter.

This misshapen globe wasn't the point of the exercise. It simply proved that the whole earth was symmetrically there, to validate what you were looking at when you spread it out to flat paper again. Then you saw the whole world in one view with minimal distortion. The departure from the shapes you see on a globe wasn't noticeable, and there's no all-at-once way to see the globe. Along the edges of the fourteen parts distortion was zero, so you could fit them together in various jigsaws to get special-purpose maps: the one-continent map with all the land masses joined, Hitler's Heartland map with the Americas on the periphery, Tojo's Rising Sun map, mid-Pacific ringed by continents.

The effect was to undermine the teachings of that One True Map, Mercator's, that hung in every classroom, with its Eurasian and American masses separated by two great oceans, across which ships moved east and west. They steamed over the broad warm Pacific to Japan, through gray Atlantic waves to England or Europe. But on the Dymaxion Map (and the globe confirmed it) the short route from San Francisco to Japan pursued coastlines and almost brushed the Aleutians, while the air route from Toronto to Berlin was never more than a few hundred miles from land.

Toward the poles, Mercator's world was grotesquely misshapen, but ships didn't go near the poles. Years later, when airlines advertised a "Polar Route" from Los Angeles to Stockholm, it seemed like a trick: clear off the top of the map and then a reentry, like Buck Rogers passing through a tuck in space. On the Dymaxion Map it seems obvious, almost as though the Dymaxion Map's inventor was foreseeing a day when hundreds of thousands of vacationers would casually cross the Arctic. (I've done it myself, more than once. I can remember when I never thought I'd fly.)

The inventor's name was R. Buckminster Fuller, identified in a caption as a man of bizarre accomplishments now connected with the Board of Economic Warfare in Washington. A photo showed him, moustached and talking earnestly. That was the first I heard of him.

After that his name surfaced from time to time. There were bits of lore about his three-wheeled car and his suspended house. There was a *Reader's Digest* filler about how he slept "the Dymaxion Way"—not piling up arrears of fatigue and then needing an alarm clock, but dropping off the very minute he needed to for just the sleep his body took, which worked out to a half-hour in every six and gave him twenty-two-hour working days. That sounded like just the ticket at exam time, but I never met anyone who could make it work. Normal mortals postponed unconsciousness too long and then slept like logs twelve hours at a stretch, which was sybaritic but non-Dymaxion. Later there was something in *Time* about the Fuller Research Foundation, and by the mid-1950's one was hearing of Geodesic Domes. They were Coming, several articles predicted, and I kept expecting to see one but never did, not in those days.

My own work, apart from teaching myself to teach, entailed trying to see around a corner in time. I was teaching literature, and I'd been taught about the great literary tradition that ran from Homer, straight as a corridor, right up to a blank wall about 1850, where my undergraduate curriculum had more or less ended. Right at the wall there was a left turn, around which was said to lurk chaos —modernity. ("There be monsters," one read at the edges of old maps.) When eventually I peeped round it, a huge pulsing extravaganza caught my attention and wouldn't let go: *Finnegans Wake*. How to come around to where it was, without losing sight of everything else?

I bought the Campbell and Robinson *Skeleton Key,* which was certainly a help but somehow wrong. When I could revel in Joyce's verbal polyphony, the logic that was running down the page seemed quite unrelated to the *Key*'s guiding paraphrase. I didn't think of the flat map and the globe, which was just as well since the analogy would have entangled me. Maps, for instance a road map, are normally OK over small areas, but the kind of help one was offered with Joyce—or Eliot, or Pound—didn't fit even patches of detail very well.

Soon I was encamped among the happenings in the "modern" angle of the corridor, from which it seemed impossible to see back. Joyce and Pound held transactions with Homer, Eliot with Shakespeare, but the real Homer and Shakespeare seemed out of sight. A friend had said you couldn't hope to think coherently about the new environment—"You just let it hit you." That was why he stayed out of it. If you didn't stay out of it, you observed a Two Literatures Policy, one traditional and discussible, one anarchic.

Such was my own route to what everyone sooner or later confronts: the generic twentieth-century problem, discontinuity. Have we still lines of communication open with Jefferson, Socrates, Christ? Or have we spot-welded about ourselves a world we can't think about? Must you just let it hit you?

What imaginative act can really unite the airplane and the horse, "artifice" and "nature"? A child leafs picture books of horses and lambs while planes from La Guardia roar over her nursery. Her first word is "air." (She is Buckminster Fuller's granddaughter.) Planes before birds, poor child. Is our pity well based?

For that matter, is "nature" dead? Many urbanites must drive miles to encounter it. Many never do. Thousands of belle-lettrists will lift up their voices like spring frogs to indict the world of technology, a chromed wasteland, soulless. Other thousands don't think it dull at all. To the moon! What a challenge! Are they barbarians? Are the others aesthetes? Having it both ways is barely possible; the strain is etched on Walter Cronkite's face. It's simpler to opt for your choice of Lord Snow's Two Cultures. (Yet Snow's sunderings may be illusory, like Mercator's oceans. He seems unaware of the Two Literatures, and his own literary habits are Victorian.)

Did values break? Did morals? Did a chasm open? Huddled this side of it, are we being paved over? If so, should I be riding a bicycle to symbolize disapproval? Or live in a cabin, eating organic watercress? But there would be no bicycles without carbon steel, and the watercress comes by truck. Take up bead-stringing, the ultimate dropout gesture, and your starter kit will contain a spool of wire drawn from a brass bar in a swift Japanese machine, and brought all the way here by ship and train and diesel. Facing up to such facts at last, you can moan, "No way," or, oddly enough, take another dropout route to a commune housed in Geodesic Domes.

Or stay with your job, and if the written word is your job you have valuable incentives, because language, even Joycean language, seems to want to make sense. The engineer can always disown the past—what did Shakespeare know about carbon steel? The painter, even, can turn naive and say he's just playing (being Titian was *work*). The city planner can plead urgent business (traffic jams won't wait). But language, in part because it now leads a classroom existence, exacts the effort to make connections. The great moderns had disowned no traditions. They extolled the past they ransacked. Pound venerated Chaucer. What *The Cantos* had in common with *The Canterbury Tales* might be the view round that corner. Bucky Fuller might have told me that I was looking for a Coordinate System.

In a book I wrote about Pound in 1949 I did manage a couple of intuitive axioms. One was that the same law governs the whole and the parts. If you can understand how a man fits a sentence together, you have a model for his way of building larger units. That was one glimpse of a continuity.

My other axiom was that everything functions as the context of everything else. This implied a difficulty I couldn't solve, since it seemed to leave no secure reference points to start from. I affirmed it anyway, because it let me say what seemed true, that an ambitious project can be sustained without what book-reviewers mean by "structure": a framework of narrative, a framework of logic, something foursquare to which the elements are fitted like clapboards and shingles. I might have adduced geodesics if I'd known about them, but in 1949 only Fuller and a few of his students did. They were playing with the concept at Black Mountain College, likewise unknown, and the Dome patent lay five years in the future.

I was discovering how much we talk by unspecified analogy, especially by intuitive analogies with architecture. Buildings, all around us, seem man's most successful creations—some of them have stood for millennia—and the idiom of architectural success seeps into our minds. (We disregard the failures.) In book-review jargon, for example, a poem may be called a "little gem," meaning apparently that it has been cut from a rare substance called "poetry," but a novel or an epic is like a building. It has "structure," sometimes even "foundations." The writer designs a "framework," and also works with "surfaces," which are less important. It is filled with "perspectives," emanating from "points of view." If it really claims attention then it is "weighty." A critic may talk all day using none of these words and still say little that's not absolutely controlled by them. They locate the conditioned reflexes by which we value reality.

Not just literature, reality; at the very least anything man-made. Could a policy be stated from Washington without the word "basis"? Conversely, buildings make moral statements, well understood by bankers. The preferred statements are static, basic, rectilinear. (There was an airy geodesic restaurant in Woods Hole, Massachusetts. The owner couldn't raise money on it till he'd blackened the translucent panels so it looked substantial.) School supervisors talk this language when they ask for "lesson plans." And beware of "the superficial," and forget that all that can meet our senses is surface. The laudable is positively dense with virtue.

We get our everyday language, hence our criteria, from what we understand of the visible environment, especially from what we understand to be the successful human gestures, the structures that *last*. But what if we misunderstand those themes? What if we've been misreading architecture, misreading the human effort? That was the question that came, subliminally, from Fuller, who continued to be a reiterative bit of environment.

Then about 1963 he suddenly invaded the print world. That year I bought his new *Ideas and Integrities,* "A Spontaneous Autobiographical Disclosure" and his first book in twenty-five years. Concurrently, *No More Secondhand God*

—poems (poems!)—was published in Illinois, and in the library a new book about him by Robert W. Marks gave the first overview of what he'd been about: the houses, the domes, the car, the mathematics. I tried to have him invited for a lecture, but the conditioned reflex of the rest of the committee was "domes," which was somehow dismissive. (The consensus was for a real sage like Erich Fromm.) It was late in 1967 before I laid eyes on him, no longer the amiable fireplug of the photographs but a tiny white-haired jaunty man, rather deaf. He was seventy-two.

There was something in him unpredicted by his writings. In ten minutes he had explained about Whole Systems, which are always unpredicted by their elements. Within half an hour those substantial buildings by which we gauge achievement had become the traces of a mistaken effort to freeze reality into cubes. Reality flowed (Heraclitus had said so), but flowed through persistent knottings so that one need feel no vertigo. (Geodesics was part of the science of knots.) Pattern persisted. (Homer was such a pattern, as Joyce had divined.) A tree—the Romantic norm—yes, that was real: both while it lasted and before and after it lasted. It was not only a process in time (Yeats's "great rooted blossomer") but an embodiment of permanent principles that preceded it and survived it. "Principles do not begin and end." They were "organic," and yet were an engineer's principles. Tension webs surrounded incompressible spheroids of water, and as the webs flexed a windstorm didn't snap the huge weight of those limbs. He swayed and spread his arms and became the tree, talking, talking. (Pound's earliest poem had begun, "I stood and was a tree amid the wood . . .")

All his cascading detail pertained to a simple, liberating theme. Our thoughts, our language are collected from the physical world, from nothing else. But the physical world of Copernicus, of Bohr, of Einstein has barely affected them; we still say "solid as a rock," we still say "down to earth." Solidity, solidarity for Bucky these are sad affairs. "Solids are the fraternity of the fallen-in-together." So much that is real, and has come from a newer understanding—much technology, much art—affronts the only words we have, and we fuss like the old lady who thought airplanes "against nature."

But nature has always contained the airplane's principles. The Universe has never changed; what is true now was always true; some people, chiefly seafarers, have always acted on certain important truths. Such truths are perfectly accessible. An outfielder running to put his glove where the ball will be has Einstein in his bones if not in his head, and Homer had the feel of molecular structures through building them of language. So there has been no radical break. Certain knowledges have simply become so central we need to stop evading them, so as to get free from not knowing what we are doing. Thus we wage wars to keep things from changing, and yet every war brings about change; despite fearful destruction the standard of living improves, most frequently for the vanquished. Thus we shrink from spending, yet spend, and yet nothing seems spent: men grow wealthier. Thus we know we cannot live without technology, and yet seem to destroy our lives with it. We need to know all the time certain things we know some of the time: things the outfielder knows, things Homer knew. This entails a new model of the physical world, public and clear, for our thoughts to correspond to. Any sensible artifact is part of such a model.

This was a new reading of the human story, not disowning nor discrediting what we experience, but rendering it all continuous. (No more time-corners, nor periscopes to see around them.) Technology was no recent affront. It had continued from the day a man first jumped on a fallen tree and discerned leverage. Still earlier, men had devised language. That took at least two men, and gave us "our first industrial tool," an industrial tool being one a single man can't devise. (A stone hammer is a *craft* tool; a carpenter's hammer—forged alloy steel—is industrial.) The very principle of industrialism is social. But mechanization —the physical working of pure principle—was older than man by far. "We are all mechanized." Which of us was not trusting mechanism to convert yesterday's lunch into hair poking through the scalp? Did we think *we* were doing that?

And Nature? "Nature is never at a loss, never wondering what to do when you or I leave off." (A coin tossed over his shoulder struck the floor. "It always does.")

These simplicities of example were Lincolnesque. And Fuller was Lincoln's countryman in his willingness to absorb any instance however trivial, accept his own egocentricity that claimed our attention for the obvious, and recast the obvious into conceptual patterns that penetrated the modern world and did not threaten the ancient. (What can a tossed coin threaten, or a tree?) In his talk all was concurrent: space travel and horsepower and horses: "ways to valve solar energy into preferred patterns"—the horse eats oats which eat sun. The jet plane's kerosene was once sunlight, caught by long-ago plants whose conversion into petroleum would cost us $1 million a gallon. And his domes, his homemade mathematics, his cherished 60-degree coordinate system. The mathematical assertions—Nature does not use *pi,* always works in whole numbers; the tetrahedron is the primary system—would seem naive but for the fact that the structures which embody them have been patented and have the qualities he claims. They are packaged, in a Fuller discourse, with other structures, meta-physical structures that may prove equally habitable.

His talk solved for me, that week, a book called *The Pound Era* I had been trying to think out for years and was suddenly able to start writing. That was one validation. Since then, on five years' acquaintance, I have found him continually interesting, without feeling I needed to choose among several ways of being interested. He has true be-lievers, who like to quote the Columbia mathematics pro-fessor after a Fuller lecture: "My only regret is that Euclid and Pythagoras could not have been here." They do their best to turn him into a cult, and don't like you asking questions. There are partial dissenters, who buy for in-stance the domes but shy off "the theory trip." There are the sporadically bedazzled, who love to listen but couldn't tell you a thing he said. There are vigorous dissenters. ("He's a dangerous man," said one ecologist—he positively encourages technology.) At the very least Bucky Fuller, his story and his artifacts, are as remarkable a piece of Americana as our rich century affords.

I don't attempt a "life." The documents are so copious the biographer will be years absorbing them. I'll try to give a sense of the man his own books may obscure—that will include some hints at his limitations—and a guide to the system of coherencies he's given us for our space-age navigating.

A guide, not an outline. His dynamisms don't submit to outline. "People expect one-picture answers," he says, im-plying that they should think of cinema sequences. There's no more a definitive arrangement than there was for the parts of the Dymaxion Map I bought at Mac's. That map, like his lectures, was meant to correct a misleading view of the world. Yet one of its arrangements can look like Mercator's—which was true enough to sail by, after all—

and one of the ways I could arrange this book would make Fuller's talk seem systematic. I could also make it look like a string of platitudes, or like a set of notions never entertained before, or like a delirium. I won't do any of those things. It's a poet's job he does, clarifying the world. That's the emphasis I understand best. Should we muff our part of the world's work irretrievably—a possibility he does not ignore, though his optimism is famous—then it will have been Fuller's achievement anyhow to show a vision of what might have been. Pythagoras, long ago, glimpsed what might have been, a harmonious civic and intellectual sanity. That vision, what survives of it, no one thinks mistaken, though Greece itself perished.

TWO

The Star-Spinner

There are times when he seems not native to this planet. The pink dome is surely not terrestrially cranial; those Coke-bottle-bottom lenses shield extragalactic eyes; plastic tubes join twin transistor-capsules to uncommon ears, attuned perhaps to the music of popping atoms; and while someone anonymous wires him up for sound, hanging from his neck the microphone whose cable snakes toward a glow of red pilot lights, he extends his arms, a cooperative automaton, hiking in synchrony the open black coat, the black vest beneath, and the gold Phi Beta Kappa key, while white cuffs shoot out of his sleeves. (Phi Beta Kappa? There are no records of earned degrees.) The face is quizzical, gnomelike, its gamut of public expressions rather slight: Intensity 1, Intensity 2, Intensity 3, and (4) a sudden furrowed blankness. There is sparse white hair, like a model-maker's afterthought. There are crisp black trousers, as though studied from the Naval Dress Code. One leg, when he walks, seems shorter than the other; or is that, as some say, a shipboard gait? Or do servomechanisms respond haltingly to the floor? He reaches both hands toward the back of his neck, where the mike cord hangs snug; he gives the mike on his chest a ritual tug; the applause is dying down; he looks suddenly, boyishly, human, with a grin like a waif surprised naked.

"A self-balancing, twenty-eight-jointed adapter-base biped," he wrote once, "an electro-chemical reduction plant, integral with segregated stowages of special energy extracts." And 62,000 miles of capillaries. And he has often remarked that its manufacture is entirely automated, incomprehensible even to the persons who initiate it. Like all parents, his parents did not know what it was they were doing.

In the years since they did it he has traveled more than three million miles, mostly for lecturing. Like the winds, which he likes to point out are not "blown" but "sucked," he is never "sold" by an agent but always invited, so his travels attest not a triumph of press-agentry but a hungry worldwide interest in his ideas. A map of them would locate, he thinks, the growth-nodes of active curiosity. Their frequency began mounting just after World War II, and in 1967 alone he kept some ninety speaking engagements, in Lebanon, Iraq, Syria; in Missouri, Iowa, Arizona; at the Association of American Geographers, at a Symposium on Design and Aesthetics in Wood, at the Esalen Institute (Big Sur, California), at Sunset Church (Sunset, Maine). He told the Sunset congregation why the word *sunset* should properly be *sunclipse*. The New York Board of Education has heard him, and the Laurentian Conference on Corporate Strategy, and a National Conference on Environmental Health Management sponsored by the A.M.A. He has stood still long enough to be awarded, at last count, twenty-nine honorary doctorates (Dartmouth, Columbia, Wisconsin, Michigan . . .), a gold medal from Her Majesty Queen Elizabeth II (who was prompted by the Royal Institute of British Architects), a gold medal (architecture) from the National Institute of Arts and Letters, four more gold medals; and (twice) the Gran Premio at the Triennale de Milan; and (five times) awards from the American Institute of Architects, although he is not licensed to practice architecture. He has sponsored such wonders as a mastlike structure that will rise and rise as high as you choose to build it, though none of its struts touches any other strut. No one knows what to do with this, though a specimen stood for a year in the garden of the Museum of Modern Art. And a nine-passenger car just one foot shorter than the space it could park in. And the lightest, strongest, altogether most economical clear-span structures known to man. The Cathedral in Seville would fit under one of these, though three of the cathedral's columns would outweigh it together. He holds patents in fifty-five countries, including the 818th patent ever granted in Korea. One of his Geodesic Domes stands over the South Pole, shielding a cluster of conventional buildings against accumulating tons of snow while rotating on the same axis as the earth. The South Pole is one of the few places where he has not lectured. He goes around the world an average of three times a year (spacemen, he likes to remark, better that in less than five hours).

Wired to recorders and loudspeakers like an astronaut to sensors, he prepares at the inception of each lecture to commence a new journey through the universe. All moon flights entail the same risks as the first one did. They are all alike and never alike. The captain's vigilance will be incessant. Bucky closes his eyes and clasps his hands an inch in front of his nose. It is a crucial instant: countdown. Improvising a flight plan, he is picking up the vibrations of the audience.

California Hall, San Francisco, a Fire Marshal's nightmare. The three-story cavern, ornate with gilt and chan-

*deliers like a Brobdingnagian bordello, is jammed with
impatient people and blue with smoke; perhaps a thousand
people, crammed onto wooden folding chairs, standing
along the walls, herring-packed into tiers of balcony seats,
squatting in aisles, forced upright along the walls by sheer
numerousness, stacked as if supporting one another erect;
seventy-five tons of bodies, extracting oxygen from tons of
air with their lungs and cigarettes; beards, headbands,
leather skirts, mother hubbards, sequins, beads, nursing
infants; closely packed denizens of the counterculture.
Spotlights converging from gilded balconies mark out a
zone of floor in front of what was meant to be a stage but
tonight is a bin to pack in more hearers. A huge red tetrahedron towers at the left, someone's notion of an emblem:
a red triangle surmounted by a ten-foot red tripod. Beside
it the black biped with the pink face confronts the blur of
multitudinous faces. His antennae, he will say, are catching subtle currents of psychic feedback. The audiotape
reels have started. The three videotape cameramen have
adjusted their angles; on a monitor screen behind the tetrahedron an engineer tends the blue flicker of what they see.
The crowd is really silent at last. Bucky commences:*

"Well . . ."

The pitch is tentative, the demeanor bashful. He lifts
his hands faintly as though about to explain a broken window.

He's described this moment, too, when the "sound-
detonating mechanism" has to be put into action. A spring
leaf diaphragm squeezes an air chamber, and an executant
called "Brain" "first sculpturally arranges the passage to
the orifice of the raw fuel-receiving hatch and shapes the
orifice as well as the wall structures of the tubes leading
from the orifice to the air chambers; then, by an adjustable
mutable tongue cone, which proportionately occupies the

orifice and has a tip which is free to vibrate gently, 'brain' causes a continuity pattern of sound control to issue forth with high variation frequency."

That's a rhetoric he discarded thirty-five years ago. Like many wordmen at cross-purposes with their culture, he perfected his satiric skills the earliest. "Wherever there is objective truth there is satire," remarked one twentieth-century satirist, Wyndham Lewis, and Bucky's passion for X-raying what really happens seemed sardonic before he developed friendlier strategies. Nowadays he keeps audiences spellbound with the utter reasonableness of meshwork balloons, collapsing cubes and cows of knotted sunlight: the normal view through his glasses. Also, world-round Utopia in his younger hearers' lifetime.

He has no wish to astonish with such things. He is only happy sharing them, and only made tart by clownish refusals to understand, which he rightly thinks discourteous. If there is one thing he refuses to believe, it is that any phenomenon accessible to human reason can really be incomprehensible, and there's a kind of dismissive shrug that gets his back up. The New England aloofness into which he can retreat at such moments, directing his magnified gaze straight past the dissident's head, is normally swamped by temperamental gregariousness. His Heaven would contain twenty-six-hour days in which to share the universe with everyone. By way of making a demographic point, he once conceived the entire population of the earth engaged in dancing the twist in New York City, with everybody sheltered from the rain.

A human face turns him on instantly. As his plane's engines die he's waving behind the window at a face recognized from fourteen months ago. As he and his wife, Anne, debark he's waving again. Stumping across the tarmac, he thrusts out a hand and raises toward his greeter a broad lopsided grin of pure pleasure. He is ready with the name, one of thousands he knows. "And your curly-headed little boy, how is he?" Last year he and the boy had shared five minutes counting the vertices on an icosahedron. Bucky had seemed pleased that there were, as usual, twelve. From their sixty-two-inch altitude his eyes look up at as many faces as they look into, one experience he and children have in common.

Still exchanging greetings, he grapples for the largest suitcase. He learned long ago, he says, at Armour & Co., how to sling whole sides of beef. No manageable weight unbalances him, despite his having only one hundred and forty pounds to counter it with. Technique, not heft, that's always his secret: doing more with less. He calls a progressive lessening *ephemeralization*.

At the parking lot he's checking times and distances. Four miles to dinner; and then how far to the lecture? Another four miles. Mary (an old friend of his daughter) has asked in a few supper guests; will there be time to talk with them? There shouldn't be, really—the plane was an hour late—and yet there is. He sits in a red chair, his plate on his lap, surrounded by young faces, and offers them perspectives on pollution (squandered assets: those skies are sulphur mines), revolutions (the ones that count are invisible), and politics ("It is not for me to change you. The question is, how can I be of service to you without diminishing your degrees of freedom?").

Having ephemeralized away some sixty pounds since the days when he was built like a Yankee Khrushchev, he adorns parlors now like an alert little clergyman, spruce and always black-suited. Listen, though, and the simile alters. That tireless voice that could harangue if it wanted, shaping brief cadences that run quickly upscale like eyebrows rising, recalls rather a Down-East storekeeper, urgent about the virtues of some lobster trap or lightning rod. His humor is laconic, evanescent. Someone's remark about Southern California zoning ordinances draws a wry phrase about "mission-style geodesics." Time, among these happy people, seems timeless. In the nick of time he has vanished for the ride to the auditorium.

And here he is, in yet another city, before that huge blur of faces, once more finding the first thing to say. Not, we are to understand, with his brain. The brain is under orders from a subtler entity, one that can commune across distances as seamen do with wireless. The whole miraculous self-servicing mechanism, brain and all, he likened long ago to a ship, a ship like a battleship in the great days of sea power, equipped for long independence of the shore by gear landlubbers don't dream of playing with, and under a captain's command, but a phantom captain.

The phantom captain has not only never passed a physical, he has resisted every effort to corner him. He has eluded even attempts to ascertain his weight at the moment he abandons ship—a moment called "death"—slipping away without the scale pointer even flickering.

(Somebody dying on a pair of scales: to such absurdities can science lead. Did any researcher *expect* to weigh the "soul"? Yet how else would we be sure the phantom captain is weightless? Might anyone, for that matter, have expected to clock sunlight? Yet we have learned that sunlight has its speed, like a Cadillac. Weighing, measuring, timing, the scientist always teeters on the brink of the absurd, and whenever he obtains a negative result we feel entitled to smile. And he replies that his results are never negative. Learning something is not so that you thought was so is not to lose but to learn a great deal more. It is impossible to learn less.)

Though the scale pointer does not flicker, we know

when the phantom captain has abandoned ship, because the vessel's temperature drops and it commences to disintegrate into its elements, the same elements as those of which the universe is composed, and in roughly the same order of abundance. While the captain is in command of his intricate mechanism, it behaves in purposive if ungainly ways. If Shakespeare, it may scribble, if Picasso, dash pigments. If Henry Ford, it may assemble a vehicle. If Charlie Chaplin, it may eat its shoe. Other phantom captains, yours and mine, are glad (for elusive reasons) of the scribbled words, the spattered canvas, the Model T, the spectacle of ludicrous ingestion.

If it is Richard Buckminster Fuller we confront, January 1972, then a mechanism in service seventy-six-plus years may be observed momentarily immobile, except for the motions of balance and of oxygen exchange, while the phantom captain deliberates how the "sound-detonating mechanism" shall be configured. What to say?

For he has no script, never has. He is committed to spontaneous thinking out loud, guided by his intuition of his audience and his occasion. Homer was often in this uncertainty while kings waited by firelight, and no more than Homer is Bucky without resources. Like Homer, he has formulae, to be uttered while he is rapidly thinking ahead.

One time Homer began,

That man relate to me, Muse, . . .

—a stock opening; then in moments of need, stock phrases. The dawn is rosy-fingered, Athena is glinting-eyed; such words fill up voids as the syllables tick by, and while lungs and chest and throat occupy themselves with rolling the sounds out, Homer's phantom captain makes a thousand determinations, busy among his paradigms of nobility. One incomparable result has come down to us, called *The Odyssey.* We now think there were other Odysseys, many,

all lost, since he told it differently at many different times.
And Bucky?

> B. Fuller never makes special preparation or prewriting
> of his lectures. He assumes our whole lives are funda-
> mental preparation. He has learned to "think outloud"
> with large and small audiences regarding his explora-
> tions, experiments, experiences and deduced generali-
> zations even as we will converse intimately with one or
> a few beings. His discourse is frequently tape-recorded
> and transcribed to typescript. Because aural syntax is so
> unlike the visual syntax, his transcripts require an aver-
> age of seven retyped reworkings. He speaks at a rate of
> seven thousand words an hour, which requires three
> written words for each spoken word. . . .

—another way of putting it, as phrased in his office in Carbondale, Illinois. Homer's agent may be imagined putting
out such a bulletin. But not, for Homer, seven thousand
words per hour! That is two words a second, and even
faster when Bucky is caught up in his discourse, at about
the conventional lecturer's stopping point. "I need all the
time it takes." By the fourth hour the pressure of utterance
has often mounted until he is barely finishing the words.
Something Delphic is happening, and caught up in his vast
integrative visions, he sends syllables tumbling like a rain
of photons.

But that lies two or three hours in the future. Just now
the phantom captain is electing a formulaic opening.

"I am not a genius . . ."

      or

"I was born cross-eyed . . ."

      or

"Suppose I have a rope here between my hands . . ."

*(Santa Barbara, December 1967, in a TV studio, under
the lights, before twenty privileged people. A videotape is*

*in progress for the University archives. He is supposing he
has that rope.)*

". . . between my hands; and I have tied it in an ordinary overhand knot; one rotation of 360 degrees, a second
rotation of 360 degrees, one of them passed through the
other. . . ."

(The hands whirl, shaping space. Through the new terminology we can see that knot. Tomorrow work with pencil, paper and string will assure us that the terminology is
accurate. One circle, 360 degrees; another circle, 360 degrees; the knot does consist of two circles, and they do
interlock. And twice 360 degrees is 720 degrees, a figure
we shall meet again.)

"And when I pull the ends of the rope, the knot does
not disappear. The knot gets tighter. Each loop prevents
the other loop from disappearing. So the knot is a pattern
in the rope, and it's a *self-interfering pattern*. The harder
I pull, the more the knot stays there. . . ."

It does indeed. Gesturing across his chest, he pulls that
phantom knot till in empathy we seem to be pulling on it
ourselves. He interrupts himself to remark that he has
used this example before audiences many times, and no
one has ever objected that there is no knot because there is
not even a rope. Something important has already happened, what he calls a first-degree generalization, one step
away from every special case. We have each of us, as we
watch, a clear and distinct knot in the mind, understood
as we may never have understood a knot before. As if by
X-ray, we can see through it, think its structure. A knot
in a rope would be a model of that mental knot, and a less
than perfect model since we should not be able to see into
it when it is pulled into a tight lump.

Now, he goes on, we might loosen the knot, and slip it
along the rope. We are then slipping rope through the

knot: feeding the rope through a pattern. And if we have a nylon rope, a cotton rope, a Manila rope, all spliced together, these materials will pass indifferently through that knot, so we cannot say that the *knot* is Manila or nylon or cotton. The knot is a pattern, a "patterned integrity." And the knot isn't the rope. (In the same way the phantom captain is not the mechanism he commands.)

". . . a self-interfering patterned integrity": and we are somewhere in the terrain commanded by Fuller's special jargon. This has gained him something of a reputation for being incomprehensible, as indeed he is if our habit with printed pages is to skim and dip.

Next we are told to imagine the great winds, molecules of air being sucked across the Pacific, and across the California coastline, and into this room, and into our lungs. And out again, after the oxygen exchange. (We have possibly just expelled some molecule that once passed through Julius Caesar.)

Sixty pounds of air each day cycles through each of us, and food passes through us, too, and water likewise. In a lifetime some hundred tons of solids, liquids and gases will cycle through a man like rope passed through that knot. The man is not yesterday's steak or this moment's lungful or his most recent martini. The man is a *self-interfering patterned integrity,* like a knot.

John Donne would have been delighted, and Bucky for his part has sensed that on a printed page the knot deserves better than encasement in a rectangular paragraph. He has arranged it into what he calls "ventilated prose."

> . . . and man is a super galaxy
> of galaxies of slipknots
> sliding sum-totally along
> in a complex of reciprocal slip-knot principles

upon a complex of associable, limitably tunable
and sensorially apprehendable
in-knottings of slippable principles . . .

The rope makes the knot visible. The food, the water, the air, make each of us visible, and audible, and heavy. They are not us. They are elements in a flow of patterned transactions, of service to the phantom captain.

(And what is that steak, incidentally? A knot likewise, tied out of solar energy. Onto Spaceship Earth the light pours, and with it the invisible radiation which we do not perceive as light. Much of it is reflected back into space, for instance by the white clouds. But some is impounded by the green leaves of plants. They are green because we see them by the radiation they reject; they are impounding the red, the hot, and in such quantities that they require to be water-cooled—if you deprive a plant of water the leaves *burn*. They tie the solar energy into self-interfering patterns which cattle—knots likewise—transmute into protein we can transmute. We say that we eat steak. Really, we are acquiring knotted sun. We cannot deal with it directly—except on a limited scale, by taking a sunbath—but the plants can, and we eat plants, and eat animals that eat plants.)

A while ago he was halting, sentence by sentence. By now the cosmos of recycling patterns has taken possession of him. The voice is rapid, as though seeking means to utter many sentences at once, so doing the cosmos fit homage. The right hand, spread as though gripping crystal spheres, is pulling in quanta of sunlight; before his chest, in tense rapid movement, his fingers fashion intricate knots. His gaze travels to some distant point along a sight line just above the listeners' heads. One node is defined and tied. To go on with the multidirectional discourse he is spinning, he must elect the filament he will follow, and locate the next knotting-point. If all goes well, it will hang, when he has finished, a mini-universe, a spun skein of stars. He collects its invisible stuff out of many minds. ("Possibly what we have always spoken of in the past as telepathy is in fact ultra-ultra-high-frequency electromagnetic wave propagation. We may find that we are doing a great deal more subconscious communicating with one another than we are accomplishing in the 'reality' of the visually tunable ranges of the electromagnetic spectrum. . . . I am confident that my spoken thoughts are greatly affected by subconscious feedback from my audiences.")

He feels an astonishing kinship with his audiences, and would have them feel it with one another. (He dislikes politics. Politics divides.) One of his gambits is to dissociate them somewhat from their bodies. ("Stick your tongue way out before a mirror. It is a strange device." And, "If you were tongueless, and someone came offering to sell you a tongue, would you buy such a thing?") And bodies are extended and modified, by inlays, by lenses, by enema bags. Automobiles are extensions of their drivers, like hats, coats, shoes and faces; so if the average car weighs 3,000 pounds, the average young American now weighs a ton and a half. And "the composite American extensible into his group mechanisms"—a jetliner, a railroad train, Boulder Dam— "is larger by millions of times than any historical animate organism." For if a car extends its driver's body, a jetliner extends 200 persons' bodies; and "industrial mechanisms so gargantuan as to be without warrant as an extension of any one person are justifiable as extensions of multitudes of persons," and all people, when they are using such extensions, are "one and the same person."

But only in a certain respect; he does not thrill, as did Russian film makers forty-five years ago, when human passions are subsumed into the massive dance of machines.

And he believes so absolutely in the judgment of the folk that for years he has been advocating some way of taking electronic votes, to provide "an instantaneous contour map of the workable frontier of the people's wisdom." In a 1971 television play for which Fuller was "Consultant for Earth" (as distinguished from another consultant whose domain was Space), the people of America, of France, of Russia and of China all voted to go ahead and colonize "Earth II" by turning on their house lights while an orbiting space-craft scanned the luminosity level. A Fuller parable: politics divides; but a shared technology, he thinks, unites.

Here is a strange man indeed, a technological frontiers-man, a small-*d* democrat. In the latter role, like the shoe-less St. Francis, he personifies a naive challenge: how many politicians, piously encomiastic toward popular wisdom, would really consent to entrust their actions daily, by day-light, to its instantaneous scrutiny? Another question comes to mind. Is the populace well enough informed to govern by daily hunch? Gullibility aside, does Fuller really believe in the transparency of the information medium through which our perceptions of politicians come? Not at all; he calls news "our most polluted resource." And finally, what of literature's long testimony to the shifting, fickle mob? Is he perhaps innocent of literature? Or does he think, like Ford, that history is the bunk?

But while we think up questions, process is streaming through self-interfering patterns. All questions except questions of principle pertain to time. ("Principles do not begin and end. Experiences do.") And any question, for Fuller, pertains to details excerpted from a Whole System, and is apt to launch one of his expositions of the Universe. On with the star-spinning. To *consider* means to group stars in one's view: the word traces back to the dealings of

Roman augurs with sidereal arrays. Where will Bucky's skein of light loop next?

That depends, night by night, on the people in the room with him.

"Every one of us is going through so many experiences. Just today, the morning's news colors the other things I have been thinking about, so as we meet there is something fresh to be talked about. I am very deeply aware of a human being's eyes. Like meeting on the street: 'Do you have time to talk now?' 'Yes, I do.' I can have conversation with a whole lot of people, and I do it through their eyes. They let me feel very strongly whether I am talking about what we ought to be talking about."

Milwaukee, Expo-Center, the American Institute of Architects State Convention. Assault of strobes, blare of rock: a scheduled "happening" has invaded the brontosaurian calm. Marchers are wearing boxes as a hint that the architects present make a living at boxing-in. In Messiah robes and beclustered with balloons, a hairy kid climbs a packing-case Mount Tabor, and amid a din from which sensitive ears pick out obscenities he is transfigured in the manner of Skidmore, Owings & Merrill ("The Three Blind Mies") while disheveled worshippers bow. If this is the Program Committee's idea of a convention, some angry delegates will boycott the rest of it, beginning with Bucky's marathon statement tomorrow. Tonight Bucky grins at the goings-on, and Anne grins at Bucky; a flashbulb catches them. "I'm sure some were shocked," is his mild comment. "And I think that is what Nature wanted to do. There are young people shocking you right now and you need to be shocked to the point where you have to come out of that eggshell. You are going to come out of that eggshell to a sense of responsibility to the Universe."

Tomorrow he will commence by evoking Wombland, the nation formed by Spaceship Earth's unborn children, sixty-six million of them at this moment, the tenth largest nation in the world. (What human group can have more interests in common? What better claim on nationhood? "They have a regular way of life in there.")

"How are things over there with you?" runs their telepathy. "Things are great over here."

"I don't know what is going on, but we seem to be going through some kind of earthquake." This one is starting to be born.

Enclosed in its egg, the chicken uses up its nutriment, pecks the shell looking for more, and breaks out. "Suddenly there is a chicken on its feet, and a new relationship to the universe." It changes the universe slightly but irreversibly to have one more chicken's consciousness sensing its patterns. What an alteration of the Universe, when Man is born!

"We have been in a womb of permissive ignorance, surrounded by all kinds of resources. Life is born ignorant. If it had been up to human beings to invent oxygen, man would have died right away. Newborn man doesn't know anything about what is on board." (Like that chicken in the egg, he pecks blindly.) "Only for two hundred years has man known what he does with air, that his lungs differentiate it. And the man who discovered that [Lavoisier] had his head cut off. That is how logical man is so far."

And now we have nearly enough knowledge to manage with, and just when the supply of resources in the egg is reaching critical lows—unbreathable air, undrinkable water, exhausted mines, leveled forests—the new Man is at last being born. . . . "Out of the eggshell to a sense of responsibility to the universe."

We are born not even knowing we are on a globe, let

alone on a spaceship. We have all been persuaded of that for only three centuries, and most of us are still unper-suaded that "materials" are really patterns, that "things" are insubstantial, that a paradigm for reality is the knot. A rope's very fiber consists of molecular knots, constel-lated amid vast spaces.

In Jorge Luis Borges' story called "The Aleph," a house in Buenos Aires contains in its cellar, toward the right of the riser on the nineteeenth step from the floor, nothing less than The Aleph, which is "a point in space that con-tains all other points." It is little more than an inch in diameter, and contains, as you gaze into it, literally every-thing: tigers, pistons, bison, tides, armies, a Persian astro-labe, all the ants on the planet.

That Aleph is the unique magical peephole. For Bucky, however, every phenomenon is Aleph-like. A virus mole-cule contains a Geodesic Sphere, a model of rational energy accounting, Pythagorean geometry, a focus of patterned transformations, anything principled. A man-made geo-desic models that molecule, and an ideal monetary system would model them both. The tremor of Jell-O in a bowl on the restaurant counter will lead him to the tensional/ compressional ultimates of the solar system, or vice versa. And that knot is one of his splendid Alephs.

Dilating on all matter as knotted energy, patterned energy, he might tell us that Einstein's $E = mc^2$ makes Energy (E) equal mass (m) multiplied by the speed of light (c) expressed as an area[2]: precisely because, when the knot is somehow untied, the energy bound up in that mass expands at light's speed, propagating a radiant sphere the surface of which expands as the second power of the outward velocity.

Or he might contrast this norm of patterned flow with the old norm of rest that seemed natural to Newton's mind.

At Harvard, when Bucky went there in 1913, rest was the norm, and attrition the typical event; the universe was leaching away, and one's obligation was to grab what one could before all the ice cream had melted. *Rest was the norm at Harvard:* he found the place so inert he contrived to get himself thrown out of it twice, the second time for keeps. But now change is the norm.

Or he might note that our senses can "tune in" on the knots, and only some of the knots (try to eyeball the stubborn knot we call a virus), but they cannot tune the flow; and "99 percent of the transactions of the universe are infra or ultra to man's sensory tuning." So man, already automated, extends his senses with further automation, electron-scanning microscopes for instance, and relies on his intellect to tell him with precision what even his augmented senses cannot discern.

Or, if he sensed a roguishness in the auditorium, he might serve it with a fanciful cadenza in which metabolic flow through the human knot runs backward: the excreta reabsorbed, the digested food reconstituted, the direction of cooking's molecular changes reversed, the vegetables leaping into the cans, the cans into cartons, the cartons onto trucks which back their way to the canneries; back, then, to the fields, and back into the ground, to be unraveled into air and water and sun. And where does man's metabolism commence? Not in his stomach. It commences many miles away from his breakfast table, when the solar energy is captured by a leaf, and it incorporates the canneries (predigesters) and the supermarkets and the trucks and the gas that heated dinner (deputizing for body heat) after having first flowed through 1,500 miles of pipeline. (That gas too was once solar energy, impounded by Precambrian trees.) As I write this, my next Wednesday's breakfast is converging toward me at various rates, in various trucks and way stations. All these things flow and shuttle the way our lungs do, and our peristalses do, man having by tireless ingenuity extended his "ecological sweep-out" by thousands of miles. A Maine lunch may employ sunlight impounded by Hawaiian pineapples.

And any of these facets adjoins more, so that if you listen to Bucky speak a number of times you hear many things twice or three or four times, never quite in the same words and almost never in anything like the same sequence. He is tireless—until lately he hardly slept—because his energies feed on his vision of universal coherence as gods once fed on ambrosia. You may be fortunate enough to hear one of his breathtaking swerves toward a quite unforeseeable focus. One day he remarked of energy distribution that it tended on the whole to collect into smaller and smaller packages. "The number of times that you encounter small amounts of energy that can do small things is very much greater than the number of times you encounter large amounts of energy that do large things." There are more mosquitoes, he added, than there are earthquakes, and encountering a very large amount of energy, such as a star, is a pretty unlikely experience. So habit concentrates on small events—mosquitoes, heat waves, getting to the office—and loses the capabilities which can deal with big changes when they happen. Hence the folly of specialization. . . . And we realize that we have passed through a keyhole, from an explanation of why mosquitoes are frequent to the shortcomings of the curriculum at Harvard. The first part of this sequence did not predict its outcome, and the whole came to more than it seemed to promise. And Bucky's talk comes to more than an inventory of its topics, and two talks that contain just the same inventory of topics do not duplicate but enhance one another, if we are so fortunate as to hear them both.

No Fuller discourse will predict any other. Which leads to a general principle, one of his branching-points. "How many of you have heard of synergy? How many can tell me what synergy means?"

Show of hands, normally not many. If many hands rise, we may assume either a large contingent of veteran Fuller-ites, or else (he says) a good many chemists.

> SYNERGETIC, *adj.* [Gk. *synergētikos,* deriv. of *syn-* + *ergon,* work.] Working together; co-operating; as *synergetic* muscles.
>
> SYNERGISM, *n.* 1. *Physiol.* Cooperative action of discrete agencies such that the total effect is greater than the sum of the two effects taken independently, as in the action of the mixtures of certain drugs. 2. *Theol.* The doctrine that in regeneration there is a cooperation of divine grace and human activity.
>
> SYNERGY, *n.* [Gk. *synergia.*] Combined action or operation, as of muscles, nerves, etc. Specif.: *Med.* A The combined healthy action of every organ of a system. B The combined effective action of two or more drugs.

Fuller's definition transcends the dictionary *(Webster's New Collegiate, 1949)*:

> SYNERGY: *The behavior of whole systems, unpredicted by knowledge of the component parts or of any subassembly of components.*

He has several favorite examples, of which the most economical is the behavior of chrome-nickel steel. Various metals have various "tensile strengths," defined as the pull that a square-inch rod is sustaining just when it parts. Iron breaks at 60,000 pounds of tension, chrome at 70,000, nickel at 80,000, "manganese plus carbon, etc.," at 50,000. What may we expect if we combine them?

Well, if we are making a chain, it will be "no stronger

than its weakest link," which is 50,000 pounds. If we plan to melt them together, what happens will depend on the proportions, but common sense expects that the strongest ingredient, nickel, will be weakened by admixture of the others.

And common sense is as wrong as when it perceives a flat earth. For "stainless" chrome-nickel steel castings can be concocted with a tensile strength of 350,000 pounds per square inch. Is this perhaps, by some unforeseeable logic, the sum of the combined strengths? No, the sum is only 260,000. Somehow the molecules have interlocked to produce a behavior unpredicted by what we know of the components. That is synergy.

More examples? Easy. Does the eyelash predict the eye? Do an inflammable gray metal, sodium, and a poisonous green gas, chlorine, predict the white crystalline sodium chloride we sprinkle on our meat? (This stuff—common salt—is not the sum of their molecules but their molecules' way of combining synergetically.) Why may the merger of a dozen economic failures produce a success? Why can a 300-pound man ride a bicycle whose wheels are spoked with wires a child could bend? (The answer to that one is that the system arraying the wires exploits their high resistance to tensile loads while putting no strain at all on their susceptibility to crumpling.) Why will a few of the most ordinary words in the dictionary lock together unforgettably—

> . . . But I have promises to keep
> And miles to go before I sleep
> And miles to go before I sleep. . . .

Why, for that matter, can a man fall in love with a few inflated dollars' worth of chemicals, chiefly water, arranged in a structure to which he murmurs "Darling"? Synergy again; his beloved is a Whole System, unpredicted by any knowledge of the hamburgers and the oxygen she metabolizes.

No other word, Fuller likes to remark, has that meaning, so the fact that most people do not know the word *synergy* means that most people do not know it is possible to get more out of a system than you put into it: to get, in fact, more than you pay for. Or rather, since all of us have confronted examples, most of us have never been taught to reflect that on principle it is both possible and common. We may dwell on unwanted synergies—called "side effects" —and not know that the same principle underlies most of what we prize. And an unknown principle isn't part of your experience, whereas you alter your experience by discerning principles in it. Fuller's paragraphs about the phantom captain were meant to alter our experience of talking to the next 28-jointed adapter-base biped we might drink with, which is one way to alter the world.

The things he talks about are, on the whole, utterly familiar. It's rarely that he recites anything as extraneous to common experience as the recipe for chrome-nickel steel. Usually he is invoking what we all remember, not to "popularize" but on principle. The universe is simply the sum total of everyone's experience, most of it experience everyone has had. We have all drawn triangles in our school exercise books. Fuller could easily utter 20,000 words on those triangles.

San Francisco, the third hour. Down front, a sleeping infant is being passed to its father. A svelte girl rises, stretches, resettles. The video cameramen, to vary their tape, are picking up audience faces. Glimpses of fatigue, of rapture, of attention, of impassivity, drift across the monitor. Pacing an area defined by his tether, the microphone cord, Bucky is gesturing toward where infinity is supposed to lie. His discourse is of triangles.

What lies outside them? White paper. How much? As much as you have. If you had all you could imagine, where would it stretch? To infinity in every direction. Your little triangle bounds a controllable space, around which infinity yawns. (Have you been to infinity? No. Has your teacher? No. Forget it.) What is real to you, part of your experience, what you can understand and think about, is inside the triangle, the bit of surface it encloses. You are in the first grade, and you have received an early lesson in disregarding the "outside." You will grow up supposing, from a thousand such lessons, that you needn't think of where the refuse goes when you've ejected it from the inside of "your" house to the vast outside. Men chewed up forests once as if they went on to infinity. (Men still do.)

But draw your triangle instead on the surface of the earth, and think of what it is you are really doing. You are not staking a claim in the midst of infinity. You are simply dividing the earth's surface into two parts: the part inside your triangle, and the part outside. Each part has its shape, each part has a finite area. ("Unity is plural and at minimum two.")

Make your little triangle larger, and you make the big one outside it smaller. A closed system works only by exchange. (When you have finished drawing, there is more graphite on the paper, less on your pencil. The graphite system is also closed.) And do not suppose, by the way, that the sides of your triangle are "straight." If it runs from the North Pole down to the Equator, then along the Equator 2,000 miles, then back to the North Pole again, you can easily see that its sides are three curves, a quarter-circle each, called *geodesics*. (It will also have, incidentally, one eighth of the earth's surface inside it, and seven eighths outside it.) There are no straight lines, of the kind you intuitively call straight; even that string you stretch between your hands is sagging infinitesimally in the middle, because though two hands are pulling it east and west, a little gravity is pulling it toward earth's center. (No straight lines? But what about the sight line from the sun to my eye? No, light takes time to travel, and the sun hasn't been "there" for eight minutes. You see it through a curved pipe of light.)

The earth is a Whole System, even the idealized earth, the 8,000-mile smooth sphere we visualize when we imagine triangles drawn on it. And what is outside the subsystem defined by the triangle is as real, and as definite, as what is inside. (And what we are not thinking about is nonetheless there; whatever we throw into a river goes someplace; infinity does not absorb it. Lake Erie is a dying lake now because men were slow to see this.)

It follows that drawing a triangle is a moral act; it follows (for Bucky) that geometry classes are one cause of industrial pollution.

Men's earth was flat once, and went on "to infinity," its world-island washed by the engirdling ocean. When Dante's Ulysses sailed out of the inland sea and turned to his left, he encountered Mount Purgatory and a great whirlpool. There was no telling what you might encounter. The Infinite Outside encouraged men to postulate an infinity of gods, mostly whimsical. The Greeks, in a land vulnerable to earthquakes, assumed that the two mightiest destroying forces they knew, the force of the waves and the force that shook the land, answered to one god, Poseidon Earthshaker, so they erected temples in his honor which, alas, he kept shaking down. You may see the remains of one at Sunion, on the headland below which the Adriatic meets the Aegean, with Lord Byron's name scratched on a pillar. Poseidon, in a fit of rejection, smashed it long before Byron came.

But Poseidon need not invade the realm of dreams, and

it was part of the splendid dream of Greece that men's minds could subject and order an imperturbable domain inside the triangles they scratched on the sand. They deduced that the sum of the interior angles of any such triangle was always 180 degrees. (That was not true; but Euclid did not know that his triangles' sides were actually curved, and that the sum of the angles increased as the drawing grew larger.) The bisectors of the three angles crossed at a common point. (They never quite do, in a diagram, but that is perhaps because it is hard to draw a diagram accurately.) And "a common point"? What is that? Tradition tells us: A point has position but no magnitude. That seems to mean it is a nothing that is somewhere. And lines? Lines are accumulations of points, innumerable nothings which manage to add up to direction without width. (And if they are innumerable, mused Zeno, how does a runner manage to traverse them all, and Achilles pass the tortoise?) Lines enclose surfaces. A surface has no thickness. (Is a leaf a surface? No, it has thickness. It has two surfaces. Let us try to imagine that they have no thickness, and yet are back to back.) And a solid? An infinite stack of no-thicknesses.

Bucky Fuller rebelled against this structure of unrealities, he says, in the first grade. The class, of course, laughed. Seven decades later there is still extraordinary feeling in his rejection of the structured classroom. "You suddenly find that there are inflexibly coupled chair-desks. You fit uncomfortably into yours. The next kid has one. Everyone is pinned to his desk. One of the children psychologically escaping his lockup wants to go to the bathroom. You try to escape to the bathroom. It has horrid smells. I immediately resented and as yet resent those stupid little bullpen desk-chair 'straitjackets' where you are put on exhibition as they ask you to say things in front of the others so that if you venture an original thought the others can laugh."

His next thought is characteristically sweeping: "I think that within the next ten years we are going to have to give up schoolhouses."

Why not? The instant response is instructive. Young audiences applaud. They are close enough to schoolhouses to remember their time being systematically wasted. Middle-aged audiences feel panic. (What if all those young energies were *let loose?* It is extraordinary how children are feared.) Montessori personnel agree. Their founder rejected "schoolhouses" decades ago, thinking that artfully designed resources impose "structure" enough. Salaried educators have mixed reactions. Some feel vertigo. Some, scenting a trend, smile suavely. (Nothing pays like *change,* if you are the one calling the changes.) Senior Administrators, wanting nothing to alter, grimace as though Bucky had advocated abolishing them. (He has advocated that, too.) The president of one institution of higher learning, the morning after a Fuller marathon, conceived hearty misgivings. Fuller had dismissed as obsolescent the structure of the state, and the president's mature query was, "What about my paycheck?" (It is a *state* check.) Whereupon Fuller, fueled by excellent morning tea, changed the subject by mentioning his recent session, in Venice, with the aged Ezra Pound; and at the mention of the genius whom it is not genteel to mention, not in Administrative sancta where paychecks during good behavior are guaranteed by the state, the silence was suddenly cuttable with a knife. Bucky seemed not to notice. "He does not see negatives," says an old friend. That is how he passes in and out of so many mortgaged, obsolescent, structurally precarious buildings without going mad.

But back to the triangles; and let us ignore the Platonic

apparatus of lines with no width joining points with no magnitude to enclose plane surfaces with no thickness on an unbounded plane stretching to infinity in all directions. (Infinity? There be dragons . . .) Let us consider a real triangle, which means, in the first place, let us construct one.

We may use three strips of wood, and pin them together. Tongue depressors will do. And we shall discover at once that two joints swivel freely until we connect the third; whereat, suddenly, all three angles become utterly locked. That is because each side prevents the angle opposite it from opening or closing. We have invented a device for guaranteeing the integrity of angles, which is no small achievement in a universe where change is normal. It is a self-interfering pattern, comparable to the knot. It is a structure; the minimum structure, since there is nothing you can build with *two* sticks. When he is using his terminology carefully, Bucky will call it the only structure, because there is nothing else that guards angles that way. Make a wooden square, and you can deform its corners at will. (Or a wooden pentagon, or hexagon, or whatever you like. More sides will get you nowhere.) But build a diagonal into the square, and it is locked, because it has suddenly become two triangles. Nothing except the triangle has that stability. Nothing.

But only in two dimensions, and real things do not have their being in Flatland. We constructed that wooden triangle in our many-ways world, and it will yield somewhat if we subject it to a maneuver not practiced in Flatland. We have only to seize one corner in our right hand, and the opposite side in our left hand, and twist. The tighter our joints the less twist, but that is simply to say that whereas its resistance to having its angles opened or closed is a product of pure geometry, its resistance to twisting depends on the quality of our carpentry, which is a different thing entirely. Can we call in geometry to stiffen it against twisting?

We may think of bracing it. Here are some braces. They subdivide it into smaller triangles. If it now twists less, that is because there are more nails, each contributing its quota. But we are still depending on our skill at banging nails into joints, and on the friction that grips the nails once they're in. So what else can we try?

At this point we may remember that the triangle bent into a third dimension. Can we carry geometry into the third dimension, and confront the problem there? We can. We might bulge the center of the triangle outward. Let us start by putting longer sticks (B) into that six-pointed star in the center of the hexagon. Just for symmetry, we may also shorten the sticks (A) at the corners.

What happens? The center of the six-pointed star rises off the plane, because it has no choice. And if we let the corners of the large triangle point their toes inward, we shall see that the large triangle has acquired an overall curve, like the hollow of your hand, or like a triangle drawn upon the surface of a sphere. It is true that those corners will still wriggle, but the whole central zone, now saucer-shaped, has grown rigid, three-dimensionally rigid. To stabilize the corners, we might give them the support of adjacent structures. As it happens, we can make four more of these subdivided triangles, a total of five, and join their edges, and we shall find that their five top vertices are now arrayed around a zenith point, and locked, and that their bottom edges make a closed perimeter which would be locked also if we spiked it to the earth, and we have made a kind of inverted skeletal saucer. It is stable, for reasons of geometry, not carpentry, and stable, moreover,

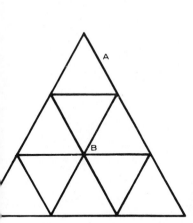

Subdivided triangle (flat)　　　　Curved triangle

in the three-dimensional world. It is stable even if all the joints are rubber. This is a simple Geodesic Dome. (Aren't you glad you stayed?)

Poseidon Earthshaker would have had his work cut out for him, shaking down one of those. Every single triangle would resist deformation, and by the synergetic behavior of Whole Systems they would unexpectedly strengthen one another, since unpredicted rings now contain the stresses. But of course Poseidon's worshippers built in stone, which would have been an unsuitable material. (How to join all those stone blocks, leaning inward?) So it's perhaps not surprising that no Greek thought of it, though they had the geometry almost within their grasp.* If you're convinced that you must build out of stone you have no ultimate recourse against earthquakes. Discerning no good

* The "2-frequency Triacon" which Fuller calls his basic Geodesic Sphere was known to them as the Pentakis Dodecahedron. But they never thought of building anything with it.

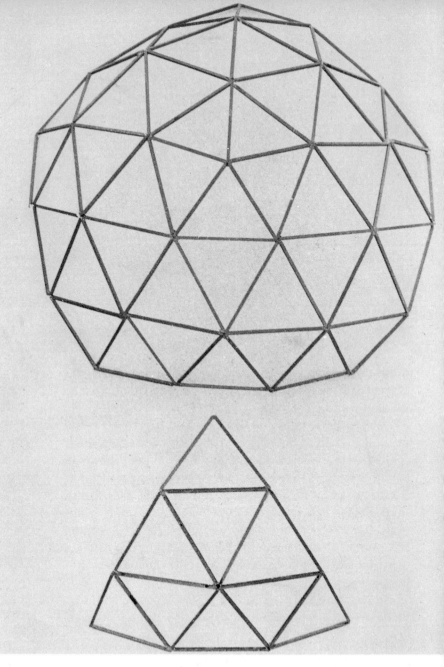

Curved triangle and dome

reason why temples need be of stone, we are entitled to call stone a Greek hang-up. It helps us not to notice hang-ups of our own.

One of these is the cube, as we shall be learning.

Meanwhile, we've isolated a useful notion: the idea of a strength that's designed in, to be distinguished from strength the carpenter hammers in. Design solves problems elegantly, but force imperfectly. Design is weightless; it costs no nails, it costs no wood; it's pure conformity to principle. We do not make "things" out of "materials"; we arrange preferred patterns (and we may learn which patterns work by studying molecules). Design is like jiu-jitsu, using the opponent's strength instead of fighting him. Design takes the air that rushes under the wings and uses it to lift the plane (the plane is in motion; there are no cables, no skyhooks). Design lets the very weight of the keystone maintain the integrity of the arch that supports the keystone. If Cleopatra must be played by a boy, then design the transformation of boy to queen as a high point in the play's arc:

> Give me my robe; put on my crown; I have
> Immortal longings on me. . . .

If a corpse must be borne off stage because you have no curtain, then design a ceremonious climax:

> Let four captains
> Bear Hamlet, like a soldier, from the stage. . . .

(Yes, the actor even says "stage.")

"Don't fight forces, use them," Bucky was saying as long ago as 1932. And when someone wants to learn, by all means let him. It's easier than "teaching" him later.

There is much, much more, but never what anyone expects. In Africa, in 1958, thirty-five senior architectural students from the universities of Natal and Capetown waited two days with pencils and notebooks ready for data on the building project they were to do with Buckminster Fuller. "In which time of continuous lecturing," their report runs, "we found ourselves making copious notes, not on architecture or engineering, but on nautical history, evolutionary patterns of the progress of man and his travels across the earth, mathematics as a science of space, juvenile delinquency, the processes of industry and mass production, his own experiences of automobile and aircraft design. . . ."

They then learned that their "project" had been sitting right in front of them for those two days. "The reason he could see it and we could not was the clearest example of the vision that has marked him from other men."

It was the world's oldest known toy, a small ball of interwoven bamboo. Youngsters have played with it for thousands of years. Bucky picked one up in Burma en route to South Africa, and immediately perceived a geodesic variant. Inspired by that, and by native architecture, he proposed that the students design and build (good grief!) a corrugated aluminum geodesic Zulu hut, interweaving the sheets. And they did, though the Zulu go on using grass.

He may have hoped to free the Zulu a little. Zulu houses die as grass rots, or can be burned down by a spark. Then grass must be again harvested, again woven. Meanwhile cattle were eating up the grass. Such a people spend a large part of their days maintaining their bodies and their shelters. Long ago men perceived that they might forcibly delegate a good part of this work to other men, called slaves, thus freeing a few to devise, for instance, geometry. The custom persisted, and the 1810 American census tallied one million families, also one million slaves. Though

Woven bamboo toy

many families had no slave at all, one per family was the average. Each family lived in a house of wood or brick, and the house was worth about $350 but the slave about $450. That was sensible, really, to set more value on directable energy than on a shell.

The energy slaveholders commanded is surprising. Using figures gathered by armies, which need to know how hard men can be pushed, Bucky once figured what a man can do with his muscles in an eight-hour day, in addition to keeping alive. Set him at building pyramids or hoeing cotton for 250 days a year (52 Sundays off, and some 50 more days for sickness and bad weather), and we get thirty-seven-and-a-half million foot-pounds of work out of him.

That's a kind of energy norm, and about 1940 Bucky used it to measure what we're doing for ourselves by design science. Periodically he updates the calculation. He sums the annual energy man is deriving worldwide from his fuels—the coal, the oil, the waterpower, the nuclear reactors; assumes that fully 96 percent of it is squandered by friction, bad design, and general fecklessness; surveys the rest of it moving us from place to place, carrying our messages, roasting our popcorn; and dividing the total by thirty-seven-and-a-half million he can tell us how many human slaves we should need to do all that. These are *world energy slaves*. At present (1972) each person on earth has 200 of these available—say 1,000 per family, to compare with the single slave per American family in 1810. Obviously, Asians aren't getting their quota; obviously, North Americans have much of the supply cornered. Obviously, "making the world work" will mean making energy slaves uniformly accessible world-round. This needn't mean enriching Cambodians by depriving Americans, since the pool of energy slaves has never stopped increasing. In 1950, with a smaller world population, there were only thirty-eight per person. Not only are more energy supplies tapped, conversion efficiency has been slowly increasing, and these factors together have been growing faster than the population of the world.

This may prompt Bucky's cadenza on inefficiencies, one feature of which is his vision of a million cars at any given moment, standing at red lights with their motors running. He assures us this is a reasonable United States figure. And back in the heady days of the Horsepower Race, how many horses were there under all those hoods, performing with all their might an invisible tap dance while a million drivers got nowhere? Quite possibly 200 million horses, from which national stable a little of the nonsense is subtracted every time a freeway bypasses a stoplight. Throwing less energy away, that's just like tapping more of it. "Pollution" is just inefficiency: something you could use, thrown into the air or Lake Erie.

The energy slaves, ever multiplying, ever more equitably distributed, the energy slaves will build the New Jerusalem, containing moreover no Dark Satanic Mills. Bucky's voice has been slowly mounting in pitch, the syllables tumbling faster but defined more sharply. Chopping his hands inward, he invokes a workable world, within the grasp, he says, of the technology we know today.

"With known technology, we can take care of every human being. We can make man a success in the universe. We can bring to every human being levels of satisfaction no one has ever dreamed of. We can do it by 1985. And don't say we can't afford it!"

As though a force field had suddenly collapsed, it is clear that he has ended. Assailed by the mounting ovation, he is giving his attention to the microphone, feeling for the fastener to unclasp it. He is suddenly minute and vulnerable. Rows of people are standing, their faces alight, applauding. Preceded by a sponsor, he limps offstage.

His back is tormenting him. Can he just get to the car and sit down? If he can't sit periodically during his talk, on a chair, on a table, anywhere, the pain starts part way into the second hour. . . . "One of my legs is shorter than the other": an apparent fault in design.

The quick walk to the car is dogged by a garrulous man stymied in his own effort to save the world. The government. . . . Detroit. . . . He scampers a little ahead, turning round trying to face Bucky and harangue him, preferably detain him for genius-to-genius summitry. "A hundred thousand people a year," and, "You can't patent it, they block the patents, and meanwhile all those people . . ." Never mind patents, says Bucky, never mind maneuvering. Publish your findings. If you are right it will be accredited to you, otherwise forgotten. It is not a satisfying answer, entailing as it does the option of being forgotten. Bucky settles into the car, relaxing as the strain comes off his back. "It takes just a few minutes . . . Better already."

Anxieties. "My slides." Anne has his slides, returned to her by the projectionist. He reaches back for them.

"Wouldn't they be safe here in my bag?" "In my inside pocket," Bucky specifies, "I have a special envelope for them." They are handed over. And, "What about my overcoat?" A rapid recheck; someone has retrieved it.

Half an hour before midnight, the waitress who had just brought his bedtime steak is back with a small bottle of champagne, "Greetings from The California Time Machine." The CTM, who or whatever they are, seem to be hidden in a darker part of the roadhouse, behind a screen of latticework and greenery. Some is poured for Mrs. Fuller, some for the friends who are driving them to their motel. Bucky instructs the waitress to convey his appreciation, and not to divulge that he himself is not drinking. He then spreads out a paper napkin and with a felt-tipped pen commences to tabulate the rudiments of the Coordinate System of Nature. Pythagoras had intuitively focused on the right-angled triangle, but had unhappily compromised the insight with talk of squares, such as the famous one on the hypotenuse. Only occasionally, as you work with squares, do things—accidentally—come out in whole numbers. He sketches a quick square, subdivides it, and numbers the subsquares: 1, 2, 3, 4. "We divide the sides into two parts, we get four smaller squares, and then we say that 2^2 is 'two squared.' But"—he sketches a triangle—"the second power has nothing to do with squares. We divide each side into two parts in the same way. . . . Count the small triangles: 1, 2, 3, 4." He numbers them rapidly. "Two to the second power, not two squared. Four is simply two to the second power. Nothing to do with squares."

Another bottle of champagne arrives; from their mysterious privacy the California Time Machine are playing *deus ex machina* to genius. Bucky's brow is furrowed with mild distress. How not to do them the discourtesy of a rebuff, and yet not let them suppose they may send more and more? Can the waitress and perhaps a friend use the champagne? Yes, they will be off duty at one. And can she, very tactfully, while thanking them . . . Wait, what can he send the Time Machine in return? A sketch of a Dome is suggested. On a fresh napkin, Bucky limns in one gesture a surprisingly symmetrical freehand circle, subdivides it with practiced arcs, and notes, above his signature, that this is the eve of his wife's birthday. The waitress slips off with this bulletin from the twenty-first century and Bucky resumes his exposition where he had interrupted it in mid-sentence.

The third power, likewise, has nothing to do with cubes. From the habit of taking a cube (based on the square) as the element to be subdivided, men have gotten into saying that eight is two cubed. But if we take the tetrahedron, based on the triangle—he sketches one—and subdivide each of its edges into two, the lesser tetrahedra we obtain will each of them have one-eighth the volume of the one we started with. . . . The drawing is a difficult maze of criss-crossing lines. "It's easier to see with a model." Here are four of these lesser tetrahedra, one at each corner of the parent tetrahedron, and a volume equal to four more of them is accounted for by the octahedron that has appeared at the center. The octahedron is nature's second primary system. And two to the third power, not two cubed, gives us a volume of eight. . . .

The waitress is back, with the Time Machine's newest offering, a candle inserted in a single slice of cake, and a napkin on which has been drawn a plain cubical house with smoke curling from its kindergarten chimney. Other late snackers catch sight of the cake, and amid an informal chorus of "Hap-py Birth-day" the white-haired lady blows out the candle. Bucky, grinning, initials the napkin dia-

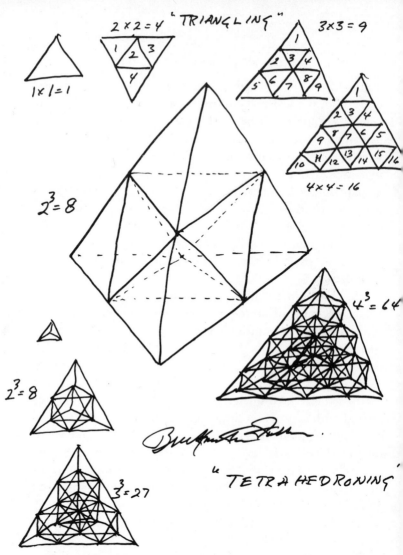

Bucky's drawings of (top) subdivided triangles, showing that second power doesn't depend on squares; (bottom) subdivided tetrahedra, showing that third power doesn't depend on cubes. Counterclockwise from 9 o'clock: (1) A small tetrahedron. (2) Tetrahedron with edges divided in two; four small tets appear at corners, and octahedron in center has a volume of four more, totaling eight. Large center drawing is same thing in a different perspective. (3) Tet edges divided in thirds; at the center of the maze is vector equilibrium, explained in Chapter 4; total volume is 27. (4) Tet edges divided in fourths; interpenetrating octahedra and vector equilibria can be sorted out to yield total volume of 64.

grams "B.F.", and as the party rises makes sure he has the overcoat from which his preoccupation is constantly getting him separated. He slips back toward the bar for a few private words with the California Time Machine. Later he does not describe them, except that they were young men, musicians apparently.

Settling into the car still aglow from the encounter, he quickly outlines the geometry that restricts the turning angle of front wheels to, at best, 34 degrees, "and usually much less because the frame interferes." By alloying the frame, thus thinning it without weakening, one or two makers, notably Mercedes-Benz, get more of that 34 degrees than does run-of-the-mill design. But front-wheel steering is inherently faulty, since the turning car is trying to lift its nose off the road. ("A holdover from the buggy, which pivoted where the horse was.") Mrs. Fuller recalls how the Dymaxion car swung its rear end into parking spaces. That, says Bucky, was because its single turning wheel—aft—could turn without limit. And the car—it was back in 1933—could execute a complete circle around the cop in the middle of the intersection, grazing his uniform all the way. Bucky did that once with a carload of magazine editors, and the cop on duty at every intersection from Fifty-seventh Street down to Washington Square demanded a repeat performance.

"I am not a genius," he says, "but I am a terrific package of experience." He has known Nehru, and also Al Capone, and seen his choreography executed at Spoleto, and had his name mispronounced by Nikita Khrushchev. No other design scientist can claim as much. The experience draws on some 28,000 days, several thousand of them very much like today. This has been a good day. They mostly seem to be, now.

THREE

The Outlaw Area

"I was born cross-eyed"—that was the first relevant experience; and not only cross-eyed, but presbyopic to an absurd degree. The usual farsighted person can focus his eyes over the distant range, and requires assistance only for near vision. But when Bucky was being gestated, some hiccup in the DNA transcription dictated that his eyes should not focus in the normal world at all. He needs glasses to see anything whatever, the moon, or a visitor's face. "Until four I could see only large patterns, houses, trees, outlines of people with blurred coloring. While I saw two dark areas on human faces, I did not see a human eye or a teardrop or a human hair until I was four." The moon he sees is like a globe of stars. He would lie in bed pondering the clusters of luminous points he saw where others saw lights. He still thinks in clusters.

Imperfect vision has shaped the specialization of more than one genius. "How is it," the adolescent William Butler Yeats asked his father, "that we are given two eyes and can see out of only one?" Instead of rushing W. B. to an oculist, the elder Yeats placed together the tips of his fingers and discoursed on the two lobes of the brain. So a certain disdain for the merely physical crystallized at the center of W. B.'s mental habits, an unwillingness to be impressed by what numerous people repeatedly said they saw, a moon merely, a cat merely. The cats and moons of his mature poetry are cats and moons of the mind; so are his swans, and so is his Byzantium. Alfred Tennyson was so nearsighted he could see the flower in the crannied wall ("I hold you here, root and all, in my hand") but was apt to turn distant blurs into the likes of

> The lone glow and the long roar
> > Green-rushing from the rosy thrones of dawn,

with incalculable effects on the imagination of Victorian England.

Bucky Fuller, though he developed no disdain for minute things, became "a student of large-scale patterns," the world having presented itself for four years in large-scale patterns exclusively. Having spent his earliest years assenting to others' testimony about what he couldn't see, he had less difficulty than most of his generation in following the leap of the scientific mind off the sensory part of the spectrum altogether. Having known about hairs and teardrops only by rumor, he had no reason to balk at the electron, not to mention such abstractions as tensile strength (you cannot tell grades of steel apart by looking). He also trusts purely mental large-scale patterns, statistical projections for example, and invisible small-scale accuracies like the machining of parts for the Ford Dome, which he likes to say transcended the visual acuity of any machinist. It gained strength from being wholly instrumented.

When he acquired glasses he took his first step toward the ready assimilation of technology. To see anything at all he relies on the expertise of the oculist, the craft of lens-shapers, the cunning of frame-makers. (Nowadays he hears with similar assistance.) His oculist's diagnostic equipment comes from Rochester and from Switzerland, and expresses in its gleaming accuracy many generations of metallurgical and geometrical lore. Glass, extracted from sand by refinements of methods first discovered in Mesopotamia, is shaped, in conformity with refractive laws written down in the seventeenth century, by machines developed in the nineteenth and twentieth; behind the machines in turn stands a worldwide technology (alloys for their gears come from all around the globe), and the frame-makers' plastics draw on the results of generations of organic chemists. More recent chemistry's scratchproof acrylic trifocals have taken a quarter-pound of glass off his nose. Much of what the human race has learned since the dawn of the Iron Age is concentrated in assisting Bucky Fuller to see a piece of string, and if anybody supposes that nevertheless all this industrialization can be bypassed, he is welcome to assault with his bare hands the resources of any island he chooses, and try if he can make us a pair of spectacles.

Bucky helps us look at it yet another way. Eyes evolving during millions of years, spectacles evolving during thousands, both are mechanisms to serve the phantom captain. To the second of these evolutionary chains countless human intellects contributed discoveries; and man's life, inconceivable apart from what many men have thought of, is uniquely characterized by the number of human discoveries that have been folded into it. Dogs have never altered their role by taking thought: only men have done that. It is *natural* for men to do that, and the line between nature and artifice is less easily drawn than the platform ecologist would have us suppose. Aluminum for instance, though a chemical element, does not occur "in nature." Every pound of aluminum in the world exists thanks to man's intervention. And man can do nothing nature does not permit.

*　　　*　　　*

When Bucky entered the human community, how was man's evolution proceeding? During the century a remarkable thing had happened: the human male had ceased being a creature that lived, on the average, about three decades. For every Lincoln who lived long enough to be assassinated at fifty-four, for every Edison whom natural causes carried away at eighty-four, enough male babies succumbed within weeks, enough Keatses at twenty-five and Mozarts at thirty-five, to hold the average down. If most of the men we have heard of lived past their thirties, that is only to say that living long enough is one of the factors that conduce to being heard of.

When Bucky's father was born in 1861, his calculable life expectancy was not much greater than a cave man's, but greater. It was under forty years. He beat the odds somewhat; he lived to be forty-nine. Bucky's own life expectancy when he was born thirty-four years later was forty-two years, a result obtained within quite recent history by improved shelter, improved nutrition, above all by a massive drop in infant mortality. So an insurance company would have bet that Bucky would die in 1937, and given him 1 chance in 100 of living to be ninety. As of 1972 he was still going strong, and an American male born this year has a 72.7-year bet placed on him. "Expectancy," Bucky used to say, "has rocketed ahead of me."

What else? A man walking and riding (horseback, coach, train, ship) might expect in 1895 to cover some 1,000 miles per year. Two men in Bucky's home town had been to Europe. "They gave talks about it each year." In Paris they had been able to move upward 898 feet, by steam lift to the third platform of the Eiffel Tower. That was as high as anyone got without climbing mountains, though the Swiss were already thinking of a tourist railway to the summit of the Jungfrau. The Eiffel platform is just a place to visit; the highest conventional rooms in the world were in the twenty-first story of the Flatiron Building at Twenty-second Street and Broadway. One could ride a horsecar or an electric trolley. Steam moved the mails, and copper wires moved messages, encoded in clicks. There were 208 times as many Americans as telephones; Alexander Graham Bell declined to have one, thinking its invasions of privacy discourteous.

In 1895, on July 12, Richard Buckminster Fuller, Jr. was born in Milton, Massachusetts, in a new house designed by Longfellow's son "Waddy." In that year Gelett Burgess published that assertion that he had not seen a purple cow. Many years later Bucky was to plot his career against an inventory of his time's achievements. In his birth year, it turned out, the first American gasoline-engined car had been designed under Charles Duryea's patent; Guglielmo Marconi, at his father's country place near Bologna, had sent messages more than a mile with no wires at all; and W. K. Roentgen had learned that rays his apparatus was emanating passed clean through opaque materials; not knowing what such rays might be like, he named them "X." If anyone in 1895 had known how to correlate these three curiosities, he might have foreseen what Bucky calls the prime theme of man's recent evolution: the transition "from tracked to trackless, from wired to wireless, from visible to invisible." But no one seems to have intuited a large-scale pattern of that order, and even when it has been clearly stated most people still have trouble remembering it most of the time, though Bucky reduces it to a single word, Ephemeralization.

The next year the Duryea brothers produced all of ten cars, and the first Ford was completed in a brick workshed. Humanity was also enriched in 1896 by the steam turbine, in 1897 by the electric trip-hammer drill, in 1898 by the electron, a truly elegant invisibility. In 1899, still not fitted with glasses, Bucky Fuller was manipulating by touch the toothpicks and dried peas on the kindergarten table. He had still never really seen what shape houses were, and having no idea it was orthodox to make cubes, he proceeded to discover the tetrahedron, a three-legged pyramid, and the octahedron, eight triangles born of interlacing three squares. Archimedes and Euclid had been among their earlier connoisseurs. His fingers told him these triangulations were rigid.

He also found that they would nestle together in structures that could be extended in four directions. A teacher called another teacher to see this space-filling doodle. One day, rethought and equipped with engineered hubs, it was to be the subject of U. S. Patent #2,986,241. By then he was calling it the Octet Truss. In 1959, sixty years out of kindergarten, he erected outside the Museum of Modern Art a giant octet structure in which the toothpicks had been superseded by gold-colored aluminum tubes. Twenty feet above the ground, its rooflike lattice cantilevered forty feet in one direction, sixty feet in the other, with no visible sag and yet with no support except a spidery off-center pier. It was a splendidly useless thing, a gesture: a gesture of ephemeralization. No one would have conceived such an insouciance during all the centuries when it was self-evident that *strength* entailed *weight*.

That principle was still perfectly self-evident when the tallest structure in the world was inaugurated a decade before Fuller's birth. That was the Washington Monument, which in getting just 555 feet five inches into the air used up more than 81,000 tons of stone. Stone is too heavy to be easily dislodged. That is its virtue when you build with it, weight. Weight is what holds the Washington Monument together, and except for containing an elevator, it

Octet Truss

embodies no design innovation later than the time of the Pharaohs, who were also impressed by weight. The New World in those days was intensely cautious about the idiom of its public gestures.

But it was the Old World that replied, just four years later, with a structure nearly twice as high, achieved, moreover, with about one-twelfth the weight. Slice Eiffel's tower (1889) where you will, and chiefly you encounter air. In fact it weighs just about as much as the air would weigh in a canister big enough to fit over it, a mere 7,000 tons, and all the metal in its lacy frame, melted down into a square the four legs could straddle, would make a plate just over two inches thick.

The Eiffel Tower, until antennas were mounted on it, was like Fuller's structure at the Museum, quite magnificently useless, yet paradigmatic. When it was still on Eiffel's drawing boards the united taste-makers of Paris disliked intensely what it portended. It would be the shame of Paris, ran a manifesto of which Dumas *fils* and Guy de Maupassant were among the signatories. It would be mon-

strous without the excuse of being useful; not even commercial America, they thundered, would perpetrate such
a thing. (And think of that graceful obelisk by the Poto-
mac!) What, moreover, would visitors say? It must be forbidden. It went up nonetheless, and commenced to sway
very slightly; its tip continually traces a dainty circle, never
more than five inches in the fiercest gale, and on a patch of
ground a chair might cover it imposes no more weight than
would a man sitting in the chair. (The Monument's pressure on three square feet of soil is twenty-seven tons.)

Eiffel's Tower was four years old when Bucky Fuller was
born, prophet of ephemeralization and performance per
pound. Had it changed the world's intuitions of how
strength may be related to weight, Fuller might have saved
much breath. But buildings, post-Eiffel, and notably in
Washington, went on being heavy, heavy.

Nevertheless ephemeralization was proceeding, and performance per pound controlling at least some calculations.
In 1900 Count Zeppelin made an Eiffel-like steel framework light enough not to burden the dirigible balloon it
stiffened. The same year Max Planck, having brooded on
the new electron, published Delphic equations whose pur-
port was that ways of giving off energy inhered in the
structure of matter, and that energy was emitted not in
streams but in discrete packets you could count, 1, 2, 3, 4,
much as you might disassemble peas from toothpicks.

The next year Marconi sent a telegram across the Atlantic, on (so to speak) weightless wires, and the Wright
Brothers, bicycle mechanics, took to gliding. (Bucky entered elementary school.) In 1902, in a laboratory demonstration, photographs were dissociated into pulses at one
end of a wire, and reconstituted at the other end; the picture weighed nothing in transit. (Bucky first saw an automobile.) In 1903, a telegram went around the world in

twelve minutes, and Orville Wright was aloft in a sort of gasoline-powered box kite for twelve seconds. The Wrights had allowed 200 pounds for their engine weight. It delivered sixteen horsepower. By pedaling and cranking at once, a 200-pound man can work up perhaps one horsepower for about as long as Orville flew, so one secret of flight was an ephemeralization factor of 16 to 1.

In the few years before Kitty Hawk, flight had somehow seized young imaginations; all over the country lads were tossing darts about schoolrooms, and paper planes out of attic windows, to loop and swoop and get lodged in the maple trees. Bucky's taste ran to biplanes and triplanes, something of a technical challenge; he thinks that by the age of nine he must have launched (and lost) twenty of them. That was fine play, said the grownups of America, but you mustn't waste all your time on impractical things. . . . A year's effort was devoted to various proofs that what the Wrights announced must have been a hoax. Indeed two years before they flew, Professor Simon Newcomb, America's foremost astronomer, investigator of the perturbations of the moon, had explained to the large readership of *McClure's Magazine* that constructing an aerial vehicle which should carry even a single man from place to place at pleasure "requires the discovery of some new metal or some new force." So it was clear that the kids were just playing.

Newcomb's argument was based on the simple law that the bigger the heavier, but disproportionately heavier. (A five-inch trout has twice the weight of a four-inch trout.) Lifting area increases fourfold for doubled dimensions, but unwanted weight increases eightfold, so in making a wing big enough to lift a man you also make it too heavy to lift itself. There is an upper limit to the size of birds;

the condor cannot even get off the ground without help from an updraft.

All those boys with their paper airplanes may prompt us to ask how such prescient fads arise. Not all adult speculation about flight was negative; had some of it filtered down, perhaps by way of magazine pictures? Had Jules Verne something to do with it? Is there perhaps some orchestration in the mind's themes, which allows us to see in retrospect that the humblest diversions were all the time in accord? Is that why the random thoughts of the audience and Bucky's thoughts are congruent? When Sigfried Giedion researched the history of mechanization, he found that the detailed study of motion, indispensible to mechanizing it, was being conducted in the nineteenth century by artists whom it is nearly certain the pioneer mechanizers were paying no heed to. And it is entrancing to discover how much detailed attention was being paid to themes Bucky would spend a lifetime developing, notably the relation of structure to weight and of geometry to natural growth.

The footnotes in Sir D'Arcy W. Thompson's classic *Growth and Form* (first version published in 1917) disclose instance after instance of seventeenth- and eighteenth-century insight leading to curious detailed Victorian researches. Thus in the 1840's a German, Carl Bergman, was showing that a warm-blooded animal much smaller than a mouse is physically impossible, since as the creature is made smaller its heat-producing bulk diminishes faster than its heat-dissipating surface: a mini-mouse could not get food down fast enough to maintain its temperature. Really small creatures therefore are cold-blooded: little frogs, little fishes. Other workers were verifying the calculations of the great seventeenth-century naturalist Borelli, who showed that similar creatures, whatever their size, are constrained by mechanics to jump to the same ceiling. In jumping 200 times its own height, a flea gets no higher than a grasshopper (20-30 times). And it was argued in 1881 (following up an eighteenth-century hint) that 300 feet was about the upper limit of growth for the tallest tree, for beyond a certain height a tree bent ever so little by the wind will continue bending of its own weight and be unable to recover.

The notion of structural limit haunts all these studies. We find for instance that most creatures smaller than mice are constructed upon radically different principles, with a hollow exoskeleton and no provision for keeping the system heated. And we do not find creatures heavier than the elephant, whose four columnar legs can just support his bulk, since the whale, though larger, is not heavier because it floats and is weightless. The swamp-dwelling brontosaurus half-floated.

D'Arcy Thompson even assigns structural limits to the dome-shaped crab or lobster: for the stresses within a hollow shell, he says, "increase much faster than the mere scale of size; every hollow structure, every dome or cylinder, grows weaker as it grows larger, and a tin canister is easy to make but a great boiler is a complicated affair. The boiler has to be strengthened by 'stiffening rings' or ridges, and so has the lobster's shell; but there is a limit even to this method of counteracting the weakening effect of size."

That is why geodesic structures similar to Fuller's are used by nature only for very small objects: diatoms, radiolaria, virus molecules. So what are we to think when Bucky affirms that his geodesic domes get stronger, more efficient, and proportionately lighter as they increase in size: that in fact there is no upper limit at all?

Had Bucky somehow evaded a law of nature? He replied that he could do nothing that nature did not permit, and then invoked anew his principle that man's intelligence is part of nature whenever man chooses to exercise it. Materials for the aluminum struts and the steel tension cables of the huge "tensegrity" structures that may dome whole cities did not occur in the Nature that lay before Adam. They could not exist until men had "differentiated" metal out of stone, and then tensional and compressional factors out of metal. Using the raw stone that raw nature affords, builders indeed encountered what the naturalist calls natural limits. Across stone columns whose finite height is set by their tendency to topple, you may lay, as they did at Stonehenge, a stone lintel whose length is limited by its tendency to break in two of its own weight. It breaks in two because the strain along its lower edge is tensile, and the tensile strength of stone is relatively slight because its particles pull apart. But separate the metal from the stone, and the tensility from the metal, and enhance the tensility . . . D'Arcy Thompson's great book, cataloguing natural limits, is the terminal moraine of a conception of nature which education still perpetuates though design science has rendered it obsolete.

On similar principles, the tension-spoked bicycle wheel had to await the invention of carbon steels. Tension struts held the Wrights' airplane together, and did not break, says Bucky, thanks to a piece of design science familiar to bicycle mechanics but to few other craftsmen. You tighten bicycle spokes by turning a threaded collar, which grips threads cut into the end of the spoke. But to cut usable threads into a thin spoke entails such an incursion into its thickness that three-quarters of its strength is cut away. So bicycle-makers thicken the spoke's end by "swaging," and cut their threads into the extra thickness. The cables that laced the Wrights' biplane wings were swaged, and had it not been for this piece of bike-shop lore they would either have snapped or have had to be made too thick, hence too heavy, for that chancy flight. So metal to fly with was segregated from rock, and tensility from metal, and the swaged wire's-end from its normal slenderness. Each of these separations meant an act of attention that can often be analyzed into many detailed acts of attention: all that attention impressed on the flying-machine that it slowly extricated from the stone.

Bucky thinks naturally along lines of separating-out. One of his most striking images invites us to envisage man

> converting one hundred tons
> of raw broad countryside
> into five tons
> of scintillating airplane-in-flight

—the plane potentially *in* the landscape, as the statue was once considered to be inside the stone (and Michelangelo had only to knock away the nonstatue). But you cannot just dig away and discard the nonplane.

In a similar way we might dig around indefinitely in the cultural history of Bucky's early years and find most of the components of Bucky's thought without finding a convincing explanation of Bucky. A genius is more than the epitome of his time: that is part of what Bucky means when he calls himself "a random element." Still, it is surprising what close analogies we may sometimes find. What are we to make, for instance, of Alexander Graham Bell's infatuation with the tetrahedron?

About two years after little Bucky's adventure with the toothpicks and the peas, the veteran inventor of telephony perceived in the tetrahedron a figure of singular virtue. It is the three-dimensional equivalent of the triangle, holding its form with invincible tenacity. It is the minimum space

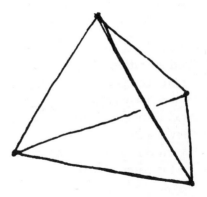

Tetrahedron

enclosure, with four identical sides; nothing simpler can be envisaged. Having of all space enclosures the maximum structure in proportion to its content, it has therefore the maximum attainable strength. Bell's mind moved to performance per pound and to aeronautics, and the very summer before the Wrights flew he wrote in his son-in-law's *National Geographic* of the virtues of a tetrahedronal configuration in kites. Such a kite will not easily lose lift, and Bell's idea that the future of aeronautics lay in a design which wouldn't tend to kill the pilot in case of a stall led him to hundreds of experiments with kites composed of many tetrahedral cells, as many as 1,300.

In 1905 such a kite, powered by a feeble breeze, lifted a man some thirty feet into the air. Bell danced about like a schoolboy while his wife developed the photographs. He was too convinced of the tetrahedron's transcendency to bother noticing its enormous aerial drag, and aeronautics consequently passed him by. (Stabilities held his attention, whereas aircraft design was to turn on velocities.) He did erect, on his Nova Scotia island, a tetrahedronal tower, its seventy-two-foot legs meeting tripod-fashion five stories above the ground. Each leg was subdivided into four-foot tetrahedral cells of half-inch pipe, and each cell could support two tons without signs of distress. Bell had effected about 1907 one of the periodical rediscoveries of the oc-tet configuration Bucky stumbled on in kindergarten, and moreover had used it in a practical structure. He seems not to have applied for a patent, and the tetrahedral tower was dismantled after a decade. Bucky had very possibly never heard of it when he came upon the principle yet again during his geometrical work of the 1940's and wrote to his patent lawyer.

In 1904, the year in which Henry James revisited America and the Ford Motor Company observed its first anniversary, Bucky's grandmother Caroline Wolcott Andrews bought an island. Bucky's formal biographer, when he gets to work one day, will ponder Caroline Andrews at considerable length. Her three-times-great-grandfather Roger Wolcott was colonial governor of Connecticut; her two-times-great-grandfather Alexander Wolcott was brother to George Washington's aide-de-camp. The wedding of her grandfather was the first to be solemnized in Chicago and is recorded on a bronze tablet on the lower southwest wall of the Wrigley Building. The next generations prospered in Chicago, and she herself, in Civil War days, married a Chicago lawyer, John Andrews. Their daughter, also named Caroline, was to be Bucky Fuller's mother, and tell him how it was to watch all of Chicago burning five miles to the south of their many-acred Briarwood Farm, where the Edgewater Beach Hotel stood until recently. Young Caroline had her unforgettable view of the orange blaze from the window of a cupola atop the house. One can nearly imagine the great house from that detail: a prosperous family's stately pleasure-dome, gingerbreaded, cupolaed, nearly minaretted. The idiom of elegance was assured in those days.

Grandmother Andrews was assured, and articulate, about her family past, and decades after her death in 1906 it was a pleasure of Bucky's to recall it in anecdotal detail. Her presence, in his first eleven years, had helped shape his world. In one photograph a large, calm woman with black mutton-chop sleeves and a lace stomacher shares something the camera has not recorded intelligibly—a piece of embroidery, perhaps?—with two grandchildren, a dark-haired girl whose attention is on something else, and small Bucky, the student of large-scale patterns, whose big-brimmed hat will not blow off thanks to that chin strap. In this comfortable vignette of a century's end, grandmother enjoys the unforced authority of a Presence.

One thing with which she and her affluent relations pervaded the family was the note of success. It went without saying that one amounted to something, earning leisure time to spend at a summer place. Which is why we find Grandmother Andrews island-hunting in Penobscot Bay early in the summer of 1904. She led what was nearly a small colonizing party: her two daughters, Caroline Andrews Fuller and Lucy Andrews King, their husbands, Richard Buckminster Fuller, Sr., and Rockwell King, and all of their tribe, a total of seven grandchildren of whom one had been born cross-eyed but was far from hopeless. They moved with the easy calm of the entitled: Boston to Rockland, Maine, by scheduled side-wheeler, Rockland to Eagle Island by chartered steamer (after six decades Bucky could still recall the captain's name— Crockett). From a boardinghouse on Eagle Island they explored by boat and with picnic baskets the purchasable domains, and by August Grandmother had selected a mini-archipelago: Bear Island, which she purchased in her own right, and Compass and Little Spruce Islands, which her sons-in-law purchased jointly.

Everything, that summer, enchanted Bucky. When the side-wheeler docked at 4 A.M. at Rockland, June dawn was commencing to silhouette shadowy islands out in Penobscot Bay beyond the breakwater. Suddenly the wilderness silence was broken by the first seagull's call, and the dawn wind touched the rapt nine-year-old's cheek. That touch, that sound, the ghostly islands and the salt tang in his nostrils—"exquisite sensorial thrill"—remained ever after his paradigm of natural beauty, a tranquillity mysteriously astir, pressure waves and photons and particles of salt composed into moving stillness.

And Bear Island, thereafter the family's summer retreat and still the chief geographical constant in his life, presented themes with which all his later speculations have comported.

For instance, the vision of special men, men on the move, who have stayed on Bear Island since before history begins: Indians, and then Norse fishermen perhaps, and since 1604 successive colonial settlers, building, moving, leaving. The underbrush conceals their overgrown foundations. Such men obeyed the natural laws of the sea, and shrugged off other laws. All seamen, Bucky eventually reflected, are "outlaws." About 1956, at San Quentin, he confronted a roomful of prisoners, each with bowed head as if he could hardly look up. "I can't tell you how shocked I was to see how young they all were. They were all about twenty, very few with any age at all." They were "outlaws" whose luck had been bad. (Only the physical laws of the Universe are self-enforcing.) He told them it was "by a tiny little hair of luck" that he wasn't locked up with them. ("My mother used to say to me very many times that she was scared to death I would go to the penitentiary.") He meditated aloud on this theme a full hour, so intently that his eyes closed tight, and he nearly fell off the platform. And all human advances, he once told a visitor, originate "in the outlaw area." If the Wright

Brothers had required permits they would be waiting yet.

In the seamen's outlaw area, where laws are real, you cooperate with powerful moving masses because there is no use getting angry with a hurricane, nor legislating against it. You design your way through it. You also treat resources as communal. Possession means use, and everyone understands that a house that is not being used is liable to removal piece by piece if some seafarer has a use for the lumber. Wealthy folk from the domain of statute law would often be surprised to find that the island buildings they had vacated last Labor Day had mysteriously disappeared during the winter, all but the foundations, no one ever knew how. The Bay folk said that such houses had "gone a-drift," like abandoned ships which are anybody's property. Human laws codify customs, which in turn secure a web of mutual convenience, and the laws of the mainlanders secured a static existence enforced by title deeds. Seamen's law defines change and the allocation of limited resources.

Then there were the seamen's crafts. Nothing afloat stayed put; twice daily a tide lifted everything fifteen feet. Combating such rhythms, and hurricanes and multitonned seaquakes, they had recourse not at all to mass and bulk but to thin asymmetrical structures kept operational by tensioned cordage. A man mastered cordage, in all degrees from heavy to delicate, and a sound splice was one of the modes of virtue. A compressioned mast held erect by tensioned cables was able to prevail because able to bend as its parent tree had bent: that was a design principle of nature, carried over to the service of human requirements. Being flexible, a tree is less often broken by wind than uprooted. A mast, being flexible, is seldom broken, and if the heeling ship makes the gesture of a tree being uprooted, it regains equilibrium as the land-based tree will not. And wind fills sails held outspread by tension systems, wind sufficient to move many tons of ship, governed by cunning systems of slim lines pulling taut.

The tendency of a tensed line to pull true pervades Bucky's feel of the universe, where the tensest lines are of zero diameter, the intermolecular bonds or the invisible cords on which planets swing. "Therefore when nature has very large tasks to do, such as cohering the solar system or the universe, she . . . has compression operating in little remotely positioned islands, as high energy concentrations, such as the earth and other planets in the macrocosm, or as islanded electrons or protons or other atomic nuclear components in the microcosm, while cohering the whole universal system, both macro and micro, of mutually remote, compressional, and oft nonsimultaneous islands by comprehensive tension:—compressional islands in a nonsimultaneous universe of tension." Earth, moon, a silicon atom, are islands like Bear and Compass, and the Universe is also like a sailing ship, with tension and compression separately emphasized and usefulness gauged by performance per pound, since every unnecessary ton of ship is a ton of cargo the less. And large interchangeable elements in a geodesic structure he sometimes calls "rafts," sensing that they are afloat above our heads on a spherical tensional sea.

If boatbuilding was the local parent technology, the primary local industry was fishing. "Such tension systems as seines, trawls, weirs, scallop drags, lobster pot heads, and traps, together with all their respective drag and buoy gear," exacted of the men who tended them "deft tension techniques as spontaneous as those of spiders."

Living things at home in that world taught one its economies. Bucky's first venture in imitating the design principles of nature resulted from pondering the jellyfish, which moves by opening and closing, umbrellalike. He designed an umbrellalike rig to go on the submerged end of a pole, and on his daily four-mile trip to Eagle Island for the mail he was able to face the way the boat was going, pulling the pole in with the folding cone collapsed and pushing it out as the cone spontaneously opened to grab against water almost as though touching bottom. It was faster than rowing, and he didn't need to keep turning his head to make sure of his course. (Not that he rejects rowing, though he prefers to see it scientifically enabled; a patent of his granted as late as 1970 is entitled "Rowing Device." *)

He also made tensionally partitioned gramophone record cabinets. They have been in use now for two-thirds of a century, preserving on edge and shielding from dust such ancient discs as long ago escaped the emphatic critique of cousin Andy King, whose way of eliminating something played oftener than he liked to hear it was to skysail it into the sea like a discus. Caroline Andrews' grandchildren were a willful brood.

A big house went up, designed, like Bucky's birthplace, by his father's classmate Henry W. Longfellow, Jr. The lumber was carried in by a two-master that had seen service in the War of 1812. Each smallest component of the house came in by ship: lumber, nails, hinges, locks, glass, bricks: a vivid enactment of what Bucky was to spend years trying to rearrange, the insane logistics of building.

The house is still called The Big House. Records were

---

* A catamaran, twin tubular metal hulls of merely six inches cross section, surmounted by a sliding seat. The water resistance is negligible, and if you should capsize you can right it unassisted: it's not like rolling out of a hollow log.

played: they still are, still nonelectrically. Water was collected—still is—by bucket and pitcher from rainwater-gathering cisterns. Books were read aloud—still are—by kerosene light. It is one of the pleasant anomalies of Bucky's existence that he schedules a month each year in a place where the technology—but for jeep and bottled gas—is still too unobtrusive for unpracticed eyes to recognize it. A cistern, nonetheless, is true technology: a valving of certain random energies into a pattern human convenience prefers.

And there was Jim Hardie, who said that the hardest thing about building a boat was the ends, and preferred to splice an enormous center section between the two ends of a wreck. At six feet one he seemed twice Bucky's size, but competed with Bucky because Bucky had schooling, while Bucky competed with Jim's strength and his seaman's skills. Few men had more effect on Bucky's early life, unless Uncle Waldo Fuller who, as an alumnus of the Klondike gold rush and a chief engineer when they built the New York subway, was for a time Bucky's greatest living hero. But not even Uncle Waldo could dream of matching Jim Hardie's feat of digging and shelling eighty barrels of clams one winter, nor of teaching himself, all alone, to read and write. Jim put together the words under newspaper pictures with the words he heard on the radio. Champollion's feat with the Rosetta Stone was scarcely more impressive. He and Bucky shared work that entailed moving tons of stone—building a road from the harbor through the swamp, building the island's first tennis court—with only the help of horses and oxen. The interaction of intelligence, character, and mobilized energy . . . one could start a dozen Fulleresque themes from that.

*　　*　　*

In 1907, Ford announced the Model T (and Bucky, aged twelve, coincidentally first drove a car). In 1909, Bleriot flew the English Channel (and Bucky, coincidentally, saw his first airplane). In 1913, Bucky Fuller went to Harvard, where four generations of Fullers had enrolled. Harvard was part of the family's commitment to stability. Its roots were generations deep in New England. The first New World Fuller, a sometime British Navy lieutenant, had come to Massachusetts in 1630, seven years before Harvard College was founded.

And yet there was a contrary family tradition, to the effect that Fullers were random elements, disruptive of New England complacencies. The Reverend Timothy Fuller, the family's first Harvard man (class of 1760) was a Massachusetts delegate to the Constitutional Assembly, but declined to sign a document which did not prohibit human slavery. His son, the Honorable Timothy Fuller, helped found Harvard's Hasty Pudding Club, but was demoted to second place in his class (1801) for being mixed up in a student revolt. The Reverend Arthur Buckminster Fuller (class of 1840) got himself shot dead while leading a charge across the river at Fredericksburg. As Chaplain of the Fifth Massachusetts Regiment he had no business leading charges, but his abolitionist sentiments were too ferocious for dissipation in mere spiritual talk. He left a son, Bucky's father, Richard Buckminster Fuller (class of 1883), who broke with a generations-long tradition of pulpit and bar to found his prosperity on tea and leather. In great lead-lined teak chests, the teas of Ceylon, India and China filled his warehouses near India Wharf on the Boston waterfront. His aunt had been Emerson's and Thoreau's liberated friend Margaret Fuller, and he had a nephew named John P. Marquand whose vocation was to be the chronicling of Brahmin tensions.

Richard B. Fuller had entered his son at birth in the Somerset Club, with an Agassiz and a Longfellow for sponsors. Bucky has not been one to disown such a heritage, though he sees no incompatibility between the Somerset Club and a card in the machinists' union. Nor has he regretted his years in Milton Academy, where young men were prepared for Harvard. He had no trouble with mathematics classes, only with Latin, and things he learned from his physics teacher at Milton have stood him in good stead ever since, if sometimes as themes for dissent. And he played football—characteristically, he speaks of "the historically differentiated family of controlled physical principles known as 'athletics,'" a phrase to put beside Henry James's summation of the spectator side of football as "the capacity of the American public for momentary gregarious emphasis."

Especially since he could not distinguish friend from foe without his glasses, his football experience contributed to heightening "the 'intuitive dynamic sense,' a *fundamental,* I am convinced, of competent anticipatory design formulations." He came to his freshman year (class of 1917) "puerilely in love with a special romantic Harvard of my own conjuring—an Olympian world of super athletes and alluring, grown-up, worldly heroes." He was to further the family tradition for dissent by getting himself expelled, twice.

Two other things happened in 1913, one symptomatic, one formative. The first was the opening of the seven-minute subway between Cambridge and Boston. The second was a talk with an uncle.

The subway served notice that the pace and quality of Harvard experience were altered forever from norms more than two centuries old. Fullers for four generations—Richard B. Fuller, Sr.; his father, Arthur Buckminster

Fuller; his father, the Honorable Timothy; and his father, the Reverend Timothy—all had passed undergraduate days at a walking pace. Their diaries and letters, carefully preserved (the Fullers, including Bucky, have been great preservers of paper), told the same story generation by generation: a life governed by the time plans took for execution, in which it was a day-long excursion to visit Boston via Watertown Bridge. You took the day off with forethought, much as a man might take off some months for a voyage to China. Now suddenly the trip could be made at whim, and in the time it takes to hard-boil an egg, very much as fifty years later China would have moved as close to Boston as a day's flight. One coordinate of the "special romantic Harvard" had dissolved away, a fact Bucky's class would be the first to experience. (Official Harvard noticed little change: did not its routines stand steadfast?)

As to the uncle: he was one of the rich uncles, and he did Bucky the favor of taking him aside to explain in Boston's terms how the world was. The world was like this: it did not contain enough to go round. This fact had stood established for a good three generations, but never been widely publicized. It was Thomas Malthus, with mankind's first comprehensive statistics at his disposal, who had shown at the threshold of the nineteenth century how population tended to outstrip resources, exactly as, by Professor Newcomb's calculations, the weight of an airfoil would always exceed its lift. Population had since done just what Malthus predicted, and men had outgrown the era of the Golden Rule, the formulation of a less crowded world. The possessions of the *haves* were now founded on the destitution of the *have-nots,* and despite Sunday-school pieties serviceable to placate women, that was henceforth the unalterable state of things.

The fittest, said Malthus' disciple Darwin, were the survivors. It behooved a man, therefore, to cultivate enough of the red tooth and the unsheathed claw to ensure that he and his loved ones should be *haves*. This was not nice, and he need not distress the innocent by talking of it, but there was really no choice. It had been established that a man's chance of passing his life in any comfort was about 1 in 100. "It is not you or the other fellow," explained Bucky's uncle, "it is you or one hundred others." To prosper in the Fuller way with a family of five, he would have to slit the throats—genteelly, of course—of 500 others. "So, do it as neatly and cleanly and politely as you know how, and as your conscience will allow." That was a new role for conscience: the lubricant of murder.

The uncle warmed to his oration, which he cautioned was for Bucky's ears alone. "I'm not going to try to educate your grandmother because she's quite happy thinking in her own golden-rule way. And of course—unknown to her—I have taken care of her one hundred alternates." She was therefore free to be grateful to God. Others, all around the world, clung to their gods and yet died off, short of their potential years, no relative having taken care of their alternates. "But they keep themselves happy by having their hopes and their infinite possibilities. So we don't tell them about it."

That uncle was the first closed-system theorist Bucky had met. The system had closed 150 years before with the implementation of the great worldwide trade routes, shuttling resources from the domain of the ignorant to that of the enterprising. Infinity no longer surrounded a triangle, nor infinite resources a dinner table. It was clear before 1800 that there were no more undiscovered lands. There were unexploited lands, but these too had limits. Malthus could think of men becoming so numerous, spreading themselves so widely, that the limits would hem them in at last: indeed, were already doing so (famines in India).

Bucky never forgot the conversation. Elm-shaded tranquillity, attic windows to launch paper airplanes out of, Bear Island summers, fanlights and alabaster and steamship journeys to see the towers of Pisa and of Eiffel, the Somerset Club and Harvard College itself, these were founded on the elimination of other claimants, a hundred dismal failures for every success. That elimination could be wholly impersonal, hence the aperture through which conscience might breathe. No Boston tea broker administered the *coup de grâce* to unnumbered Chinese whom starvation tended to take care of. Yet that they should covet his living standard was unthinkable (and was anyway a problem for the Emperor of China).

From the Harvard debacle a few themes emerge. One was Harvard's conviction of a static world, at variance with intuitions sharpened on Bear Island. This conviction both shaped the curriculum and underwrote a system of social boxes, impressed upon Bucky at the threshold of his freshman year when his best friend at Milton Academy chose to room with someone more affluent. (What had Four-Eyes Fuller been doing at Milton Academy if he hadn't the cash to sustain an appropriate style?) There were even three automobile owners in that class, one of them Ray Stanley of the Stanley Steamer family, and the clubs which structured social life seemed not open to a boy whose presence on campus derived from a family decision to pool such money as would suffice to keep him there. (His father was three years dead. It was only the relatives now who had money.) Meanwhile his courses—English A, Government, Musical Composition, Art Appreciation, German Lit, Chemistry—seemed as dull as the Latin in which he had not achieved an A at Milton. On the eve of the midterm exams he suddenly resolved to spend as much money as the next man. He withdrew his semester's stake, entrained for New York, and lived it up. A Ziegfeld star, Marilyn Miller, was his dinner guest, and the entire chorus line also. The waiters at Churchill's were deferential when he signed the check.

As to how he had first caught the eye of Miss Miller, there is an instructive story. Being too short to be noticeable at the stage door, he equipped himself with a white wolfhound and had no difficulty standing out. His knack for the appropriately arresting gesture—the personal symbol, "Dymaxion," "geodesic"; the model home with the nude doll in the bedroom—is inextricable from his story. It puts off people who excuse themselves from paying attention because they think his chief talent is for publicity. ("A punk," snarled a retired dean of engineering, "who has appropriated the icosahedron.") He is the century's most tireless explainer, and whatever is explained is dramatized, and in the course of the drama subtly taken possession of. At one juncture an uncomplicated routine subtracting of 2 is called "applying the Fuller Synergetic Treatment," which is a kind of mathematical white wolfhound. He is publicity agent for the universe, and unfriendly folk are discoverable who feel that he explains it as though he had invented it. "I've gotten leery of meeting him," wrote another structural innovator. "He'd tell me so much more about my own ideas that I'd end up thinking they were his."

Then there is the sense that one is *entitled* to money. He explains why the Industrial Equation entitles everyone, and while he arrives at this view with such careful logic that there need be no question of the wish fathering the thought, it would likely have been an unthinkable conclusion had he not been temperamentally pressed toward experimenting with what it would be like to do what one wanted. He has also recalled that until 1928 Robin Hood was his mythological ideal. He discarded Robin only when he perceived that affluence might be distributed without expropriation, from a cosmic bank account design science has accumulated.

In the early winter of 1914, however, it was the family bank account in Milton that was liable for the champagne charges. Back in Cambridge, he was not surprised to find his family agreeing with the Harvard authorities that Buckminster would have to leave. The following fall, having demonstrated acumen and reliability in a textile mill owned by a cousin, he was readmitted and promptly reexpelled as generally irresponsible. This terminated his connection with Harvard until, at the instigation of Dean McGeorge Bundy, they appointed him Charles Eliot Norton Professor of Poetry in 1962. T. S. Eliot had occupied that chair.

"I am the opposite of a reformer," he told an academic audience forty-six years after his second expulsion. "I am what I call a new former. The new form must be spontaneously complementary to the innate faculties and capabilities of life. I am quite confident that humanity is born with its total intellectual capacity already on inventory, and that human beings do not add anything to other human beings in the way of faculties and capacities." (He might have been remembering that no one taught Jim Hardie to read.)

"What usually happens in the educational process is that the faculties are dulled, overloaded, stuffed and paralyzed, so that by the time most people are mature they have lost many of their innate capacities." An old priest once spoke to W. B. Yeats in a railway train of "ignorance spreading every day from the schools."

Bucky's belief that the school is an ignorance factory distills a half-century's reflection on the fact that, essentially, he educated himself, and to such effect that fifty years after his class graduated without him, Phi Beta Kappa, to repair an oversight, awarded him the key he is never without.

In missing formal higher education he missed the advantages and liabilities of being initiated into a shared culture. That is perhaps the most that college accomplishes. George Santayana, a sometime Harvard instructor, was to reflect that the precise books young aspirants might read mattered less than that they should read the *same* books. Homer in some such sense had been the educator of Greece, and the biblical authors the educators of Western Europe. Whatever misinformation these works may contain—and the Bible for instance seems to assign to pi a value of 3.0—everyone who was familiar with them enjoyed the enormous advantage of a shared terminology. (Biblical quips pervaded demotic English speech as late as Victoria's time; a pub-keeper was a publican, and a cabby a Jehu, after the man celebrated in II Kings 9:20 for driving "furiously.")

When President Eliot late in the nineteenth century made Harvard's curriculum a smorgasbord of electives he sacrificed that principle to some extent, but not wholly, the curriculum having ceased to be really central. College youths whether they major in Education or Egyptology proceed for the rest of their lives from a shared rite we may call the College Experience. It hardly matters what college. An alumnus of Wesleyan and an alumnus of Iowa

State will have more in common than will two Vermonters of whom one has gone to college and one not. In a country without a capital as the French and English understand a capital—for Washington is not so much a capital as the place where the government is kept—intelligence flows and experiences are shared through the College Network. Places otherwise inconspicuous are points on that network: Hanover, New Hampshire, Charlottesville, Virginia, Bennington, Vermont, Poughkeepsie, New York. But on such a map, for instance, Sacramento, the capital of the most populous and richest state, is invisible, though its neighbor Berkeley is marked with the circled star which mapmakers reserve for major centers.

Time spent in a node on that network means many things. It means, for one thing, that shared idiom. Lacking this, Bucky has developed a curious jargon of his own for discussing the universe. He would be quick to point out that he also escapes a shared idiom's liabilities. What is known is apt to be identified with what the common language readily describes, and novel combinations are so difficult to achieve that people gifted that way are given the special name *poets,* and run the special risk of having their communications thought insubstantial.

College also brings classifiability. You are apt to *be* what you have majored in: an engineer, an historian, a linguist. This promotes acceptance. Real impediments attend life outside the authorized box. Is Bucky an architect? No, say the architects, an engineer; no, say the engineers, a mathematician; no, say the mathematicians, but perhaps some kind of poet; no, say the litterateurs, a jargon factory. In any case listening to him is somebody else's responsibility. He calls himself "a comprehensive anticipatory design-science explorer," and moreover has said "I seem to be a verb," but there is no major in verbhood.

Another thing a man may get out of college is a sense of what the faculty agrees has been found out. Let us postulate an idealized case. Let us roll back time, and reenroll Bucky Fuller in Harvard, and remove the social and financial pressures, and put him in mathematics classes where he may indulge his great aptitude. Let us graduate him in 1917, appropriately oriented in the advanced reaches of that subject as 1917 understood it. He has complied, unresistingly. He has approached the known themes by the orthodox routes. He is no verb but a noun: "a mathematician."

One impression may be that such an experience would have saved him years of time. "I found . . ." he says repeatedly, describing his tireless investigation of geometrical models: and what he found was time and again some detail established long ago. "He doesn't know anything Archimedes didn't know," whispered a bright student during one of his expositions. That isn't true, but it points toward a certain truth.

Working with models, he has kept his mind on the parts of mathematics that cope with forces, counterforces, changes. A Fuller triangle is something that will twist if it isn't braced, a pencil-line triangle isn't. By staying at Harvard he would have acquired the habit of deducing from postulates—those unreal postulates, the point, the line —quite as though nature, like Harvard, kept mathematics in a separate department where two lines can pass through the same point even though in the physics department two electrons can't. And he would have inherited the orthodox conventions as to which are the main themes, which the details. Rediscovering the subject by his own curious route, he has had no reason not to emphasize what are normally considered details. The cuboctahedron, for instance, is a detail in most expositions of solid geometry, one of the so-called quasiregular or non-Platonic solids. Bucky, who calls it the vector equilibrium and for a while even called it the Dymaxion, encountered it not as a "solid" but as a system of equipoised thrusts, and was not inhibited from perceiving "the Grand Central Station in the energy system of Nature." Ignorance of the orthodox hierarchies was as liberating as his kindergarten ignorance of cubical norms.

Ezra Pound, aspiring to musicianship, drew encouragement from a performance of Debussy's *Pelléas,* "ignorance having no further terrors if that DAMN thing is the result of what is called musical knowledge." Let it pass that his own *Le Testament* did not revolutionize opera: the attitude is intelligible. In appraising Fuller's relationship with the academy, the experience of Pound's literary generation may help us.

Though Pound might seem to have been a more likely candidate for expulsion than a fifth-generation Harvard man, he nevertheless persevered to take not one degree but two (B.A. Hamilton, 1905; M.A. Penn., 1906). He had the advantage of knowing what it was he wanted to become, a man of letters, and could see the use of various sorts of classroom knowledge. Indeed his career is unintelligible apart from his classroom work in what would now be called Comparative Literature. Yet he was to spend much of the next two decades putting the facts he had been taught together again in a historical pattern of his own, and excoriating the academic system. What his complaint amounted to was this, that the system imparted the facts but had only a received and inert sense of the relations between the facts. These were dynamic relations, whereas syllabi are static affairs of language and period. When everything has become "evidence" the lecturer can no longer distinguish the unique *virtù* of Arnaut Daniel, Dante's high estimate of whom becomes one more fact, a curious one. The lecturer has the Provençal syllabus to get through, and Daniel is difficult anyhow.

The experience of Pound's friend T. S. Eliot is subtler. Like Fuller he attended Milton Academy. Like Fuller he had family ties with Harvard. Unlike Fuller, he graduated (class of 1909). Later, like Fuller, he occupied the Charles Eliot Norton chair, and his was, like Fuller's, a somewhat daring appointment, for in the years since his graduation he had become known for poetry that seemed not to answer the seminar definitions of poetry, and for historical pronouncements the likes of which had been heard in no classroom anywhere. In classrooms opinions of Shakespeare were imparted; and, "Who," Eliot asked a few years after he graduated, "has a first-hand opinion of Shakespeare? Yet I have no doubt that much could be learned by a serious study of that semimythical figure."

His seminal theme, like Pound's, was experience, experience of the literary work. Classroom schemata did not incorporate experience. The critic, Harvard had taught him, sets facts in order, historical facts. No, Eliot rejoined, quoting Remy de Gourmont, the literary critic's job is to start from the impressions literature makes on him, and to erect those experiences into something like a structure of laws. Appealing to experience, he and Pound seemed mavericks. In this respect their story is much like the story of Fuller's disdain for mathematical postulates. When Fuller first heard a teacher discourse of the cube, he wanted to know how long it had been there and how warm it was, and was reproved for impertinence.

The difference between the literary and the mathematical maverick stems from the fact that literature offers experience to anyone who will heed it. Great talent may therefore survive classrooms, and even profit by what classrooms impart; *Hamlet,* the *Divine Comedy,* will still be there after graduation day, summoning attention. But the experiences mathematics proposes to set in order are easier to disregard and more difficult to heed, lost as they are in the subject's prehistory, obliterated under the majestic structure of deductions from postulates no one can any longer have the experience of making. To postulate a dimensionless point was daring once; mathematics forgets that daring. Bucky was perhaps lucky not to know how daring it was to be pondering the equilibrated thrusts his little wooden models contained.

FOUR

Modeling the Universe

Something to astonish, made of sticks and wires. Here's one of the sticks. It has a little piece of wire fastened through its middle. It also has a little screw eye at each end, to attach things to. We have thirty of these ready.

Next we can join two of them together, using (screw eye to screw eye) the wire that passes through a third. We can hold the outside sticks and watch the middle stick dangle. Nothing remarkable yet.

Next stage: We can keep this up till we have a closed loop of five, a pentagon, with a dangler at each joint. If we had enough hands, we could hold the pentagon upright, as in the picture, while doing things to it. Since we haven't, the picture idealizes what is really a floppy mess.

On. Let's use the dangler at the top of the picture to start a second pentagon. It will cross the first one again at the bottom, and can be hitched there, using the piece of wire that's hanging available. We now have two intersecting pentagons, like a pair of great circles on a globe. At least that's the idea. In front of us, on the worktable, the mess is getting floppier and more complicated.

Keep this up, completing great circles. In the diagram you see the general pattern we're aiming for. As more and more sticks get wired in, we have to be extra careful about what goes where.*

And, surprise! Just when the confusion verges on hopelessness, it's as though unexpected forces were suddenly released. It's like a physical encounter with synergy. For no clear reason, the contraption mounts up off the table and starts to support itself. The last struts don't fall into place, you press them into place, against hidden powers. And when the last joint is wired fast, a queer kind of spiky sphere stands free in space.

Bucky Fuller, who invented this in the early 1950's,† calls it a *Tensegrity Sphere:* tensional integrity. No stick comes anywhere near touching another stick. Really there's no sphere there, no continuous surface: just a connectedness, alternately wire and stick, enclosing empty space, and penetrated moreover by empty spaces, roughly pentagonal or roughly triangular. Look at a pentagon edgewise, and the pentagonal alignments dissolve into a jumble of unrelated sticks. (The Big Dipper in the sky would also disintegrate if we could inspect it from another part of the universe.)

A bee might pass right through, or a canary; not a partridge. (And you understand how a balloon's meshwork traps molecules of air, too large to pass through the holes.)

Everything seems to be hanging from everything else. Common sense says it ought to collapse in a jumble. It doesn't. And look near the bottom: are those sticks hanging *up?* One man stared at it hard for five minutes, and christened it The Suspension of Disbelief. It seems hardly a *thing.* It's a whole system, its behavior utterly unpredicted

* For construction details see page 321.

† An associate named Lee Hogden seems to have made the first one. Rubens in the same way supplied the vision for pictures he signed though apprentices painted them.

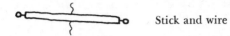 Stick and wire

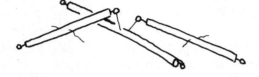 Two sticks joined
by a third

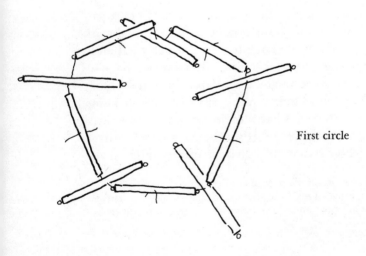 First circle

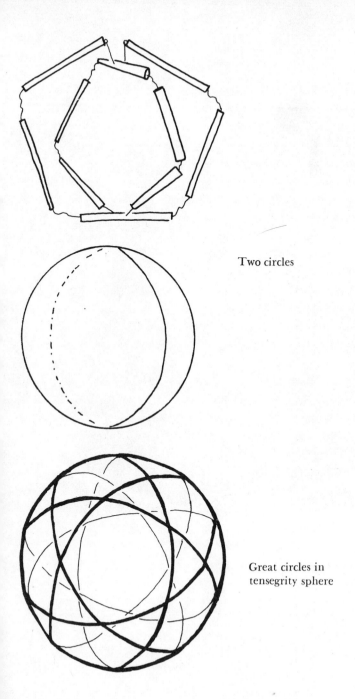

Two circles

Great circles in
tensegrity sphere

Tensegrity sphère (*William Acker*)

by its parts, and as dramatic an example of synergy as we are likely to find.

Magic, obviously. Everyone wants to touch it, and is afraid to. It looks about as stable as a cardhouse. Yes, it's quite safe to touch it. In fact, pick it up and even squeeze it. It's not the least bit delicate. Between the hands it yields like a rubber ball, and pops firmly out again. A really determined squeezer would break something, a wire or a stick, but short of that you won't damage it.

One's intuition is that a wire would break first, one of those gossamer wires. But another invisible synergy is at our disposal, the tensile strength of metals. From a metallurgical catalogue it would be easy to specify wires stronger than the sticks. And then stronger sticks, of metal tubing possibly. And better fastening than twisted wire affords. Any force we are likely to apply, a good engineer could defeat by specifying components and details. His attention would be on components—wires, struts, fastenings—not at all on the system, which is simply invulnerable. Yet at first glance it was precisely the *system* that looked so precarious. Not at all. Things break. The system abides.

The Tensegrity Sphere is a remarkable discovery, in many ways Buckminster Fuller's most profound. Not that it has yet been put to practical use, our conceptions of practicality lagging in a different order of experience.* The U.S. Patent (#3,063,521) which describes its principles contains the remark that a fine enough tensegrity meshwork, spun from billions of ultralight components, could vault over whole cities. It would be perceptible only as a faint darkening of the sky. In 1965, Bucky described an "Octa Spinner" to mass-produce the weave.

Getting oriented to this object takes a while. It seems to be posing a question you're not sure how to formulate. "Why doesn't everything fall?" is a first approximation. We may learn part of the answer by unfastening one wire

* As we'll see, the Geodesic Domes do use this principle, though less showily.

from one screw eye. The stick we've freed doesn't fall, it springs *outward,* and everything nearby relaxes a bit. When we press the freed stick back where it belongs, our fingers encounter a powerful springy force, all the tension on all the other sticks, each flexing slightly like a little bow. Bow and bowstring, that's a partial analogy. It helps us grasp the kind of force we're dealing with.*

But each bow is another bow's arrow, and no archer in sight. Intuition still says it ought to collapse.

So we'd better ask what's guiding intuition. Obviously, some notion we've never formulated, about what makes structures stable. A notion we've never formulated is apt to be called "common sense," and common sense tends to forget about *tension* (pull), attributing stability to *compression* (push). A stack of bricks or blocks is in compression; every child knows that at a certain height it gets unstable and every adult tends to suppress this knowledge, adults having access to nails, spikes, brute-force fastening devices. Even Maria Montessori omitted tension from her inventory of fundamental experiences. A porch swing hangs, and seems frivolous; what we'll *trust* is a platform rocker. This may be because tension networks, however strong, have no shape unless they are stressed, and common sense is comfortable only when shape inheres. This "common sense" is a conditioned reflex which we mistake for insight into the universe.

Chains, wires, ropes, tension elements, can only *pull taut.* They have no other useful property. Since all the wires in the Tensegrity Sphere are taut, everything is being pulled. Since the direction of the wires seems to

---

* The sticks bend because they are members of the tension network, this particular sphere being somewhat degenerate. I chose it because it's easy to construct. In the mature Tensegrity Spheres the wire network is continuous, and the struts receive no bending loads. They have nothing to do but hold nodes of the mesh apart: pure compression afloat in pure tension.

make no difference, the important pull isn't gravity. (That's part of our trouble. When we see a tight wire, we think, "weight.") Forces are pulling outward, away from the center, trying to pull the structure apart. Counterforces are restraining them. The interplay between force and restraint settles into a spherical pattern.

The same is true of a balloon. The expansive forces that are trying to burst it meet the restraining network in the rubber envelope. The equilibrium between explosion and restraint is spherical, pretty nearly.

A balloon is a successful restraint of an explosion.

This covers much of Fuller's sense of things. His most important model for reality is *energy radiating from a center, and being restrained.* (The center may be just a point of reference. In our Tensegrity Sphere there is nothing important happening at the center. The action is around the periphery.)

Stubborn folk, having grasped all this, still feel it works against nature. One man called it an insult to God. Bucky gives us the theme to remember: "I cannot do anything nature does not permit." Since the Tensegrity Sphere exists in the natural world, it's our sense of nature that we'd better rethink. The conviction that its pieces ought to fall down rests on a conditioned reflex as old as Aristotle, who thought that "down" was the place for heavy things.

When Aristotle's concept of "heavy" and "light" is expounded, every science student smiles. Poor deluded old Greek! Nevertheless that concept sleeps in the student. Only he does not know it as a concept of "weight." It lives within him as a concept of "down."

"I don't know why I am talking to you," said Bucky, "because you are all so ignorant." He was trailing his coat before a roomful of scientists. Their ignorance consisted in knowing that the earth rotates, and yet saying that the sun rises and sets; also in knowing that the earth is spherical, and yet speaking the flat-earth words "up" and "down." ("How are things down there?" the astronaut over Australia asked the Controllers in Houston, his words contradicting everything he knew.) Since the learned consensus about the spherical earth dates from the fifteenth century, the learned "have had 500 years to organize themselves in relation to their fundamental information and have done nothing about it." Men's conditioned reflexes may lag half a millennium behind what they know.

It is not the experience of being alive in one's body that conditions those reflexes, it is the ease with which we learn words. Words have been a preoccupation of Bucky's since his 1927 crisis, when legend has him keeping silent till he'd learned how to talk sense. (It took some two years.) In 1932, when C. K. Ogden had just reduced the English vocabulary to 850 molecules, called Basic English, Bucky's magazine, *Shelter,* immediately featured the system, no doubt to subscribers' bewilderment. And Korzybski's General Semantics, demarking the word from the thing, the map from the territory, appealed to Bucky as soon as he heard of it.

Body-knowledge, being exquisitely complex experience, is by definition never wrong, though our minds can misinterpret it. Bucky claims he can feel the earth's spin with his body. "At Bear Island I drink a great deal of tea, so at night I have to go outside a lot. And standing there facing the Pole Star, seeing how the horizon since my last visit has blotted some stars and uncovered others, I can orient myself and feel the earth turn, slowly, like the hour hand of a clock." That turning earth uncovers and covers the sun; *sunsight* is the morning word, its fellow *sunclipse.*

"*Eclipse,*" said a philologist, "an abandonment, a dropping out. So *sunclipse,* when the sun goes into hiding?"

"Is hidden," Bucky corrected.

"You will teach me accuracy yet."

In the same way, the body-knowledge of aviators teaches them that they go *out* and *in: out* in any direction, an omnidirectional word; *in* to home, a concentering word, a locator. Though opposite in feeling, they are not really opposites. The universe contains no mirror images, as according to Bucky the Nobel committee attested when it awarded the 1963 Physics prize for the overthrow of "parity." So one has reason to be suspicious of those mirror-image words *up* and *down*. Fliers, avoiding these words, intuitively say "in" and "out," and Bucky wishes the rest of us did too. This is one theme the Tensegrity Sphere forces on us.

"Why doesn't it fall down?" is a meaningless question. The question we can answer is why struts don't fall *in* or fall *out,* which is what they are trying to do. *In* and *out* are the relevant directions, not *up* and *down*. This is one way of saying that the tensional forces running through the sphere are so powerful we can forget about earth's gravity. The system doesn't use earth's gravity; weightless in deep space, it would behave just as it does here.

Tensional forces, applied through the little sling at the middle of each stick, are pulling the stick *out*. It would fly out except for the tensional forces applied to its ends, which are holding it *in*. When you tighten the wires the thing gets larger, not smaller, which is perhaps its most unnerving bit of behavior.

In a whole system the directions are always *out* and *in*. When we gain an inkling of this fact we may grasp why the words "up" and "down" annoy Bucky.

Those tensional forces are strong and stable. To rupture them we have to break sticks, or break wires: which means that the network which holds our tensegrity sphere is modeled in the tensile strength of the wires, the cohesive forces that bind the wood of the sticks. These are, when we come right down to it, intermolecular bonds. That's what the system harnesses, chemical bonds.

To be quite clear about this, take a few minutes off and build the Great Pyramid, in your mind of course. You do this by hoisting great stone blocks outward against earth's gravity till they clear the blocks below them, and then sliding them into place. They settle where you put them, pulled snugly against other stones by earth's gravity, a pervasive in-pulling field.

Inside that field the pyramid is stable, and has been stable for millennia. The field is wholly indifferent to the pyramid; its tug is on the separate stones. Occasionally a corner of stone erodes loose from the system, and gravity, feeling no responsibility for the system, tugs the loose pieces to the desert floor. If you could flip the pyramid over onto its apex, the same gravity which had been holding it together would instantly pull it apart. If you could move it away from earth's gravity, out somewhere in the direction of the moon, its uncohered stones would gradually drift in separate directions.

This means that the pyramid, standing there near Gizeh, is not a Whole System. It depends for its cohesive integrity on a force that is not part of it, a strong reliable force but extraneous to the pyramid. A complete balance sheet would show "materials" and "gravity." The denser the materials, the more massive the stones, the more gravity's effect. Mortar will keep stones from slipping, but will not support them. Only other stones will support them, and only when gravity pulls load against support. That is why, for so many thousands of years, *weight* has meant *strength*.

*   *   *

Gravity pulls inward toward a center, like the wire sling that pulls each stick toward the center of the Tensegrity Sphere. Other wires are pulling each stick outward, and the system of pulls is in delicate equilibrium. There's nothing delicate about the pulls, but the equilibrium is delicate, and the system responds to disturbances by trembling slightly. Pick it up, it elongates minutely, gravity pulling the system away from your hand. Set it down, it spreads and flattens minutely, gravity squashing it toward the table. At the instant of changeover a tremor of rearrangement spreads through all the sticks and slings as they regroup to accommodate the new vectors of stress.

Like the Tensegrity Sphere's two-way pull, forces in the great world counter gravitational forces, else the universe would gather into a point. One countering force in the universe is centrifugal: the force you can feel pressing water against the bottom of a bucket, if you swing it round and round at the end of a rope. These two forces in balance keep a satellite in orbit. These two forces in balance cohere the solar system, the outward plunge of planets in equilibrium with the inner tug of solar gravity. The planets neither escape nor fall into the sun. That's another restrained explosion.

In the solar system as in the Tensegrity Sphere, the operative forces are strong and reliable but their equilibrium pulsates a little. That is why the planetary orbits are not circular, as everyone assumed for so long, but elliptical. Now they move further from the sun, now they are dragged closer: it's like a tensegrity trembling. And while the system never settles down into circularity, its way of not settling down is so regular we can plot the track of Mars and obtain an ellipse, which is like a circle vacillating between two centers.

*   *   *

Though equilibria pulsate, their norm is stable. Nothing in man's experience is as stable as "sea level," a norm to which we refer the heights of mountains. Ancient wisdom says "water seeks its own level." Yet sea level is a mathematical average, pulsing twice daily with the tides and moment to moment with the passing waves. Wave motion, that is what ripples the surface of the Tensegrity Sphere, just as it ripples the liquid surface of the earth. (And the solid surface too; a seismograph trace is never still.) The pattern called "wave" sweeps along the ocean's face, but the molecules of water move in and out, only in and out, in toward earth's center and away again. (So do the tensegrity struts.) It is the ordered succession of these movements we see as a wave.

Offshore, a mass of submarine kelp rides on its little pneumatic floats, in buoyant equilibrium, lifted and dropped by the vast heave of passing waves, yet not swept shoreward until a storm drags it there. Down the wave's face planes a surfer, in toward earth's center, always toward earth's center as he glides obliquely along the wave, yet no more lessening his distance from earth's center than a planet lessens its distance from the sun, till he runs out of wave and is beached. "I seem to have been only like a boy playing on the seashore," said Isaac Newton, "diverting myself in now and then finding a smoother pebble or a prettier shell than ordinary." Bucky Fuller on the Malibu shore in December stoops to collect a stone worn by aeons' pounding. "A truncated tetrahedron," he remarks. It is. Most of them are. He tosses it seaward, and a set of airborne waves brings our ears a *plop*, while a slower set radiates on the heaving swell. A great wave obliterates it. "Yet it had an integrity of its own.

"The wave is not the water. The water told you about the wave going by. But the wave has a patterned integrity of its own—absolutely weightless.

"Just really great," he marvels. "Every wave in the universe has its own integrity.

"And look at all this whiteness and all those bubbles. Beautiful, beautiful bubbles, every one of them. They tell you spheres use *pi,* and *pi* is irrational. 3.14159 . . . , and on goes the number. Every time nature is making one of those bubbles, to how many places did she carry out *pi* before she discovered you can't resolve it, and at what point does nature decide to make a fake bubble?"

(Having no curved surface, the Tensegrity Sphere is not even described by *pi,* let alone generated by *pi.*)

"Nature has formed relationships that are just to me unbelievably magnificent."

The surfer out on his wave—"a neat matching of rates" —is "spending his gravitational advantage" yet never approaching earth's center, trading gravitational advantage against the outward motion of water molecules.

"Spending is a fallacy. Nothing is spent in Universe."

With strength, luck and skill he could surf clear across the Pacific, always spending his gravitational advantage yet nothing he spends ever spent, for he would never reach the low point of the wave. It is steadily regenerated beneath him. He moves *in;* at the same rate exactly, water molecules move *out.* "His pattern of movement, along the face of the wave, is at ninety degrees to the lines of in-and-out action. That's called *precession.* A gyroscope uses it. Press down on a gyroscope's rim. It tips away 90 degrees from where you press it." Likewise the "centrifugal" tug on your arm when you whirl a weight is at 90 degrees to the weight's circular track. It vanishes the instant you let go, and the weight instead of flying outward goes "off on a tangent." And the planets' effort, which gravity restrains, is not to move outward from the sun, but laterally. That outward pull is precessional. The solar system precesses. Modeling it, under Arctic ice, a spinning gyrocompass' precession registered changes of course, guiding the *Nautilus* with exquisite accuracy through hours of darkness. Bucky still cites with pride his exposition of precession to the readers of the Sperry Gyroscope story in *Fortune,* as long ago as 1940.

The surfer's body understands the universe better than does his mind, which is programmed with *up* and *down* and with worries about *spending.* Black in his rubber wet-suit, he plods ashore unaware. Bucky's mind is on another tensegrity, the air-ocean's tensional force drawing the sea-ocean's wave-tops into cresting curls of spindrift, which move—precessionally—at 90 degrees to the drag, sidewise along the wave-tops. Nature models all principles. Years previously—1956—his mind leaped from surfers and spindrift to porpoises:

> and porpoises are the royal protagonists
> of the synergetic precessional surfboarding realms
> for porpoises employ and enjoy
> these purely abstract and integratable principles
> as they languidly, almost effortlessly coast
> in lovemaking couples
> around the cresting waveslopes encompassing earth.

At home in the forces they "employ and enjoy," porpoises presumably know nothing of precession, of tensegrity, of wave propagation and patterned integrities. That is the human mind's unique function, to extract principles. A man, not nature, designed the Tensegrity Sphere, which models so much of nature.

"I'm not trying to imitate Nature, I'm trying to find the principles she's using."

"Islands of compression"—like those sticks—"in a non-simultaneous universe of tension"—like that net of wires: that's apparently Nature's way when she has "very large jobs to do, such as cohering the universe or the solar system." Or ourselves, for that matter.

Or a tree, in which compressional spheroids of water—nothing that we know is as incompressible as water—are packaged in a "cellulose tension network," whose flexing allows limbs to bend while the liquid globules keep them from collapsing. (Nothing in his repertoire is more wonderful than Bucky's exposition of a tree. Talking faster and faster, arms spread, he becomes the tree, heaving his chest, arms in wave-motion as the tensional fibers hold tons of outspread limb in undulant equilibrium. For anyone who sees it, no tree will ever be a "thing" again.)

And Jell-O, trembling, is a molecular tensegrity.

Countering all our intuitions by not collapsing, that Tensegrity Sphere is not after all more marvelous than the universe it models: empty space, mostly, through which energy events are oscillating with so repetitive an equilibrium our senses can tune them. One kind of energy event is vibrating 600,000,000,000,000 times per second; and we are so constituted that when this kind of event solicits the retinal structures of our eyes we perceive "blue light." Another kind, pulsating 261 cycles per second, is registered by our ears as "Middle C." The stable pulsing of molecules against the molecules in a fingertip is likewise registered, through electrified nerve ends, as "solid table." *We*, so far as our senses go, are a network of responses to pulsations. Amid this network, unlocatable, the phantom captain is constantly monitoring, intuiting, guessing, deciding, willing.

When Lieut. R. B. Fuller, U.S.N., was consorting with Navy captains, a small ship under his command was put at the disposal of Lee De Forest, whose recent invention of the triode vacuum tube had made the Navy wonder if its planes might now talk to its ships. Since the primitive tubes had little "gain" to deliver, De Forest had recourse to *regeneration,* a strategy for getting more boost out of the tube by passing the signal through it more than once.

In practice this was so ticklish an operation that regenerative receivers are no longer met with. Currents tended to flywheel pell-mell around the system, and the operator jerked the headphone from his ears to avoid being deafened by a self-sustaining howl. A burp of static could initiate this howl. Chasing its amplified image round and round, it discovered a resonance at which it could cycle comfortably, each pulse from the output presented again at the input exactly in time to catch the system off balance.

What plagued De Forest seems to have fascinated Bucky, whose writings are filled with the word *regenerative.* The sky out over the Atlantic pulsed with lurches of electromagnetism: pure invisible principle, its patterns so large-scale one might loosely call them random. But sweep the skies, funnel those randomnesses into the regenerative receiver the technician was struggling with, let the flywheel effect but commence, and the earphones are filled with a sustained banshee tone, stable in pitch, stable in loudness, and "permanent" until something breaks down or a plug is pulled. It corresponds to no sound locatable "out there." Rather, regeneration has so organized energy that the ear receives sustained stimuli as physical as a steel block.

It is in just this way that "things" make themselves known, when they are presented to hearing or sight or touch. They are patterns of recurrence, patterned solicitations of the senses: light interfered with steadfastly, for the eye to detect as a colored surface, or the fingers bom-

barded just here (not over here) so that they report contact
with something "solid." These stimuli are our experienced
reality. They interact so reliably that we speak of in-
habiting a world of "things."

But these "things" are regenerative patterns, like that
steady howl in the ship's radio shack, and when common
sense speaks of the fundamental nuclear *particles* of the
iron atom, constituting a bar of iron we can see and touch,
the knowing mind should think accurately, as it knows
how to, of "purely regenerative abstract principles," in-
substantialities, but sustained.

> and the predominantly associative resultants
> of self-interference patternings
> which precessionally regenerate as almost exclusively
> inwardly shunting chordal patternings
> of systems of periodic self-interference
> are known to man's "common sensing"
> in superficial, solid-thing-apprehending terms
> as the "basic building blocks of universe"—
> the "chemical elements"

—though these elements are not "blocks" but pure knottings of energy. How the mind does run on blocks, when
it designs houses of blocks! But the Tensegrity Sphere has
no blocks.

It has not even palpable sphericity: no curved lines,
and no surface whatever. Only our Platonizing minds say
"sphere." It is an ordered system of Energy Events, and
these energies at least are palpable. You can locate them
by applying a fingertip and sensing the yield and recoil.
Energy (what else?) is pulling all those wires taut. The
same energy is holding those sticks in place, and you can
see it restore them to place when they are disrupted.

Since it trembles, "place" is an average, which resembles what we are told about atoms in a molecule, never *exactly* located from instant to instant. What is stable, in this closed system, is the sum of forces. The forces have not only intensities, they have lengths: the force along a wire reaches from anchor point to anchor point, just the length of the wire.

Lines of definite length and direction, which do not go on to infinity because they represent forces, are called *vectors,* a key word in Bucky Fuller's scheme of things. In the Navy Academy classrooms, in 1917, they drew vector diagrams, modeled on a procedure of Galileo's, to represent what happens when two ships collide. Each line's direction represents a ship's direction. Each line's length represents its ship's momentum, made up of two realities, its speed and its weight. Where the lines meet the ships will meet.

Complete the parallelogram, draw its diagonal, extend the diagonal by its own length, and the extended line is supposed to show what happens next: the speed and mass of the two ships being violently united, they "waltz gayly north-north-east twelve miles together," and drift to a halt where that vector comes to an end, all passion spent.

Bucky, as usual, protested that this was idealized. One ship, we don't know which, will likely plunge toward earth's center with a hole in its bow, and we can't be sure what will happen to the other. Anyway it will glide a good deal less than twelve miles: perhaps a few yards.

The direction toward the sea-bottom isn't in the diagram. Nor is the direction outward from the center of the earth, which is the direction both ships are trying to pursue as they accelerate. If they speed fast enough they will go "off on a tangent," into orbit. When they collide, their combined momentum lifts their bows outward against gravity, absorbing most of the energy in one mighty heave. Then the survivor drifts "downhill" a few yards. The real vectorial diagram is tetrahedonal.

So much for plane geometry, which we teach beginners because it's simple and easy. It excludes important energetic realities even when it claims to be mapping energies, and for Bucky the effort to ignore the excluded realities was much more difficult than the geometry, which therefore seemed to him not simple at all but a highly specialized case of "pure mathematics," i.e., an idealized fraud. "Plane geometry is the most special case of 'not true at all.' "

Nevertheless there was nothing wrong with vectors, if you drew the right ones. They were very nice lines, he thought, because they didn't "go on absurdly forever to the nowhere of two infinities." They literally didn't have time. Time determines a vector's length: the time it takes an energy event to happen.

"I wondered if nature might have a set of omnidirectionally operative vectors that represented all our experiences."

I wondered, in short, if everything might be modelable.

"Vectors are like *spears*. I could 'massage' any object into a spear shape, point and thrust-throw it in a discrete direction. I intuitively liked those directional vector 'spears.' I felt that they tended at least to embody all the energetic qualities of represented experiences."

Since we've been experiencing the Tensegrity Sphere, we might try our hand at a vector diagram. It will have to represent the way everything is trying to escape from the system, and is being exactly restrained. On page 108 some vectors head outward. I could have drawn more, but

Ships

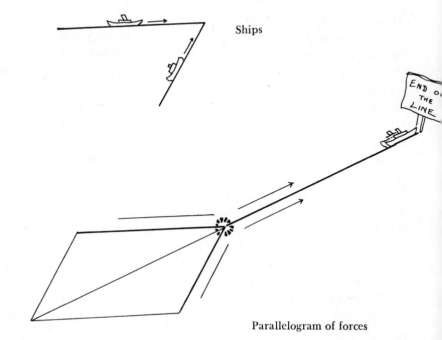

Parallelogram of forces

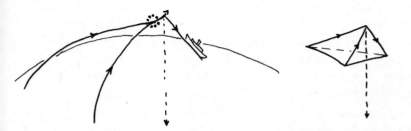

Tetrahedron of forces

twelve seems to be the right number. If you turn the sphere around and look at it, you see that its symmetry repeats twelve times, around twelve pentagonal arrays, so a vector running toward each of these will represent the out-thrusts.

Now bind these vectors together with in-closing hoops, and what we get doesn't look like the Tensegrity Sphere but does map its equilibrium of forces. We've drawn twenty-four lines to make the in-closing network, and if it weren't for the perspective flat paper imposes, you could check that each of them is the same length exactly as the spears that radiate out. Same-length lines mean the forces balance, which is correct: the Tensegrity Sphere neither explodes nor collapses. We can call this figure a *vector equilibrium,* and take note that nothing will turn up more often in Fuller's model of the Universe. Since most things are neither exploding nor collapsing, the vector equilibrium will model any of them: a football, a cat, a parked Volkswagen, what have you.

Lines mapping energies led Fuller to his energetic triangles, in which the three lines are not just lying there but are busy stabilizing the angles opposite them. We can see this if we put a triangular truss under a roof, and rely on its lower side to keep the roof from collapsing. (The triangle has six events: three compression sides, three tension angles.)

Energetic tetrahedra also map forces. They bear weight: their own at least, or perhaps that of a camera on a tripod. They map forces in the real world, and include the direction the unlucky ship took to Davy Jones' Locker.

If all the sides and all the angles are the same, all the forces a tetrahedron represents are equal. If we wanted to represent stable energies thrusting through space in all directions, we might try to do it by filling up the space

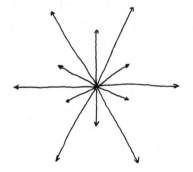
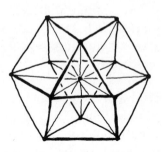

Two radiating vectors   Vector equilibrium

with tetrahedra. But we find we can't, because octahedral gaps turn up between them. We can fill as much space as we like with octahedra and tetrahedra alternating: we are back in a Milton, Massachusetts, kindergarten, 1899, and have discovered the *Octet Truss*. It's easy to model, maddening to draw. Yet anyone can draw a cubical lattice, which fact is as cogent an explanation as we may need for our intuitive recourse to cubical models.

Still, cubes are appealingly symmetrical. It would be pleasant if the oc-tet structure disclosed some module symmetrical in all directions the way cubes are. If we go into it and explore we shall find one. It's the vector equilibrium again. Any node in the Octet Truss lattice is the center of one: a point from which twelve vectors radiate into rings of restraint. That's where the Octet Truss gets its great strength: every stress is dissipated twelve ways, and caught in those rings.

So we come back to his interest in equilibrated explosions, like balloons which are trying to burst and also trying to shrink, and strike a spherical balance. You can

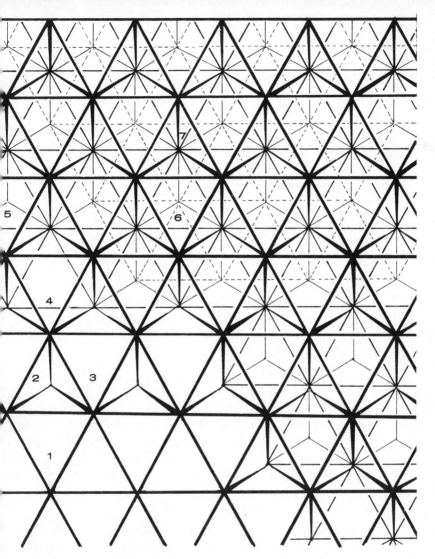

The Coordinate System of Nature, alias Octet Truss. Thickest lines are elements nearest you and (despite effect of perspective) all members are the same length. Start at bottom left. 1. First-level triangular grid. 2. Tetrahedra, pointing away from you, with octahedra (3) appearing between them. 4. Second-level grid joins tips of tetrahedra. 5. Next array of tetrahedra. 6. Dotted lines show third-level grid. This can be continued indefinitely. Twelve-way vertices (7) in second level are centers of vector equilibria.

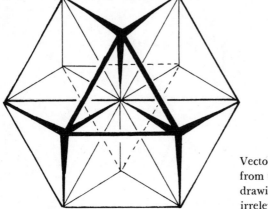

Vector equilibrium extracted
from the grid in previous
drawing, and shown with
irrelevances omitted.

see that a vector equilibrium would make a sort of stress
diagram of a balloon. Its four crisscrossing hexagonal rings
represent the tensile skin, restraining twelve different outward thrusts that represent the compressed air. And we've
seen that if you filled up your room with an Octet Truss
latticework, every junction point would have twelve rods
radiating from it, restrained by the rings of a surrounding
vector equilibrium. Energy radiating along those rods
would collide with the energies radiated from neighbor-
ing junction points. The vector equilibrium around each
point models the resulting pattern of restraint, and the
Octet Truss lattice, extending in all directions, models the
whole system's equilibrium.

Standing inside it, you would know what it feels like
to be inside a bar of some idealized metal, watching the
attractive and repulsive forces between all the atoms equilibrate. (It's idealized because atoms themselves are complicated; but copper or gold will come pretty close.) Each
atom, in this model, is surrounded by twelve others, restraining it. Each atom occupies a junction point in an
invisible Octet Truss. Held in place, they cause us to say
that the metal is stable, massive. If the attracting forces

could be cut like tension wires, the energy (E) locked into that mass (m) would radiate at enormous speed (c²).

The knot we have heard Bucky talking about models the same kind of phenomenon: a self-interfering pattern of energy and restraint. The more you tighten a knot, the harder it resists tightening.

So "matter" itself is a contained explosion, and the vector equilibrium is its austerest image. *I* am a contained explosion. So is my thought. So is my cat. So is a star, from which radiation streams out, but not faster than it is generated. None of these *looks* in the least like a vector equilibrium, but it models these energy systems.

It is not chosen by accident. No other model is possible. It's true that a cubical lattice will fill all space, like the boxes in a warehouse, but it won't give us equilibria outward from centers. If along each edge we have a force of 1, then from center to corner the force is $\frac{1}{2}\sqrt{2}$, which seems meaningless as a description of real events. You can't have an unresolvable fraction of an energy event, and $\sqrt{2}$ is unresolvable.

Since the model has exactly twelve outward vectors, you will not be surprised when symmetrical enclosures have something to do with twelve. Bucky's Geodesic Domes are sliced from spheres with twelve key points, which stand out amid the intricate array because the eye can pick out pentagons surrounding them. All the other configurations are hexagonal. If you turn back to page 42 you'll see the pentagon where the five big triangles join. A complete sphere would disclose twelve of these.

When he made his Dymaxion Map in about 1940, he modeled Spaceship Earth as a vector equilibrium, and projected the continents and oceans onto its squares and triangles. Sure enough, if you fitted the thing together, you found twelve points of intersection, symmetrically

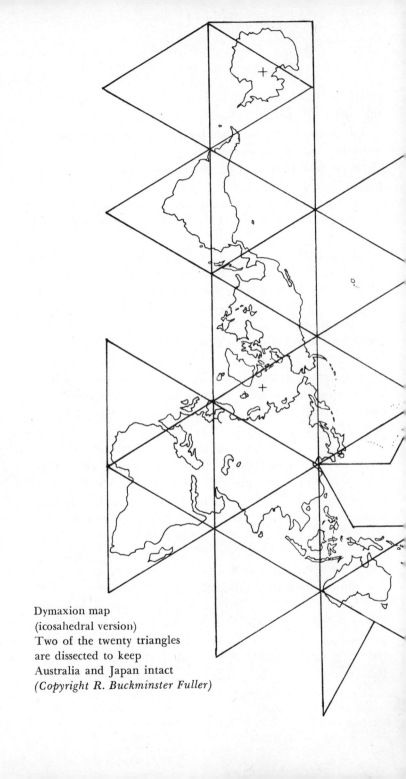

Dymaxion map
(icosahedral version)
Two of the twenty triangles
are dissected to keep
Australia and Japan intact
(Copyright R. Buckminster Fuller)

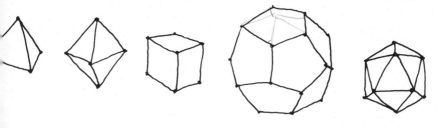

The five platonic solids

spaced. Current versions of the map use the icosahedron instead. Its jigsaw puzzle uses six more components, but it has the advantage of yielding identical pieces, all triangular. And it still has twelve gathering points.

Bucky was so enchanted with the vector equilibrium that he called it by his copyright name, Dymaxion. Later he had second thoughts about egotism. Anyway, he was not the first to gaze on it. Under the name cuboctahedron, it has been around since Archimedes' time. We find it officially listed among the Archimedean Solids, a collection of miscegenated objects whose equal edges surround faces or angles of more than one kind. This fact chilled the Greek imagination. Greek connoisseurship singled out the Platonic Solids, five aristocrats that flaunt perfect equality everywhere: equal edges, equal angles, equal faces: the tetrahedron, the octahedron, the cube, the dodecahedron, the icosahedron. But the cuboctahedron presents both six squares, like a cube, and eight triangles, like an octahedron, and in Plato's Republic it is obviously a second-class citizen.

Yet it has extraordinary qualities. Bucky enjoys showing us how it will fold up, if we make it with rubber joints. He sets one triangle on the tabletop, and holds the top triangle in his hand, and lowers it. Immediately the rest of the system commences twisting. It twists a little till its vertices occupy just the position in space of an icosa-

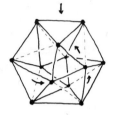

Vector equilibrium folding to octahedron

hedron's vertices; "and I keep lowering, lower, lower, and suddenly it becomes the octahedron." It does indeed, a perfect octahedron, and all the sides are doubled.

He pulls it up again, to the vector equilibrium configuration, and invites us to imagine its vertices as a huge star group, majestically symmetrical, revolving in space; and "suppose another great star group made a mass attrac-

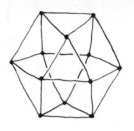

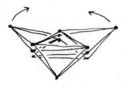

Vector equilibrium folding to tetrahedron

tion, and simply retarded this thing, then it would be forced to contract." And the edge drag from the second great star group interferes with its orderly progress toward the octahedronal stage; it folds in a more complex manner; and behold, the tetrahedron! The edges are aligned in fours; "all the vectors are fourfold."

"This is the way we go from carbon, which is relatively

lightweight and soft, down to the very hard diamond—by getting down into the doubling-up of the vectors of the edges."

No boy's concentration on an electric train was ever more intent. "Now we'll unwind again, up we come, back again to our friend the vector equilibrium. Sometimes it's called the jitterbug. Pumping, pumping, but the center is not twisting. So the whole system is contracting symmetrically. All twelve points approach the center at a symmetrical rate."

We are to think of pressure on the roof of a building. "You're used to the idea of the building flattening." (Cubical buildings flatten.) "But you put pressure on the top here, it means that the whole building contracts symmetrically." (Geodesic Domes do that.)

"The vector equilibrium contains the whole phenomenology of the universe. The vector equilibrium is never witnessed by man. It is as pure as God. It is truth which is approached; it is exactitude that is approached."

When he spoke of the forms of carbon, the graphite crystal and the diamond crystal (which every schoolboy knows are chemically identical) he had in mind another route by which the vector equilibrium may be approached: the closest packing of spheres. In classrooms atoms are often modeled by spheres, and in 1883 an Englishman named Barlow proposed that the ways they pack might underlie the geometry of crystals. Ping-pong balls make good models, and there was a time when Bucky Fuller lived surrounded by ping-pong balls. The aluminum trailer he took to lectures in those days seemed full of them. He would stack four and demonstrate the invisible tetrahedron whose vertices are their centers, and then point out that when spheres are piled high, like oranges in a

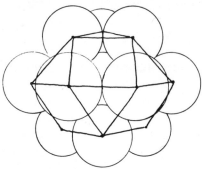

Spheres packed as vector equilibrium

grocer's bin, the array "goes on triangulating in all directions," which suggests the Octet Truss. Sure enough, if we
take three layers we can find the vector equilibrium,*
which suggests that it may have something to do with
atoms when they nestle in closest proximity.

In fact, this is the minimum symmetrical array we can
build around a center: twelve balls, all touching every
neighbor and touching the center ball also. If you could
make the center ball disappear, the remaining twelve
would shift slightly, like Bucky's "jitterbug" commencing
its collapsing act, and an icosahedron would join their
centers. If six of the twelve balls each absorbed one neighbor, the octahedron would result.

So the vector equilibrium, *né* cuboctahedron, stands
out among the Archimedean Solids. As to why the Greeks
didn't make more of it, the obvious explanation is that
the total symmetries of the Platonic Solids infatuated
them. The word *solid is* perhaps another clue. If you think

* Though not if we rotate the top layer so that its balls lie above the
balls in the bottom layer, instead of above the spaces between them. In
that case we won't get the vector equilibrium but another square-and-
triangle construction. Bucky seems to brush this aside as an unimportant
variant, but when a chemist expounds spherical packing he dwells on
the choice you make as you commence that third layer. One option—
Bucky's—yields "cubical close-packing," the other "hexagonal." Both are
oc-tet coordinated.

of the cuboctahedron as solid, you concentrate on its surface, where the irregularity strikes your eye, and dismiss its interior as a featureless putty. So you won't reflect that it has a natural center, and that the vectors radiating from the center are exactly equal to the vectors that bound the faces. No other structure in space can make this claim.

For that matter, if you're a Greek you won't think in vectors. Vectors map events; Greek geometry was eventless. Euclid spoke of "points" and "lines."

This is all such fun that we may forget to ask what it may mean. One thing it means is that we can now make a model for energy events distributed uniformly through space. Atoms, might they arrange themselves like the intersections of an Octet Truss? Atoms are energy events, united by energetic bonds; the oc-tet, with its minimal and uniform distances, would be the most economical and stable arrangement.

The fit between reality and Bucky's abstractions seems not to be quite that neat. There is only one kind of oc-tet intersection, with twelve radial vectors to the corners of the vector equilibrium that surrounds it, but there are ninety-two different kinds of atoms. We should not be surprised that the compounds of these atoms are structured in an enormous number of ways. Nevertheless, certain Fulleresque themes recur and recur. Every scrap of living tissue, for example, whether the polio virus or the elephant, contains molecules that are tetrahedronally structured.

That is because living things use carbon compounds, and the carbon atom presents four opportunities for other atoms to attach themselves. In 1874, two chemists independently suggested that these might be tetrahedronal vertices, which was scoffed at as a Pythagorean notion

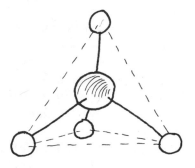

Methane molecule

until evidence grew overwhelming. Thus the methane
molecule, diagrammed on flat paper

$$
\begin{array}{c}
H \\
| \\
H - C - H \\
| \\
H
\end{array}
$$

—carbon and four atoms of hydrogen—is a tetrahedron
with the carbon atom at its center. There are thousands
upon thousands of other carbon compounds, every one
tetrahedronal.

After that, things get complicated. Linus Pauling, the
Columbus of molecular realities, has found tetrahedronal,
octahedronal, icosahedronal structures in profusion, as well
as far more cubes than Bucky prepares us for. A glance at
the diagrams in his *Nature of the Chemical Bond,* or
the beautiful colored drawings in his *Architecture of
Molecules,* discloses tantalizing approximations to Bucky's
a priori system, but little of the neatness of fit Bucky's
audiences may be led to expect. He has none of Pauling's
zest for inconvenient data, numbers that don't fall into
the sequence of integers his dogmatizing calls for, angles
that are skew, unassimilable cubes. His lack of interest in
such data seems radical, and confronting the Platonic
perfection of what he claims is "the coordinate system of

nature," we may wonder what happened to the boy who asked of a classroom cube what it weighed and how hot it was.

Such grit on the interface between theory and data gives him no pause at all. One morning he responded with a pair of maxims: "Don't try to make me consistent. I'm learning all the time"; and "Principles are more of a reality than the qualities they produce."

Notice his phrasing: the principles produce the qualities, not vice versa. The principles are generative forces, like Tension and Compression. They are rather numerous, and they interact. They never produce exceptions to one another—if they had exceptions they wouldn't be principles—but they produce fairly complicated reactions and resultants. In one order alone, the order of energy knotted into mass, they produce not simply "matter," that primal world-stuff minds have lusted after, but ninety-two different regenerative chemical elements. (Why just ninety-two? Bucky thinks he knows. If you keep packing more balls round a vector equilibrium of balls, there will be ninety-two in the third layer.) With so much complexity, so many local principles to equilibrate, you may expect to get many patterns that look like exceptions: local systems like the camel, the aardvark, the cube. Bucky's attitude seems to be that someone else can wrestle with them.

Meanwhile, piecemeal confirmations keep surfacing. About 1963, it turned out that many viruses were icosahedrally configured, and moreover geodesically subdivided, like Fuller domes. The geometer H. S. M. Coxeter summarizes: "In 1955, Fuller built a dome as bachelor officers quarters for the U. S. Air Force in Korea. This seems to be the shape of the REO virus. His 'thirty-one-foot geodesic sphere' at the top of Mount Washington in New Hampshire is like the *herpes* virus and the *varicella* (chicken pox). His U. S. pavilion in Kabul is like *adeno-virus* type 12. His 'radome' on the Arctic DEW line is like *infectious canine hepatitis.*" Geodesics and Tensegrity Spheres are first cousins. The Tensegrity, we have seen, helps us model the very large, and the virologists' correlation with the very small is suggestive. Perhaps nature does use a single system after all.

We can transfer the Tensegrity Sphere to the domain of the very small if we perform an operation on those sticks. The sticks are a little misleading anyhow, their solid appearance concealing the presence of important tensile as well as compressive forces within them. We have only to replace each stick by a linear structure in which tension and compression have in turn been differentiated out.

Such a structure exists: it is called a Tensegrity Mast. The sculptor Kenneth Snelson discovered it when he was a student of Bucky's at Black Mountain College in 1948. It fitted into the Fuller System so patly that a large one was exhibited, with Snelson's name attached, in a Fuller Special at the Museum of Modern Art, in 1959. It climbed up and up like a space-age Indian Rope Trick, evidently suspended from wires which were nevertheless not hanging from anything.

One cell shows how it works. The two V-shaped sticks are held fast in a sling. Points A and B cannot move together (inward) because of circumferential restraints, and cannot move apart (outward) because of the vertical wire. By stacking these cells we can go as far as we please, within the limits of wire strength. Exactly as the Sphere refutes the principles of the Great Pyramid, the Mast refutes the principles of a brick chimney. Unlike a column of bricks, the Tensegrity Mast models all the forces that hold it together, and can be turned on its side or suspended or

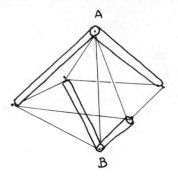

Cell of Tensegrity Mast

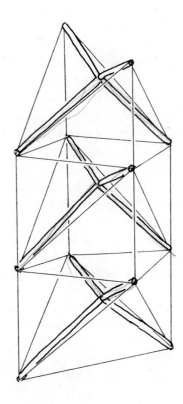

Tensegrity Mast

pointed at the sky. It behaves like a stick, not a brick-pile, and restores itself if you flex it. But whether you pull, push or bend, it is tension you are working against.

Now, suggests Bucky, imagine that each strut of the Tensegrity Sphere is replaced by one of these masts. (This exceeds my model-making skill at least. I don't know if it's ever been tried. Anyway, imagine.) The "solid" sticks are gone, each replaced by a system that is mostly empty space, through which run tensile forces that hold in position little floating islands of compression shaped like children's jacks.

Now remove, one by one, those little jack-shaped islands of compression, and replace them, one by one, with arrays of ultraminiature Tensegrity Masts. The V-jointed compressive members are now very numerous, and also very small indeed. And the percentage of empty space is rising sharply. Next, under a microscope, replace each tiny strut in turn with a Tensegrity Mast yet smaller . . .

No one's fingers are clever enough, but the mind can follow. Finally, under a scanning electron microscope, the last struts would be replaced by the last set of sub-sub-miniature Tensegrity Masts, down at the order of size where we speak of an atom's diameter.

Step by step, before the mind's eye, in stages each one perfectly discrete and conceivable, we have dissociated a wooden stick nine inches long into "the inherent discontinuous compression, tensional integrity of the nonsolid atomic structures themselves." The last tensile wires will be simply the chemical bonds.

As the empty space in the system multiplies, its crisscrossing tensional members also multiply, until they start interfering with the ambient light. The rays that passed through it in the earlier stages are diffracted by many wires as the wires get smaller and closer. Next the rays are absorbed and reflected the way a substance like wood absorbs and reflects. Finally, as we reach the microminiature stage, the assemblage will look "solid": this despite the fact that we're taking solidity out of it. It will feel "solid" too, poked by an inquiring finger. We should not be surprised if it looked and felt rather like a piece of wood. But now we know what to think of wood's "solidity." We can understand too, thinking of those tension bonds, why the wood behaves as it does, flexing and restoring itself.

So the payoff for a lot of work is a synthetic wood. Components, each one too small to be seen or felt, have come, collectively, into our senses' domain. It is not hard to understand that they were perfectly "real" when we couldn't see or feel them. Nevertheless an inherent prejudice, like the one that responds to words like *up* and *down,* equates reality with the visible and palpable. Very well, Bucky urges, rethink the domain of "reality." Reality is a broad spectrum of energy events, across a small portion of which our senses can "tune."

Like "regeneration," this image of "tuning" comes from his radio days. The room you are sitting in is filled with the patterned energies of what you see and hear, and also with the patterned energies generated by thousands of radio and TV transmitters: ham calls, quiz shows, weather reports, satellite transmissions relayed from collars round the necks of polar bears. Instrumentation gives access to some of these. A simple American AM broadcast receiver will tune anything between 550,000 events per second and 1,600,000, but nothing beyond: no police calls, no astronauts' chatter.

Your eye in the same way responds to a restricted band of the spectrum, the wavelengths between what it sees as "red" and what it sees as "violet." Your ear picks up neither bat cries nor the slow beat of an eagle's wing, but only air disturbances midway between those in frequency. A touching hand passes unheeding through air whose impact at a higher velocity will lift a 747 into the skies.

Being restricted in bandwidth, each of our senses resembles a radio, and whatever is "infra or ultra to man's sensory tuning"—one of Bucky's "mental mouthfuls"—we tend to discount as imperfectly "real." Extending the senses with instrumentation is like equipping a radio with additional tuning bands. In this way the electromagnetic spectrum was slowly explored, the entire bandwidth of energetic events. Bucky says that the map of that spectrum in its totality was published only in 1933. In that year men supposed they were deep in a Depression, when in fact they had acquired their first full chart of the areas where significant history would thenceforth be transacted. Through fully 99 percent of this reality, our senses with their limited tuning range give no guidance.

None of this is new. Everyone knows that his dog hears sounds he cannot. Everyone has read of the interatomic spaces into which, for the physicist, "solid" reality vanishes. But hardly anyone knows what to do with such knowledge. It enjoys a kind of Sunday-supplement reality, after the brief astonishments of which we return to the really real, for instance television. We have learned this attitude from a long tradition of using the scientist's reality to startle, thus stressing its incompatibility with common experience. Fifty years ago Sir James Jeans and Sir Arthur Eddington, founding fathers of this tradition of popularization, were making their living from elegant mystifications, and since then the scientifically literate have been mostly split men.

Bucky puts it differently. Science, he says, lost touch with nonscientists, and engendered the famous "two cultures," when it gave up the use of models, thus letting us suppose it was talking about nothing real. His own principal contribution to humanity, he thinks, has been to restore modelability. That is what he claims for his coordinate system, where for instance you can go in four directions from the faces of a tetrahedron, or pack twenty

units of volume round the center of the vector equilibrium. Cubes have just three axes, not four, and around a
point you can pack just eight (or 2^3) cubes, restricting you
therefore to three-dimensional space and allowing you to
model no equation that goes beyond x^3.

For years a big book has been promised, spelling out
with proper rigor the transition between Einstein's reality
and the oc-tet coordinates. Meanwhile Bucky has been
contenting himself with lecture-hall metaphors that tend
to raise more questions than they answer. While we wait
for the book, we may fondle the Tensegrity Sphere, and
ponder the rhetorical plight the mainstream scientific pop-
ularizer has gotten into.

Arthur Koestler, for instance. In *The Sleepwalkers*
Koestler showed us in brilliant detail how a sequence of
great cosmological discoveries really got made. But when
he came to his last chapter, and a confrontation with what
had been discovered, he succumbed as readily as a Sunday
supplement to the rhetoric of mystification.

"Each advance in physical theory, with its rich intellectual harvest, was bought by a loss in intelligibility." That's
his theme sentence. For, "compared to the modern physicist's picture of the world, the Ptolemaic universe of epi-
cycles and crystal spheres was a model of sanity." (Bucky
Fuller would here ask what can be expected of scientists
who say *up* and *down*, their verbal reflexes 500 years out
of date.)

Koestler presses on. "The chair on which I sit seems a
hard fact, but I know that I sit on a nearly perfect vacuum." (Gee whiz.) So small are its atoms' particles, so wide
their orbits, that "a room with a few specks of dust floating
in the air is overcrowded compared with the emptiness
which I call a chair and on which my fundaments rest."

To dispel any notion that the substantial is somehow

resting on the insubstantial, it would be helpful to examine the corresponding composition of the author's fundaments. Instead of doing that, Koestler tells us how
electrons in fact do not occupy space at all, how reality is
mathematical, mind-stuff, and how we must deal not with
transcendental vistas but with the imperatives of a dismal
peroration:

> Thus the mediaeval walled-in universe with its hier-
> archy of matter, mind and spirit has been superseded by
> an expanding universe of curved multidimensional
> empty space, where the stars, planets and their popu-
> lations are absorbed into the space-crinkles of an ab-
> stract continuum—a bubble blown out of "empty space
> welded onto empty time."

Bucky likes bubbles, in fact the Tensegrity Sphere models
a bubble, and Time gives the measure of its vectors'
lengths. Koestler however likes nothing he feels compelled
to say. On his showing, the world which science opens up
is therefore unexperienceable, unintelligible, unthinkable.
We are consequently—this is the old political revolution-
ary's closing flourish—immersed in a sort of permanent
darkness at noon, at the mercy of "the new Baal, lording
it over the moral vacuum with his electronic brain."

But this is not the tune that Bucky sings. Bucky has
certain bridges to and fro between the world of patterned
energies and the world where one feeds the dog, bridges
he crosses and recrosses freely. Some of these are bridges
of homely analogy, for instance the knotted rope, which
he uses the way Lincoln used proverbs and frontier anec-
dotes. Others are substantial technological bridges, like
the one Lee De Forest built between the electromagnetic
spectrum and the deck of Bucky's ship. Still others are
devisings of his own, like that way of building spheres

which we shall be calling technological when someone has imagined a use for it.

All technology models principles. The radio set puts into everyone's hands a sensory patterning of invisible inaudible energies. Since Bucky perceives in its tunings a special case of the sensory encounter, and in its regenerative circuits a special case of the reiterations that will sustain a bar of steel, he finds all these invisibilities and impalpabilities quite domestic. His complaint that expounders of science stopped using models about a century ago is matched by his observation, from as long ago as 1932, that technology is the popularization of science. Every gadget is a model, and a virtually perfect model since it really does grapple with the mysterious principle and bring it into the domain of experience.

This took less expounding once. The radio sets of 1919 kept their tuning condensers in plain sight, the brass plates interleaving with as physical a demonstration as a piano tuner twisting a peg, and when regenerative circuits were being peaked, rather large coils came cautiously into proximity. You could watch a steam engine's pistons on any train, or an airplane's propellor blades chopping back air and its ailerons responding to taut piano wire. In those days before everything was enshrouded and encapsulated technology was a public flirt, inviting a Bucky Fuller by quiver and wink to tarry with its incarnations of pure principle. Its devices still accelerate his mind. And his own eyes and ears are "tuned," for that matter, with lightweight gadgets, and nothing in the universe, he is convinced, lies outside human experience. Hence his cheerfulness.

FIVE

Bubbles and Destiny

Bucky's peculiar fervor, preaching these themes—there is only one vector equilibrium, and he is its prophet—sweeps us past simply being comfortable with the atom. His vocation is nothing less than to save the world. Stark beauty and simplicity allure him—those Platonic constructs, those gratifying round numbers—but he has too New England a mind to rest in beauty. Beauty has an allure beyond itself, the promise of rightness. Can anything be so neat and not be right? And it is supremely important to be right, because finding what Nature's working principles are is the key to "making man a success in the Universe."

Vocation is the right word: it is like a saint's. And his life, like a saint's life, contains crisis points of conversion. As he tells it, there were two conversions, the second completing the first. He was converted (1917) to a new mathematics, and converted again (1927) to a new mission. Each event involved gazing at water. We may call them the Vision of the Bubbles, and the Vision of Destiny. It is possible that neither of them happened.

Not that he deceives. He mythologizes, a normal work of the mind. The mind, like the Universe, has contracting and expanding phases. It expands to embrace multitudinous perceptions, making thousands of separate statements about different things. It contracts to utter summarizing statements, out of which *time* tends to be squeezed. A man says, "I fell in love," as though it had been instantaneous. If he teased what actually happened into its elements, he would talk for hours, to little effect. "I fell in love" is a mythological statement; it is not "untrue."

"Cadmus gave men letters" is a similar statement. "Pericles built the Parthenon." "The emperor Seu-Gin taught the breaking of branches, the knotting of cords." More recently, "Lincoln freed the slaves," and "Lenin overturned Russia" and "The United States lost China." All these are useful myths. And everyone knows the story of Washington and the cherry tree, or Newton and the apple, or Watt and the teakettle. They are mythological statements; they concentrate truth.

Thus, that uncle we have encountered, talking of Malthus: did he indeed take Bucky aside just before the 1913 Harvard term? That was how a 1965 audience heard it; the version is printed in *Utopia or Oblivion,* pages 121–22. Or was it in the Navy, four years later, that the Golden Rule was denied on principle, and did the talk with the uncle occur still later than that? So runs the version in the 1963 *Ideas and Integrities,* page 60. And why does *Utopia or Oblivion* put "uncle" in quotation marks? Was there really a single uncle, holding forth on a single eloquent occasion? Or does "uncle" mean "the elder generation," reinforced for purposes of exposition by remarks remembered from one man in particular, perhaps not remarks all spoken on one day but collected from a span of memories? Such questions do not challenge Bucky's purpose in telling the story, which is to establish his elders' Malthusian postulates. They do serve to cast doubt on an illusion his talk often generates, of thought suddenly crystallized on red-letter days when he went to bed knowing a fundamental thing he had not known at breakfast, thanks to some epiphanic experience that occurred at 10:32 A.M.

What a myth squeezes out is linear time, reducing all the fumblings and sortings of years to an illuminative instant. We can see why Bucky needs myth. The vision that possesses him eludes linearity. To present it sequentially is a technical problem, like geodesic design, and a true solution, if one were ever found, ought to merit a U. S. Patent. (A patent on Linguistic Arrays? Why not? He already holds the only patent on Cartography, to spread the earth out flat.) For his is a Whole Systems Vision, and the ultimate Whole System (and only functional perpetual motion machine) is nothing less than the Universe. How to spread that out?

He can talk it through, he says, in fifty-five hours, 385,000 words, a discourse half as long again as *Ulysses*. But even the fifty-five-hour exposition has to proceed word by word from somewhere to somewhere else, and one should grasp it whole. One solution is to seem to be uttering many strings of words simultaneously; warmed up, he will generate this effect by sheer pace. Another is to extract local clusters for inspection, and since "no man has ever seen outside of himself," the clusters tend to fit into an autobiographical myth.

This myth is anecdotal; its unit is the Germinal Moment, with place and time specified. Aboard a ship, in 1917, he had a great insight. Beside Lake Michigan, in 1927, he made a pivotal decision. These are patterns danced into being by his speech, as Orpheus' music moved stones. He believes that we partly create experience by talking of it, and extend the Universe by thinking of it. "Intellect may be 'creating,' finitely extending and re-fining universe as it asks each next good question," and it is in the act of creating, thinking-out-loud, that Bucky is being uniquely Buckminster Fuller.

Imagine him then, standing, age twenty-two, at the stern of a running ship, gazing at its white wake on the dark water. Millions of little bubbles compose this whiteness, each one a little sphere or partial sphere, each exemplifying the mathematics of spheres, including presumably the famous *pi* which enters the mathematics of anything circular.

Pi is a very old scandal. Generations of circle-squarers attested to the persistent intuition that it ought to have a rational value, but nobody ever found one. Eventually it was proved that none was findable. The decimal sequence for *pi,* circumference divided by diameter, commences 3.141592653589793 . . . and will go on forever. This appears to mean that infinity will invade any circular system, which feels wrong since circles are closed. In practice the embarrassment is slight. Human dexterity encounters limits, and the specifications for making anything practical, like airplane engine cylinders, can accept an error of one part in 10,000, four decimal places, 3.1416.

Being unhampered by a machinist's finite eyesight, Nature need not stop at a rounded-off fourth place. At what place then?

"I'd learned at school that in order to make a sphere, which is what a bubble is, you employ *pi,* and I'd also learned that *pi* is an irrational number." So "when," he recalls asking, "does nature have to fudge it and pretend it comes out even and then make some kind of compromise bubble?" And millions of them per second. "I think it's too many decisions for nature to make."

And now the insight, and the vocation. . . . "And I

reached the decision right at that moment that nature didn't use *pi*. I said to myself, 'I think nature has a different system, and it must be some sort of arithmetical-geometrical coordinate system, because nature has all kinds of models. . . .' And I decided then, in 1917, that what I'd like to do was to find nature's geometry."

What makes this an especially beautiful story is that just fifty years later the world was to be enriched by what is still the most spectacular geodesic structure ever erected, a giant 250-foot steel and plexiglass "skybreak bubble." It is as free as a soap bubble of internal supports, the load on its foundations is less than the weight of its separate materials, and had it been a half-mile in diameter it would have been capable of drifting away.

Still, the Vision of the Bubbles invites query. We shan't learn if it really happened quite as he tells it, though our legacy of Romantic introspection, commencing with Wordsworth's *Prelude,* may remind us how recollection in tranquillity, and still more recollection in excitement, shapes what is being recollected. We can safely say that as of the mid-1960's, when the Bubble Story began turning up in Bucky's talks, it seemed to him that his quest for Nature's geometry has been on his mind since 1917, and that its origin was entangled with a memory of watching bubbles. Many reflections about *pi* and vectors were no doubt later refinements. It resembles the story of Newton and the apple in being an incident only *potential* with meaning.

We may next ask what it may mean. Its explicit yield was, "Nature does not use *pi*," which has the ring of perdurable crackpottery, of flat-earth dogmas and other sturdy defiances of book learning. *I can draw a circle with a compass,* we may think of retorting, *and draw it well without giving a thought to pi.* Ah, but the challenge was not to draw a circle, the challenge was to make a sphere. *Well, I can massage clay until it feels right, and if my clay ball is not perfectly spherical, very likely those bubbles are not perfect either.* But nature makes bubbles too fast for any such trial and error, and by the million, changing and disintegrating.

Still, we can describe how this is done. Disturbance, for instance from a passing ship, folds a little air into the water, and the air bubble, being light, shoots toward the water's surface. At the surface, it is enfolded by *surface tension,* which we may envisage as an elastic membrane, met with at the boundary layer of liquids. (Water bugs walk on it.) The surface tension is uniform, closing in. The air's thrust is uniform, shoving out. The two reach equilibrium in a surface of minimum area, which is a sphere though not a long-lived sphere unless there is soap in the water to cohere that membrane. It's the contained-explosion principle once more, and the vector equilibrium is its model.

A balance of tensile and compressive forces, then, and nothing to do with 3.1416^+. If Bucky was taught at school that you use *pi* to make a sphere, then he was simply mistaught. More likely he is doing what we can sometimes catch him at, scoring points off a phantom adversary. Nature is not alone in not employing *pi*. It is difficult to think of even a man-made sphere you need *pi* to undertake. And if geodesic spheres occur in nature, as Bucky affirms they do, you might well object that designing a geodesic sphere entails much tedious spherical trigonometry which nature hasn't time for either.

No, the real principle involved is somewhat different. What the Bubble Vision illuminated was the difference between generating spheres and answering questions about them. They can be generated without *pi* and described without *pi*. But the minute someone fixes his attention on the linear distance straight through the bubble's middle, and commences phrasing questions that entail that measurement, then *pi* starts turning up. Since the measurement can't be made without destroying the bubble, these questions are apt to be rather fanciful. That distance is the bubble's diameter. What is the distance clear round the bubble? *Pi* times the diameter. If I slice the bubble in half, then—quick before it vanishes!—what is the area of the circle I expose? Fanciful indeed, since that circle has no surface; but if it had, its area would be *pi* times the second power of half the diameter. And the area of the bubble's whole outside surface? Four times that. And the volume of the air in the bubble? Four-thirds of *pi*, times the third power of half the diameter.

None of these questions has the least pertinence to making a sphere, whether in the wake of a ship or in a bowling-ball factory. Nor does any of them enter the explanation of how it hangs together, since if you graph the forces a bubble equilibrates you draw straight lines with little arrows on the ends to denote thrusts. *Pi* has nothing to do with those lines. We might even say harshly that they are such questions as would only occur to idle curiosity, doodling in a static universe of ideal forms. What Bucky means by "nature's own geometry" is *a set of economical statements about the way patterns come into existence and then hold together*. This means, statements about *forces*, which always interact with maximum economy, as in the triangle. By the criteria of "nature's own geometry," the greater part of formal mathematics is elegantly irrelevant game-playing.

Part of the game is the game of definition. There's a classical definition of a sphere. "A sphere is a surface equidistant at all points from a central point." Bucky delights to tell us what such a thing would be like. "That means, you see, that it couldn't have any holes in it, because as you went over the edge of a hole you'd be getting closer to the center. So it's a perfectly closed system, and it divides the universe into two parts, the part inside the system, the part outside the system. No communication between them. So no energy could pass through the barrier, hence no entropy. A local system totally conserving energy: that would be a perpetual motion machine."

But we know, he says, that there are no real surfaces; there are molecular meshes full of holes. And if the air stays inside a bubble, that is because the holes in the bubble's skin are smaller than the molecules of air. The bubble is a tension network, and the compression system within is an agitation of air molecules. The ones near the outside, being crowded by the ones toward the center, keep hitting the molecule-thin mesh and stressing it outward.

The mesh, for that matter, has not even continuous threads. The nodes of the mesh are " 'Milky Way'-like constellations, great energy aggregates cohering only 'gravitationally' to act as the 'webbing' of the pneumatic ball's net." The skin of the sphere is a discontinuous network of energy events, interspersed with vast spaces which are nonetheless not so large as the molecules of air that blunder against them.

And the shortest distance between two energy events is not an arc but a chord, so a diagram of the intermolecular tension network would consist of tiny straight lines. There is no "real" curved surface; hence no need for pi. Any three of these boundary events make a triangle, so the bubble is omnitriangulated, hence (surprise!) geodesic.

We've hinted that the questions pi answers tend to be frivolous questions. In the real world they don't even get accurate answers, since they postulate curves, which in fact are nonexistent. Which is not to deny the great usefulness of *pi* as a rapid-calculating device for getting answers as good as we need. (It got us to the moon.) That's what it is for Bucky, nothing more.

A world freed of *pi,* it is not too much to say, seemed freed of a deep scandal. For millenia it has seemed wrong to numerous minds that seams of irrationality should run through the universe. At Kroton, about 500 B.C., the Pythagoreans encountered such a seam when their beautiful sets of whole numbers pervading all creation collided with the diagonal of the square, which will no more yield a whole number than will *pi*. This quantity they named *alogon,* The Unutterable, and when initiates were told of its existence they were sworn to secrecy. They executed a man named Hippasos for babbling it.

The Pythagoreans had good reasons for their veneration of whole numbers. They had discovered that when the seeming randomness of sound was zoned into concords, the octave, the fifth, the fourth, then the lengths of the lyre strings bear simple numerical ratios: 2:1, 3:2, 4:3. They had learned that if you group stones into squares,

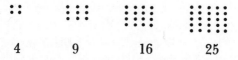

| 4 | 9 | 16 | 25 |

then you can pass from square to square indefinitely by adding the successive odd numbers. To go from 4 to 9 you add *5*; to go to 16 add 7 more; to go to 25, *9* more. You might expect to get the next square number by adding *11,* and so you do: 36. This was marvelous; the bare number system itself generating orderly patterns the senses can caress.

And they had discovered a remarkable piece of Synergy, behavior of a whole system unpredicted by our knowledge of its parts. The Whole System is a right-angled triangle scratched accurately on the sand, with a square jutting out of each side; and behold, the two smaller squares taken together will always enclose as much sand as the largest square does. This is still called the Pythagorean Theorem.

It works backward too. Now that we understand the three-parted Whole System, knowledge of any two parts will yield exact knowledge of the third. Here is a triangle, with shorter sides 3 and 4. The square on 3 has 9 units, the square on 4 has 16. Sum them, 25. Then the square on the longest side has 25 units, and by arranging 25 stones into a square pattern we can see that the length of that longest side is 5. We learn this without measuring; we need not even draw the figure.

And here the trouble arose. Let us have 10 units for each of the shorter sides (meaning that our right-angled triangle is half of a square). Then 10^2 plus 10^2 is 200, and by arranging 200 stones into a square we can discover the length of that remaining side. But 200 stones will not arrange into a square. 196 will give a square 14 to a side, and 225 will give one 15 to a side, but 200 is impossible.

Or put the problem another way. Lay uniform counters along the two short sides, 10, and 10. Then lay them up that diagonal: 14, plus an awkward little gap, like a gap in nature: The Unutterable.

For while it is not surprising that numerous right-angled triangles should yield numbers we cannot manage, so infinitely variable are the proportions of triangles, we are not here confronting just any triangle. The triangle we are struggling to rationalize is one-half of the sacred Square itself, and it seems unthinkable that the Square should fizzle in this way. What to do?

The Pythagoreans might have decided they were asking an empty question. (What meaning has the diagonal of a square?) They chose instead, with what anguish we can only guess, to accept an inherent unreason locked into the beautiful world their researches had been revealing. They also chose to conceal the fact from casual enquirers. They left two traditions, the tradition, extending forward twenty-four centuries to Einstein himself, that one could expect tidy relationships of number in the very depths of the universe, and the tradition, seldom dwelt on but always obscurely suspected, that scientific thinking at a certain point will always stop making sense.

Subsequently, alongside the system of whole numbers, 1, 2, 3, 4, and their fractional parts, 1/2, 1/3, 1/4, a new compartment was opened up for the irrational numbers to be kept in, the numbers no finite fraction can represent.*
Such numbers are as plentiful as any other kind. They need not give pleasure except to special tastes, but being on the census rolls they need no longer embarrass. They describe innumerable physical facts, for instance the lengths of geodesic struts, figured from trigonometry tables crammed with irrational numbers. Whether they pertain to nature's cohesive forces remains a different question.

For remember, there "are" no surfaces: just meshes. And there "are" no solids, just molecules. When it's hot enough, the molecules swarm like bees, and we speak of a gas. When it's colder their aggregation starts being shapeless but incompressible, which is what we mean by a liquid. When it's cold enough—which means room temperature for most things—they usually arrange themselves into symmetrical

* When 1/3 becomes .333 ... it's non-terminating but not irrational. The fraction is perfectly good, it just won't reduce to tenths. The fraction for an irrational number is non-existent. *Pi* is nearly 22/7, not exactly.

lattices, where they keep ranks but wriggle in place like itchy soldiers. Then we say "solid." In any case we have the same molecules, therefore the same *number* of molecules.

This means that in the real world there's always something to count. When we talk of "lengths" and "areas" and "volumes" we might instead be counting molecules, and always getting whole numbers. You can't have 3.1416 molecules. One of Bucky's Geodesic Spheres has a countable number of components, and so has a soap bubble.

In 1811, a chemist named Amadeo Avogadro announced the surprising discovery that identical boxes filled with any gas you like will all contain exactly the same number of molecules, if temperature and pressure are kept constant. Hydrogen molecules, oxygen molecules, molecules of gas from the cookstove, all diffuse themselves through space with identical uniformity, keeping identical average distances as though fitting into a uniform invisible system. Bucky cites Avogadro's Law repeatedly. It helps anchor his intuition that describing reality is based on counting, as Pythagoras counted stones, and that nature's arrangements permit an orderly count. School mathematics, he tells us, inherits a very old tradition of asking the wrong questions, and has drifted off in another direction where it mostly handles abstractions based on squares.

To understand this, look at a bathroom floor covered with hexagonal tiles. Here's a piece of it. An appraiser wants to know its area. For this piece, a sensible answer would be eleven tiles (count them). But that's not what the schoolteacher told the appraiser to mean when he asked about areas. The schoolteacher told him areas were measured in square somethings, square inches, square feet. This means, here's a grid of one-inch squares. Fit it over the tiles. (To make it easy, the tiles are one inch to a side.) Now, how many squares cover tiles?

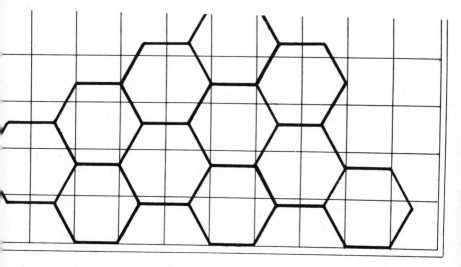

Hexagons in square grid

No, nothing fits. We can count the whole squares—
eighteen—and then keep lumping part-squares together,
estimating as best we can. Or instead of fussing with the
grid we can apply a mathematical jiujitsu based on squares,
and say that the area of that piece of floor is 28.6 square
inches approximately. We have to use $\sqrt{3}$ to get this result,* and since $\sqrt{3}$ is an irrational number you can see
why we have to say "approximately." When we call $\sqrt{3}$
irrational we are saying that no piece of luck, no accident
of dimensional fit, will ever express a hexagonal reality in
squares. Yet there is a whole number of tiles, exactly eleven.
If we talked in hexagons instead of in squares we could
get a whole-number area, or at least a finite fraction.

---

* Each hexagon consists of six equilateral triangles. The area of each
triangle—you can get it from Pythagoras' Theorem—is $\sqrt{3}/4$. So the area
of a hexagon is 6 times this, or $3\sqrt{3}/2$, or about 2.598.

Floor tiles might be just a beginning. Frank Lloyd Wright built a house with hexagonal rooms, opening onto a hexagonal-contoured patio. We might imagine it on a hexagonal lot, abutting other hexagonal lots laid out in hexagonal blocks. In fact we can imagine a country in which everything is structured in hexagons. Let's infest it with insane tax assessors who insist on thinking in squares. Every time they want to survey a potato patch they solemnly drag out tables of square roots, muttering about the mysteries of their craft, and get unwieldy numbers like 23.1786⁺ square yards. Though simple uniform unbroken hexagons abound for the counting, the hex-squarers are too snobbish to count. Mathematics isn't *counting;* that's for kindergartens.

The square grid they impose is a *coordinate system,* which simply means the system you count with to say where anything is. Four-cornered city blocks fit a square system, and you can send a stranger three blocks east, five south. In Hexland, where three streets meet at every corner, you'd need to guide tourists differently.

The assessors in Hexland are using a coordinate system that doesn't fit the nature of things. It would be a trial, doing official arithmetic in a country like that. Bucky Fuller tells us we are in a Universe like that, and teaching our children just such a mad arithmetic.

Nature—look at the honeycomb—favors hexagons and three-way intersections. Even dried mud cracks in a three-way grid. "Surfaces" are layers of events. In the top layer of a honeycomb all the events are hexagonal. "Volumes" count the events distributed through a cup of water or a bar of steel: how many molecular happenings go on in there? To extend hexagons into the domain of volumes, we have only to interlock four of them, obtaining our old friend the vector equilibrium, which models an ideal distribution of molecules in three-dimensional space.

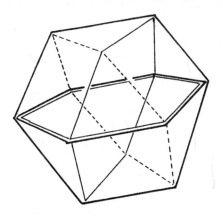

Six hexagons make a vector
equilibrium

We call space three-dimensional because three measurements will locate a fly anywhere in the room. But though
space needs a three-way coordinate system there is no reason why its elements need branch at 90 degrees, to-fro,
left-right, up-down. The vectors that radiate from the heart
of the vector equilibrium are at 60 degrees to their neighbors, and a 60-degree coordinate system is perfectly workable. Its grid in space will look like the Octet Truss, and
unlike the squares the surveyors used in Hexland, it will
map the structural lines of chemical and biological events.

A few years ago Bucky began attributing two awkward
numbers, Planck's constant and the gravitational constant,
to the lack of fit between the 60-degree system and the
cubical. Since the gram in which mass is measured is defined as the weight of a cubic centimeter of water, a hidden
cube enters equations dealing with mass, to infect with the
irrational any statement about energies radiating from centers or concentrating toward them.*

Each of us carries in his mind a phantom cube, by which
to estimate the orthodoxy of whatever we encounter in the

* A vector equilibrium's volume is 20 / 3 or 6.6 times that of a cube.
Delicate empirical measurements for both the gravitational constant and
Planck's constant give something pretty close to 6.6 preceded by appropriate strings of zeroes. I don't know if any physicist has commented on
this, nor what we are supposed to make of the fact that Bucky gets his
neat ratio, 20 / 3, by measuring the cube's diagonal instead of its edge.

world of space. We note "squareness" or lack of it, "up-rightness" or lack of it. This is a moral terminology as well as a geometrical: a coordinate system for assessing satisfactoriness. And because a brick stack topples if it does not rise at 90 degrees to the plane, a system of construction is implied as well, wholly compressive, disregarding tension. So deeply does geometry pervade our minds, sponsoring whole families of conditioned-reflex judgments.

But Nature, Bucky is telling us, works not by piled bricks but by systems of radiation from centers, for which the appropriate coordinate system uses vectors radiating at 60 degrees. What we should carry in our heads to understand reality with is not a phantom cube but a phantom vector equilibrium, and the sooner this figure gets installed in kindergarten curricula, the better. Speech radiates from centers; *Finnegans Wake* radiates from nuclear phrases; light expands spherically; an oak tree is a system (below ground as well as above) which has radiated from an acorn and stopped one kind of energetic transaction—growth in space—only to specialize in another kind, photosynthesis, self-renewal. There are no "things," no "building blocks," none of those phenomena the cube connotes.

If we make the vector equilibrium by packing spheres, the spheres are the component "events," and "area" means the count of surface events, "volume" the total count clear through. We impose no squared grid nor cubed lattice, and Bucky will happily tell us we are looking at a model of how Nature actually works.

In nature, for instance, a microscopic sphere will somehow become a frog or a cat or a man. The microscopic sphere is the fertilized egg. We were all spheres once—close-packed concentrations of exquisite energy events—and during nine months some transformational system that always dealt in whole numbers turned a long-ago close-packed sphere into *you*.

The instructions that came with the egg were coded into DNA helices. (Bucky has a model for these, made of chained tetrahedra, and had it before the DNA double helix was discovered.) The patterned integrity did its orderly business with local air, local water, local nutrients, and structured them into its patterned transformations, which began with a cell splitting into two, then four, then eight.

To be less personal, we may talk about a frog.

If you could see a just-fertilized frog's ovum you might be excused for calling it a "point." A "point," for Bucky, is not "position-without-magnitude," but an agglomeration of events we have not resolved. From a transcontinental jet, eleven men in a football huddle look like a "point." From my window, the rose a quarter-mile away is a pink point. From your back garden, a star looks like a point. They are all systems of energy, and the star is a huge one.

The ovum divides, divides, new cells clinging in a spherical conformation. There are two cells, then four, then eight. Later the spherical form is growing outward in layers. Cells are packed upon cells, and we can see the ones in the outer layer nudging one another into hexagons. "Perfect fit" is one principle of nature's design, and the hexagon is now the economical shape.*

It happens that a sphere inscribed with hexagons is mathematically impossible. A few other shapes must be mixed in. Pentagons—since we're idealizing—will be the most economical, and if they appear there will be, by inexorable law, exactly twelve of them.

We now have (1) a spherical system of closely packed

---

* Electron-scanning photomicrographs of the eye's cornea show a hex pattern like the surface of a geodesic dome.

cells; (2) the surface hex pattern; (3) an even dozen pentagons. The dozen may remind us of the twelve balls that
would pack around one ball. Sure enough, this system is
projected from the vector equilibrium, that module of radiating growth. It is also a very young frog.

Having followed its progress as far as the blastula, we
may leave the frog to develop by itself while we ask what
the model has to do with it. The model, first of all, is highly
idealized. The frog is going to be hollow, and hollowness
has already invaded the upper part of the blastula, which
isn't as closely packed as it looks from outside. And there's
no guarantee, let alone probability, that the layers of cells
have been added in an orderly fashion, permitting an off-
the-cuff mathematical statement of how many cells there
must be. What the frog and the model have in common
are a general configuration, and the theme of growth.

Or think of a flame emitting photons, another energetic
transaction. We may imagine little radiant globules packed
round it, filling space with a fast-growing sphere of radi-
ance. That sphere expands outward at the speed of light.
In four and a half years its wave front will sweep past a
planet of Alpha Centauri, where they may suddenly note
that we have lit a candle. At any moment we can talk about
the number of photons on the radiant surface, or the vastly
greater number that fill space between the surface and the
flame: a sphere, an area, a volume, and no *pi*.

The Pythagoreans, it would seem, were right all along.
All things are number. All arithmetic derives from counting. The principles of the Universe answer to a triangular
way of enumerating. And when we collide with an irrational number, we have asked a question that does not
pertain to the interaction of energies.

Pythagorean faith in number is a mystical tradition.
Bucky inherited it because everyone does in the Western

world: every watchmaker, every bookkeeper, and everyone who believes that Kepler and Newton accomplished something important. So pervasive, so unexamined is that faith that we seldom think to be surprised by the extreme simplicity and neatness of physical laws, though we have no a priori reason to expect anything as tidy as gravitation proportional to the second power of the mean distance, or the second power of planetary years proportional to the third power of their mean distances from the sun.

And Bucky inherited a second mystical tradition too, not numerical, this one, but rhetorical and visionary, and apparently to be traced to Eastern sources. This was the transcendentalism of his great-aunt Margaret's friend Ralph Waldo Emerson.

If Pythagorean numbers bound together the orderliness of crystals, planetary orbits, vibrating strings, and figures scratched on sand, transcendental insight bound together absolutely everything, though with no promise that all truth was penetrable.

Penetrable or not, it was *there*. "Things admit of being used as symbols," wrote Emerson, "because Nature is a symbol, in the whole and in every part." (So bubbles may be a vehicle of revelation.)

"Throw a stone into the stream, and the circles that propagate themselves are the beautiful type of all influence." (Bucky was one day to devote twenty-five dense pages to what those propagated circles may portend; they explain vision, substantiality, surfers, porpoises, knots, galaxies, the ninety-two elements and man's role in the universe.)

Not just a few poets, Emerson went on, but man himself is always an analogist, and studies relations in all objects. "He is placed in the center of beings, and a ray of relation passes from every other being to him. And neither can man be understood without these objects, nor these objects without man." (Here is authority for Bucky's repeated insistence that man has a function in the universe, indeed completes the universe, which consists of "all that is not me, and me.")

Hence only the Whole Systems view is worthy of man, who has better things to do with the language he has derived from the whole cosmos than expedite pot-and-kettle affairs with it, quite as if it was *he* who did mountains and waves the favor of using them for his figures of speech.

> Have mountains, and waves, and skies, no significance but what we consciously give them when we employ them as emblems of our thoughts? The world is emblematic. Parts of speech are metaphors, because the whole of nature is a metaphor of the human mind. The laws of moral nature answer to those of matter as face to face in a glass. . . . The axioms of physics translate the laws of ethics. . . .

All natural things image all others, and image invisible laws, and ethical laws. Bucky Fuller's whole generation of genteel New Englanders shared the heritage of such sentiments, but few had his incentive to ponder whether statements Emerson made about the physical world might be physical truths as well as ethical metaphors. "Everything good in man leans on what is higher": New England repeated that maxim, but tended not to notice Emerson's example of it: that when the force of gravity brings down a carpenter's axhead, "the planet itself splits his stick." Morality and technology always rhyme. Alone among Emerson's inheritors, Bucky Fuller has kept this principle steadfastly in sight. Both morality and technology derive from the largest patterns of the Universe.

Man's wisdom, Emerson said, is to hitch his wagon to a star. It would astonish ten thousand commencement speakers to learn what prompted that famous sentence:

the spectacle of harnessed tidal power, which "engages the assistance of the moon, like a hired hand, to grind, and wind, and pump, and saw, and split stone, and roll iron." (And since coal is solar energy, for that matter, railway wagons are hitched to a star.)

It is hard to find a sentence in Emerson that Bucky Fuller would reject:

"The most advanced nations are always those who navigate the most. The power which the sea requires in the sailor makes a man of him very fast, and the change of shores and population clears his head of much nonsense of his wigwam."

"The ship is an abridgement and compend of a nation's arts."

"As our handiworks borrow the elements, so all our social and political action leans on principles."

Emerson's mind was open to science and technology as his friend Thoreau's mind was not. On an Atlantic crossing he stood marveling at how the engine that drove the ship was also made to desalinate 200 gallons of water every hour, "thereby supplying all the ship's want." The economy of good design thrilled him. Fresh water as a by-product of the ship's powering, like "the man that maintains himself, the chimney taught to burn its own smoke, the farm made to produce all that is consumed on it," exemplified in their tidy economical recyclings a highly moral conformity with principle.

He drew on the science of his day to support a Whole-Systems vision in which all phenomena repeat one another at different rates and with different degrees of subtlety:

> The law of harmonic sound reappears in the harmonic colors. The granite is differenced in its laws only by the more or less of heat from the river that wears it away. The river, as it flows, resembles the air that flows over

it; the air resembles the light which traversed it with
more subtle currents; the light resembles the heat
which rides with it through Space. Each creature is only
a modification of the other; the likeness in them is more
than the difference, and their radical law is one and the
same. A rule of one art, or a law of one organization,
holds true throughout nature.

He seems to be inviting us to find that law. Combine
his vision with the Pythagorean vision it so intimately resembles, and we have Bucky's mandate for his lifelong
quest after what he calls the Coordinate System of Nature:
that economical geometry sustaining all structures, the
icosahedronal viruses, the tetrahedral carbon molecules.
And when he slips from number and structure into a mys-
ticism that annoys scientists, or from man's affairs into
geometric talk that bewilders literary folk, he makes a
transition not only natural to him but faithful to a kinship between the traditions of Emerson and Pythagoras.
Emerson himself moves toward Pythagoras at the end of
the long paragraph we were just quoting:

> Every universal truth which we express in words, im-
> plies or supposes every other truth. *Omne verum vero
> consonat.* It is like a great circle on a sphere, compris-
> ing all possible circles; which, however, may be drawn
> and comprise it in like manner. Every such truth is an
> absolute Ens seen from one side. But it has inumerable
> sides.

A sphere, inscribed with great circles, yet many-sided:
Emerson might have been glimpsing the Geodesic Sphere
from which the famous Fuller domes are sliced.

The Pythagorean vision could live with *pi*, albeit
grumpily. The Emersonian vision, serene in its conviction
of vast interreflective order, would have responded to such

an anomaly like a buzz saw to a nail, and it was well for Emerson's psyche that he did not trouble himself deeply with number. To eradicate *pi* from nature was a true transcendentalist deed. It is not surprising that Bucky's next Mythic Experience had to do with his obligations to the Oversoul, and crystallized a nearly prophetic mission.

This experience is dated 1927. Once more we have Bucky gazing at deep water, but this time he is deciding whether to throw himself in. The ten years since the Vision of the Bubbles have been crammed with experiences, of which the economic balance is alarmingly less than zero, and he is wondering whether a world from which he has subtracted himself and his capacity for getting into trouble would not be a more hospitable world for his wife and his infant daughter. Dr. Johnson remarked that knowing one is about to be hanged "concentrates the mind wonderfully." "So standing by the lake," as he puts it, "on a jump-or-think basis," Bucky Fuller elected to think.

I have, he remembers thinking, if no fiscal wealth, yet a wealth of experience, uniquely mine.

The double expulsion from Harvard had initiated a many years' pattern of diverse employment. A man with no degree takes what jobs he can get, and his first job, the one in the textile mill, became a point of reference for many industrial insights. He learned how cotton-mill machinery is constructed and installed, and seems to have glimpsed, for later understanding, a large-scale pattern wherein the factory—run by shafts and pulleys from a single powerhouse—was adding "a rich synergetic admixture of *technology and energy*" to the intake of raw cotton. The energy (obtained from steam in boilers) was ultimately solar—the mill hitched to a star—and as for the knowledge, gathered over many decades, less of it was discoverable in the workers than in the cunning design of their machines. (And replacing broken parts, he learned how to recapitulate the machine-designers' strategies.)

It's a typical Fulleresque gamut, from the cotton mill's Whole System to the logic of single metal parts. There's a twentieth-century aesthetic implicit here too, reminding us that the scope of aesthetic matters was even then growing increasingly operational, less contemplative. Fuller's elder contemporary Ezra Pound has recalled young lads of his generation poring over machine catalogues, excited by configurations of parts and wholes they had no prospect of owning, perhaps no ambition to own. (Two generations later, the *Whole Earth Catalog* with its chain saws and beekeepers' manuals was to prove a surprise best seller.) Elsewhere, fragments of destroyed Greek poems were becoming no longer the poor remains of loss but excitements for minds that were learning to discern, all round the torn edges, traces of the energies that had animated and structured the onetime whole. Pound happens to have been working on Sapphic fragments in London just about when Bucky was learning to cope with parts that arrived broken from the factory.

Any object in space is a memory system. Gazing at a piece of metal like an archaeologist, Bucky "had to rediscover the economic considerations and production strategies" that had helped shape it. Then he had to find ways of realizing British or French conceptionings with the resources of Sherbrooke, Quebec. ("I came to know shop foremen, molders, machinists, . . . the beginnings of metallurgical procedures.") Performing a function anew by substitute processes, with local means: it was more like translating a poem than he need have realized. Pound at that time was elevating translation into an archetypal poetic act. And Pound soon after, in a book about sculpture, was quoting Whistler's "Nature contains the elements," and affirming that the artist "is not forbidden any element, any key because it is geological rather than vegetable, or because it belongs to the realm of magnetic currents or to the binding properties of steel girders and not to the flopping of grass or the contours of the parochial churchyard."

Pointing as they do to Brancusi's aesthetic and George Antheil's, these words are worth our pondering. They suggest a way of de-jargonizing Bucky's talk about a Whole-System view. It is the *aesthetic* view. Or so it is once we understand the artist to be a man with simultaneous intuition of both a Whole System's energies and its crafted parts. At a similar point in time James Joyce was trying to make such a thing clear with the aid of a scholastic jargon he seems to have lifted from Bosanquet's *History of Aesthetics*, the purpose of this terminology being to keep us from thinking we understand before we do. In the first place, Joyce instructs us, the whole system (*integritas*) is grasped; then the fitting of the constituents (*consonantia*); the reward is called *claritas*. This meant that the old preoccupation of poets and critics with Unity required modifying. Instead of resting in connoisseurship of Unity (and testily checking the contour for violations), the mind works from it inwardly to details, multivalent details, and then fortified by its encounter with details returns outward for a refreshed encounter with the whole. It can do this whenever a whole system is identifiable, as well in a cotton mill as in reading *Ulysses*.

Then another distasteful experience at Harvard; then Armour and Company, where eventually he had worked at twenty-eight branches and risen to be Assistant Export Manager. At Armour and Company, where there was less machinery to study, there was still much system, all of it in motion. Meat had to be moved, from barnyards to dinner tables. And it was perishable, so the systems could afford no hitches. *Turnover* was a key concept: the time dimension, which by 1928 was obsessing his architectural thinking, ousting a millennial architecture of achieved stabilities, like the Great Pyramid. This stability is illusory, since the purchaser is in for a lifelong battle against dilapidation, blandly called "maintenance." Even the Pyramids have decayed considerably.

And one reason the computations of Malthus were lagging behind actuality was that less and less food got spoiled uneaten. Design science underlay this, designing refrigerators, designing systems for moving the beef. Bucky learned, he says, "of the economics of abattoirs, refrigeration, by-product chemistry, and high-speed cross-nation perishable tonnage movements impinging endlessly on sidewalk market trading"; also "of distribution shrinkage, of comprehensive premechanical accounting and auditing methods, and, most importantly, of broad-scale, high-speed, behind-the-scenes human relations in the give and take provisioning of men's essential goods."

One way of summarizing this is to say that he did not need to guess about details when he began thinking, long afterward, about ways of feeding the world.

His time at Armour was interrupted, from 1917 to 1919, by the Navy, where he learned perhaps more than from any other span of experience. Ships more intricate, more sophisticated, than anything dreamed of in Penobscot Bay were concentration points for the most advanced technology of their time. They used anything that might prolong their independence of land: oil heating, air conditioning, mechanical refrigeration, systems no one yet had in a house.

Even electric light bulbs were first used at sea. Such a ship was a life support system, a whole community sustained by mechanization.

And naval captains had to be "comprehensivists," since they were solely responsible for a self-contained world no higher authority could get in touch with, once they had slipped over the horizon with perhaps the nation's destiny in their keeping. Ever since Lincoln's time, land-bound militarism had been linked by telegraph with the Commander-in-chief, and had grown technologically indolent. Armies scavenge. A corps commander can seize a farmhouse if he needs billets, or some horses if his guns are mired down, and if he must get instructions he can send a runner. But there is nothing to scavenge at sea, a navy must take its habitable environment with it, and its equivalent of a runner would be a futile man bobbing in a rowboat. So the thrust to develop laboratory curiosities into working inventions was apt to come from sea warriors, and it was not surprising to find Marconi's wireless being made reliable under naval auspices. (Ironically it was wireless, by linking the captain with the shore, that destroyed the need for him to be a comprehensivist. "I was fortunate," Bucky says, "in belonging to the last generation that received comprehensivist training at Annapolis." Being a ninety-day course, this was more a metaphor than an education, but many thoughts were later spun from its node.)

Since the Navy, his experience had been largely managerial. He had been, in just three successive years, assistant export manager at Armour & Company, national sales manager of the Kelley-Springfield Truck Company, and president of the Stockade Building System. Milton, Massachusetts, might have noted with approval that the wild Fuller boy was after all making his way: a Company President at twenty-seven, and even taking out patents. That was the Alger way, to apply oneself. Had the truth been known, he was spending money as compulsively as his exact contemporary Scott Fitzgerald, who confided to a million readers in 1924 how easy it was to go broke on $36,000 a year. He was also learning the rationale, such as it was, of the building industry, whose procedures, he decided, belonged in the Middle Ages.

The Stockade Building System turned on an invention of Anne Fuller's father, the architect and painter James Monroe Hewlett. It was one of those inventions on which, with luck, fortunes are built: a simple component, easily mass-produced, for which there ought to be unlimited demand. (Hooks to hang gutters from roofs—spike and a half-circle, patented—had made one early twentieth-century fortune, and the patent on the valve atop an aerosol can today maintains its inventor in Switzerland.) That is one aspect of the American Dream, that with something very simple you can hope to coin money.

Mr. Hewlett's patent invention (1923) was a substitute for the common brick: a "Stockade Block" cement-bonded from excelsior or straw and pierced with two vertical holes. The blocks were so light they were not hod-carried: a workman could throw them up to a second-floor scaffolding, and if they fell the tough fibers did not break apart. (One building firm in one city typically broke a million common bricks a year.) They constituted the key to a building system which Bucky and his father-in-law co-patented. You stacked them, omitting mortar but lining up the vertical holes. Then cement poured down the holes gave your wall a concrete frame, and a plaster on both surfaces yielded two walls, the inner and the outer, bonded to a fibrous insulating substance, eight inches thick, which would neither burn nor pass moisture. Bucky devised the machines and the processes to mass-produce the bricks, and gradually through a network of five companies got the system into operation in a total of 240 structures, a disappointing sliver of the potential market.

Requiring no hod carriers and no mortar, such a system interfered with the bricklayers' lucrative choreography. And what union should do what? That had to be negotiated every time. And were the newfangled structures even legal? They were declared not legal in Glencoe, Illinois, "where not even an engineer was on the excluding committee." When they were approved, as well as when they were not, time was wasted explaining things to the building commission. Every house meant starting this dismaying routine all over again.

And the brick industry felt threatened. At one "Own Your Home" Exhibition the president of the Common Brick Manufacturers' Association showed up drunk and commenced to smash the Stockade exhibit.

This was a prime discovery for Bucky, that the building industry is wholly irrational. Men who know how to do what they have always done, locked into craft unions that perpetuate their specializations, stumble through sequences immune to violation. Typically, everything possible is done on the site, as though Ford's crews were to build your car in your garage. Men with saws measure and cut, one by one, hour after hour, dozens of identical framing studs which it would be more rational to square off in a jig at some factory. But that would be *mass production,* and and builders pride themselves on not duplicating designs. Uniformly dimensioned lumber they will tolerate, notably the "two-by-four" which really means one and a half by three and a half, and machine-made nails, but little standardization beyond that. Each house "is a pilot model for a design which never has any runs." That is how roofs are gotten over people's heads; no wonder the mortgages burden them half their lives.

Such realities interfered with the working of one of Bucky's intuitive faiths, that if you found out how to do something better, and worked out the details, it would receive a spontaneous and simple acceptance. (Emerson had said something similar of mousetraps.) No, cheaper-and-simpler did not at all prevail; too much standard operating procedure was threatened. Nor were the shareholders of the Stockade Building System aflame with Fulleresque zeal. They simply wanted their dividends. In 1927, a crisis forced Mr. Hewlett to sell his stock, and the Celotex Company, on purchasing the controlling interest, instantly pronounced Mr. Fuller's services no longer essential.

If it was managerial skills they valued they were probably right. Not only did Bucky let larger vision distract him from pursuit of this week's dollars, he had also been coping throughout his entire Stockade period with a depression triggered by the death of his only child. Alexandra had successively contracted influenza, spinal meningitis, and polio in her second year, had come to require round-the-clock nursing, and had died toward the end of 1922, just before her fourth birthday.

Such a death, Bucky came to believe, was "design-preventable," but instead of attending to comprehensive design the whole world was pursuing short-term goals, with ensuing collisions and gear-strippings such as the wars that fostered the influenza epidemics, not to mention the houses that sheltered microbes more efficiently than they did people. There were still outhouses in Brooklyn, and Bucky had seen New York secretaries give their parties in the office buildings because of the gleaming marvel of indoor plumbing. There was a complex liaison, he was slowly to decide, between the scandalous irrationalities of the housing game and the Whole-System irrationality of which war was the culminating expression, and today's lecture audiences frequently hear of Alexandra's death as a catalytic experience. The most visible things it catalyzed at the time were sustained depression and heavy drinking. "The minute I was through work for the day I would go off and drink all night long, and then I'd go to work again. I had enough health, somehow, to carry on."

In 1927, he was stranded with Anne in Chicago, jobless and with the stigma of having been ousted from a top position. From there, the normal curve points further down. He surveyed himself: a gestalt of "manifold ineptitudes." "I had not been vicious; yet even to myself, I appeared, in retrospect, a black, horrendous mess. I had wanted to give, not take, but I seemed to have converted the opportunities to give into negative waste." Against the rot of a tenement district they were sheltering, on no funds, the health and mind of a newborn second daughter. It seemed to Bucky that Anne and little Allegra would be better back east with relatives, and he himself better canceled out by Lake Michigan. He was thirty-two years old.

According to legend, the crisis took place at the very lakeside, where in a dialogue with himself he turned his life round. This makes an acceptable symbol, though as with the story of the bubbles we can never be sure how many subsequent clarifications he has read back into it. The principal insight appears to have been that he possessed a remarkably diverse inventory of experience and no reliable knowledge whatever. If he destroyed himself the experience would all perish too, and be lost to others whom it might benefit. He had no right to take it from them. "You do not have the right to eliminate yourself, you do not belong to you. You belong to the universe. The significance of you will forever remain obscure to you"—this sententious phrasing is of a much later date—"but you may assume that you are fulfilling your significance if you apply yourself to converting all your experience to highest advantage of others. You and all men are here for the sake of other men."

He has phrased it another way: "Whether you care to be or not, you are the custodian of a vital resource." This resource, his inventory of experience, might help him provide bridges for mankind, "to span the canyons of pain into which you have gropingly fallen." Sometimes his big-picture rhetoric can be tacky.

Contingent resolves, according to later legend, included giving up speech until he was sure he knew what he said when he spoke, and giving up all thought of making a living, in the faith "that one of the rules of Nature is that she permits us each day the integrity of that day's thinking." They survived somehow. Some day a biographer will ferret out the details.

Since he had no schedules, he commenced sleeping whenever he needed to, like a dog. This worked out to a half-hour every six, and gave him twenty-two thinking hours a day. "I was trying to find out how much I could get done, and noticed that a dog when he gets tired simply lies down and sleeps. So it could be that if the minute you're tired you just lie down, you'd need far less sleep. So I just tried it out." (He still goes to sleep in about thirty seconds, and feels a little defensive that in his seventies he needs to absent himself from the waking world for five or six hours, even eight, a night.)

The next project, as he tells it, was to put his thoughts in order, which was difficult because while he had always been a fluent talker he had never had any confidence in his mind. Here the narrative is drifting past great archetypes. Thus another connoisseur of geometry, René Descartes, had sat a whole day in a room with a stove and resolved to think all knowledge out afresh, commencing from the mere certainty that he was thinking. This had entailed the provisional rejection of everything he had picked up in his formal studies. It had also entailed the certainty that God must exist because he was a necessary thought, and the ambition of ordering a structure of certain knowledge not for the delectation of philosophers, but for practical use, to improve the human estate.

We can make many parallels, if we like, between Fulleresque and Cartesian aphorisms; we can note that both of them evolved geometries based on dissatisfaction with a geometry in which nothing *moved;* we can account for the similarities as we choose; but we shouldn't fail to register a fundamental difference. Descartes encountered a great theoretical difficulty in switching from the track of deduction to the world in which men breathe and bodies move, whereas Bucky's starting point was what he had experienced, breathing and moving: not "I think, therefore I am," but "I experience, whatever I am."

Making what he calls "a blind date with principle," he compounded his ten-year-old resolve to discover Nature's system of patterned principles. What he could discover he would ease across the design gap into practical application, for everybody's benefit. It is wholly unsurprising that he turned his attention at once to housing.

And it was the year of Lindbergh's Paris flight, of Heisenberg's indeterminacy principle, of the Holland Tunnel under the Hudson River, of Henry Ford shutting down the Model T production line, so that during months of retooling for a wholly new model there were, for the first time many people could remember, no new Ford cars at all. It was therefore natural for Bucky's thoughts to be guided by analogies with aircraft, with massive industry, and with the automobile production line. These were clearly the day's themes.

SIX

Dymaxion Messiah

From his silence, he emerged talking of everything at once, and was barely intelligible. Amid the hubbub, a publicist hired by Marshall Field's to give focus to a Fuller exhibit coined the word *Dymaxion,* a useful word resonant with suggestion. It became Fuller's property, and for decades his trademark. It combined parts of words the publicist heard him use frequently: *dynamism* and *maximum,* and (for some reason) *ions.* If we should want a working definition, Bucky, who long ago decided what the word ought to mean, will tell us that *Dymaxion* means getting the maximum performance from the technical knowledge we have: the most from the most, which also (come to think of it) means the most from the least. (Since your knowledge is never enough, it is always a minimum.) If we never hear the definition, still the word has a fine modern sound. It has probably scared as often as it has lured.

Everyone, like the publicist, heard parts of words. From a nonstop presentation in St. Louis, the American Institute of Architects heard the words *mass production,* and blanched. Bucky had come there to make them a gift of his patents, and instead heard them pass a resolution stonily opposed to "peas-in-a-pod-like reproducible designs." (A few months later, he remarked, St. Louis tornadoes made headlines by toppling the kind of brick walls architects designed.) Other people heard fragments about four-dimensional prosaic and harmonic integrity, and went away muttering. The editor of *Nation's Business* sent back an article as incomprehensible to "most of our 300,000 simpleminded business readers." (*Nation's Business* was the organ of the United States Chamber of Commerce. Was "simpleminded," Bucky wondered aloud, the Chamber's considered opinion of its members?) An architect who had blinked at one magazine article wondered if there existed a single person (other than the typesetter) who had gotten through it, or would, or *could*. Was Mr. Fuller's welter of words "due to his hexagonal researches having fractured his intellectual processes?" Another questioned his knowledge of engineering principles, and thought his view of human nature "far from rational."

The Total Thinking was simply too much. We have been decades getting used to his separate themes, and now that we have them—mobility, pollution, industrialization, recycling, waste, finite resources, planetary brotherhood— we are apt to wonder if they can be reconciled. Men stake out, each one, a single theme, and decry one another, and are apt to decry Fuller too: as a spokesman for smokestacks, if they are conservationists, and as a Bolshevik if their cause is industrial.

We need not be surprised that his first writings are unknown. Their expression had a midway's randomness of emphasis. A sentence would gain momentum like a cast-off wheel, bounding down ideological hillsides, entangling random clotheslines, frightening the chickens. The next sentence seemed to start t'other side of the creek, and zoom away out of sight while straw hats spun. In 1928, his first manifesto, 30,000 words long, sought to orient its readers with a brief introduction: ". . . in it Lord East and Lady West are married, with much necessary solemn music and jazz symphony—the various ceremonies, civil and otherwise, are progressively blended. Look sharply." Since it turned out to be, more or less, a tract on housing, this introduction did not really introduce. Moreover, having had to pay the printer himself, he had economized by combining minuscule type with lines so long the eye gets lost in mid-scan. With half a novel's wordage crammed onto twenty-eight pages, the pamphlet was as unreadable physically as it was psychically. It went off to 200 recipients, "deemed to be a fully representative group of altruistic thinkers."

This work, first called *4-D* and later *Timelock,* contains all Fuller in potential, but obscurely, like a cloud of gas just condensing into a galaxy. No cliché was eschewed, no swatch of jargon. "One of the most impressive of recent 'about faces' of the medical profession, that is amply justifying itself in its results, is the new school of baby doctoring, very broadly based on the 'stitch in time' or progress by creation theory." Stumbling through sentences no more graceful than that, we are apt to feel that worse prose is barely conceivable. Yet, paradoxically, inescapably, it is energized, end to end. Encumbered by deadweight, still the sentences *move.*

What moved them was the governing intuition he was later to identify as belief in synergy, a word he did not have available in those years. Start with parts, and when they come together they will interact unexpectedly. Professor Newcomb, starting with parts—existing metals, existing forces—had predicted the immediate future of aeronautics, and gotten it wrong. He was fooled by an unforeseen union of gas engine, bicycle and box kite. Someone attending to man's evolving mobility—foot, horseback, railway train, then the lightweight bicycle—might have felt confident that man would next be flying, though unable to guess how. Only by starting with wholes can you hope not to be fooled by synergy. This means identifying very large trends, and ultimately starting with the Universe, which is not at all remote but all about you. Starting there, though, you may easily sound windy, and *Timelock*'s effort at Whole-System rhetoric contained large pockets of imprecision and bluff, as though to locate what would need to be ordered later.

Another paradox was the pervading altruism, propelled as it was—and no one could fail to sense this—by a highly mobilized ego. Bucky's is a curiously innocent egocentricity. To watch him sign, date and pocket the scrap of paper on which he has sketched nothing more arcane than a triangle is to see in the septuagenarian the undying boy. In childhood, while his brother was collecting stones, he had collected pieces of paper with his name on them: letters, postcards, pictures, bills, programs, school reports. They carried their collections back and forth between Milton and Bear Island, and Bucky characteristically remarks that his, consisting of paper, was the less bulky.

In 1917, he made what he now calls a Grand Strategy Decision, which was simply to throw away nothing of this kind. He would even file it chronologically, as (mark the conversion into altruism) a unique document of the life of one twentieth-century man. (If anyone, anyone at all, anyone in the seventeenth-century, say, had kept Everything, what a window for historians! We should be still more grateful than we are to Pepys.) By 1960 his Dymaxion Chronofile had amounted to 250 volumes, 80,000 letters, 3,500 clippings, innumerable hearsay reports of uncollected items. He has graphed the frequency of news items about himself, "a wave pattern of ever increasing magnitudes, with the valleys never going quite as low as previously and the peaks going ever higher." He has smoothed the graph and obtained a ski-shaped curve, almost horizontal for many lean years, but rising at last in the accelerating-acceleration profile. This means that Buckminster Fuller is becoming ever more explicitly a part of everyone's experience of living in the twentieth-century, and we need not feel superior to the satisfaction this gives him.

In a similar way, the *Timelock* pamphlet both flaunted and concealed its author. Its first words, in large type, were "STRICTLY CONFIDENTIAL—property of 4D." No other name was visible. Yet four pages in we find the unobtrusive line, "B. Fuller, 739 Belmont Avenue, Chicago, Illinois." Respondents, after all, had to know where to address their replies.

"4D" was a piece of mystification. It stood for the rumored Einsteinian Fourth Dimension, and seemed to conceal a "4-D Control Syndicate," which possessed many solutions to the world's problems and proposed to release them at times it judged appropriate. This pamphlet was the first installment, the treatise on the House. "The authorship and directing control of 4-D is and will be kept anonymous," lest criticism be deflected from the ideas to the author.

In cold fact, the "4-D Control Syndicate" was Bucky Fuller, working furiously in a Chicago slum and sustained by the trust of various people his enthusiasm or his talk persuaded.

The need to seem numerous and organized is understandable. He had dreamed up nothing less than an industry, and needed the kind of capital that wouldn't come to "B. Fuller." The word *Syndicate,* though, suggests a curious whim, conveying as it does from that city and from those times a whiff rather more of gangland than of the boardroom. A gunman of Capone's also lived at 840 Belmont, and often helped Anne carry out the garbage. Did Bucky mean his smoke signals to hint at the Outlaw Area?

They must have seemed smoky indeed, to men with T-squares and briefcases. "The spirit is not temporal," he wrote. "Mind is of the spiritual; the brain is temporal." This was no casual distinction. A decade later mind had become the phantom captain, and brain an electrochemical resource. Forty years after *Timelock,* in the 1967 Harvey Cushing Oration, Fuller was expounding with all his resources of analogy the distinction between Mind and Brain to 2,000 members of the American Association of Neurosurgeons. That piece of "thinking-out-loud" underlies the longest poem in his 1972 *Intuition.*

"No time may be lost in meditation," he continued, "so long as it involves earnest search for the betterment of mankind, beyond which no conscious thought may go. This is a strange but absolute truth." Scattered through the treatise are many such riddling sentences, clear now that we've heard his talk of the 1960's and 1970's but surely Sibylline then.

He mentioned Margaret Fuller, and Emerson, and his own "protracted isolation for mental research," and described the "4-D House" (we'll look at that later), and suggested, here and there, three governing principles:
—Truth is one.
—The unborn are uncorrupted.
—Nature governs design.
We can look at these separately.

1. *Truth is one.* Since truth is one, all sincerity tends in the same direction. Hence there is no need to fear "pure individualism." This recurrent American premise has sel-

dom been stated. The usual statements about Individualism affirm that it glories in ferocious competition, which weeds out themes having low survival value. This version, called "Social Darwinism," figures in intellectual histories as one of the less lovely by-products of the evolutionary vision.

But Bucky Fuller's idea of the Individual is not Gouldian or Vanderbiltian, but Emersonian. He believes that Character is by definition disinterested, and that conflict does not arise unless through selfishness, a corruption of character. Emerson toward the end of his essay on "Civilization" directs our gaze to "the constellation of cities which animate and illustrate the land," and invites us to notice "how little the government has to do with their daily life, how self-helped and self-directed all families are." He perceived—this was about 1861—"knots of men in purely natural societies, societies of trade, of kindred blood, of habitual hospitality, house and house, man acting on man by weight of opinion, of longer or better-directed industry." Moreover, "each virtuous and gifted person . . . lives affectionately with scores of excellent people who are not known far from home." But no one feels it necessary to *institutionalize* this affection, virtue, and cooperation; that is what Emerson means by the minimal role of the government.

A brave dream gone? We may wonder if it was ever real. Yet Emerson does not claim to be predicting it, he claims to see it before him. Let us bear in mind, for later examination, the fact that Bucky Fuller believed in it, and continues to. That may have been what the man meant who found his view of human nature not rational.

Communities, so structured, are metaphysical, not geographical. If I can get to Munich in the time it once took a man on foot to reach the horizon, there is no reason why the people with whom I feel community should not be distributed world-wide (and in fact I have friends in Munich, and friends across town). The nuclear neighborhood was natural when *place* defined community of interest: on the frontier, on the waterfront, in the village where men use one another's produce. But, "The world," Bucky says today, "is my backyard." As long ago as 1927 he had perceived that the very houses might as well be picked up and moved. Decades later the vogue for mobile homes has endorsed him, though they are still cramped to the width of a highway lane. He envisaged air delivery.

2. *The unborn are uncorrupted.* Nevertheless if they are born into our environment they will turn out like us. That is how the sins of the fathers are transmitted: surroundings which model a deficient imagination impress its deficiencies upon the impressionable. The jailer's son believes in jails. The slum child grows up coping with slums. Squares live in cubes, cubes shape the next generation of squares. The *house* is the most immediate environment, and hovering in Bucky's mind midway between metaphor and reality, the house became his prime theme when he talked of regenerating man. "Children are born naturally to truth or reason. Protect them in it mechanically and they need never lose it. The new industrially produced home will accomplish this."

Mechanically and *industrially:* those words can alarm, in that context. Something possessed him now and then, sweeping him past caution, even rhetorical caution. He waxed Messianic about the House. It was folly, for example, to hire an architect and bid him express your individuality: that way lay "aesthetics," "the snobbish gymnastics of the formula champions." That way lay cast-iron deer, fake Tudor, fake Cape Cod, fake affirmations about the unique self. (All that was in fact affirmed was affluence.)

Think of the man, Bucky said, who must wear a special shoe: we do not call him individual, we call him deformed.

Being in the business of tailoring "individualism," the A.I.A. had naturally recoiled from "peas-in-a-pod-like reproducible designs": as though the pea were not a design triumph, as though any two phantom captains did not manipulate nearly identical bodies.

Were houses mass-produced, where would architects' commissions go? But we hardly think to impute to them self-interest, so strongly are we conditioned against the phrase "mass-produced."

Yet books are mass-produced.* Milton was not offended by the sameness of any two copies of *Paradise Lost*. Sheet music is mass-produced. Prints are mass-produced. The writer, the composer, the designer, each brings his prototype to the best perfection he can manage, and then entrusts it to a factory. Indeed by the 1960's a constructivist in steel could instruct the factory by telephone. Such things shape our intellectual environment, and our bodies too are produced by automation.

The refined prototype, mass-produced: that is nature's way with trees and cats and human frames, and the poet's way and the shipbuilder's. The prototype works as well as can be managed, and gradually, as parameters are refined, designs from different industrial drawing boards will converge on a norm. Airplanes have evolved like that. If you can tell a Boeing 707 from a Douglas DC-8 or a Convair 990, you are a connoisseur indeed. "Material affairs can be handled in but one best mechanical way." So the house should *work*, and given working houses, "even localism and nationalism will soon disappear." (What hubris!) The working house frees the life it shelters;

* Thirty years after Bucky had noticed this (*Timelock*, p. 13), it still seemed shocking when Marshall McLuhan reiterated it.

neutral itself, it should foster individuality. The house meant to "express" individuality conceals its absence.

This trust in the benign environment was a nineteenth-century theme, its orchestrations thoroughly Romantic. The romantic who believes in forests and in nature is trusting to a fit environment to free the soul.

Romanticism recoiled from "the busy hum of cities." So did Bucky Fuller, but not—save for Bear Island—into the arms of untouched Nature. He thought the busy hum of cities not natural, indeed declared that cities were obsolete. They had been herding places for animal man, or "ignorant mob protection against unknown foes." They were also agglomerations peculiar to a primitive stage of world transport, when raw materials were unloaded at docks, warehoused near the point of unloading, and processed near the warehouses. Hence the jam-packing of New York, and the building of tenements, to house workers close to where their work was. (They are human storage-bins now, for the economic overflow.)

"It is surely no love for work that fills a New York subway so full that it is necessary to employ muscular guards to literally shove men and women into the cars by placing their feet against the backsides of these so-called 'patrons.' " It was no love for work; it was stark mechanical necessity, now obsolescent. "The great city, necessary before transportation and distribution, is losing its advantage. It will have lost it all with the advent of the industrially built home."

For such a home would be "natural," one phase of nature being man's valving of cosmic laws. Valving laws, not fighting them; especially not committing one's time to "a rotting thing of wood, built after a billion different patterns, two-thirds of the cost of which is labor, for which there is practically no resale value in the material." It meant building according to the design principles of nature.

3. *Nature governs design*. This was the third theme, and in 1928 the most chaotic. Behind a rhetoric of space-time, expanding spheres, fourth dimensionality, we may detect a governing intuition and a good deal of bluff. It would be twenty years before the principles of Energetic Geometry were statable with any precision. When they were clear at last, they yielded Tensegrity and the Geodesic Dome. So Bucky was finally vindicated.

But in 1928, having at his disposal neither the tetra-hedron nor synergy, he zeroed in on the fashionable new theme, Time. We were to conceive of Time in the man-ner of a sphere expanding, like the sphere of sound around a man who has just shouted. The automobile engine or-dered a time ballet, its expanding spheres of pressure in a timed sequence impinging on metals whose time-line was far slower. The interaction meant "a transition into motion, as we can perceive of it, within the material or conscious sphere." Is the word *sphere* deliberate there? The sentence sounds cranky. Others sounded still crankier: "As long as we have time, we may have as many powers of time, times the whole or angular segmentations of the sphere, as we may wish. So-called gravity is but the ex-pansion of this earth sphere keeping up with the units of nonamplified time-control. As we control time, so may we fly off the earth."

Here we catch one indigenous American accent, that of the crank mouthing his words of power. Every mathe-matician receives now and then long unintelligible trea-tises written like that, offering to solve the universe. The authors are commonly quasiliterate, solitary, Messianic. They have not hitherto been understood, they claim, and this is a willful refusal of the power structure, guarding its expensive monopolies. In a raw land whose artists make homemade worlds, the solitary is very apt to suppose that all truth is accessible through some single aperture, now located by him. His rituals are not traditional, like those of witchcraft; their arcana are novel. Nor is his style, like that of the European eccentric, a patterned deviation from a norm it acknowledges; it is devised from the inside out, the projection of some Idea.

In Poe's time a man named Symmes * announced that the earth was made up of five concentric spheres, with huge openings at the two poles. This was hard to refute before men had been to the poles. Late in the century a certain Teed demonstrated with much mathematics and even experiment the proposition that we live, cosmos and all, inside a hollow earth, the concavity of which we mistake for convexity. That gets rid of infinite spaces very nicely. Other cranks get rid of complex mathematics, sustained by the premise that nature always works simply. Some dispense almost wholly with mathematics.

$$F = \frac{gM_1M_2}{D^2}$$ gives many of us less insight into gravity than the vivid statement of a crank named Gilette, that it is "the kicked back nut of the screwing bolt of radiation." The unwary might take that detail for something of Bucky's. Or this: "Any formation moves in a multiple direction according to the movements of many increasingly greater formations, each depending upon the greater formation for direction and upon various changes caused by counteracting influences of Suction and Pressure in different proportions." This last is from the explanation by Alfred W. Lawson, founder of Lawsonomy,

* The substance of this paragraph is collected from Martin Gardner's *Fads and Fallacies in the Name of Science*. New York: Dover Publications, 1957.

of how movement can be described after we have discarded the unnecessary concept of energy. Yet Lawson, who also set out to reform the economic system and the educational system, was not impeded by his crankery from designing, building and flying the world's first passenger airliner. In 1908, he also coined the word *aircraft*.

Such rainmakers have abounded in America, cheek by jowl with the sellers of wooden nutmegs and the decipherers of Shakespeare's epitaph. Their systems empower them to pronounce on many topics, they frequently have stocks of invented words, and they burn with the need to evangelize. They resemble American geniuses so closely that the inattentive cannot distinguish the species. Genius may overlap crankery, even charlatanry—think of Poe. Or the genius will pass through a crank phase en route to self-command, or will lapse into crankery after he has matured. It is like the way the vector equilibrium finds and loses stable states.

Why American Crank and American Genius should be so closely akin no doubt partly derives from a peculiar quality of American civilization. It is a notably *verbal* civilization, bound together not by local stabilities but by shared understandings which discussion may modify. Talk, which won't modify an Englishman's Englishry, may turn an American 180 degrees, and he'll often protect this remarkable vulnerability by making antiintellectual noises. So the reformer's tactic is to modify what somebody else believes. Citizenship is virtually defined by allegiance to a Constitution, which incorporates a Preamble, seven Articles with subsections, and a growing list of Amendments. The candidate for naturalization is supposed to demonstrate that he understands this document, which means that the very process of Americanization entails catechistic learning. The meaning of various sentences in the Constitution is subject to continual debate. The ritual American conversation commences with the question, what do you *think* of something. The town meeting was an indigenous unit of polity, people saying what they thought and sometimes hearing what visitors thought.

On sheets of paper, weighing every phrase, the Founding Fathers specified a New World, and nothing less than a world has been ever since a natural unit of American thought. What other people would have reached for the moon? No other people worries so much about schools, where the world itself, not merely the three R's, is daily shaped anew in many million new minds. No other people spends so many years in classrooms, or listens to so many lectures. So the crank comes by his evangelical habits naturally, and as for the genius, he is expected to teach. The standard way of finding him an income is to find him a teaching job. Gertrude Stein, irritated by a fellow American in Paris, dismissed him as "a village explainer, all right if you were a village, but if not, not." She too was apt to treat callers like villages. It is a national failing.

Had *Timelock*'s author died in 1930, *Timelock* would exist, if at all, as a prime piece of crankery, tied up with the legend of a man who was never really educated, failed in business, and emerged from seclusion with a barely intelligible scheme for saving the world with prefabricated houses. Since he is still with us forty-five years later, loaded with fame and honors and deferred to, we can read *Timelock* (if we can find a copy) as a blurry first sketch, and also wonder what saved him from the crank's destiny.

We may note that Bucky had not the generic crank's capacity for being satisfied with the sound of his own first thoughts, nor the crank's disinclination to learn more than he knows. So in the next few years he filled in many of the scribbled areas with sequences better thought out.

Within a decade the man who had babbled of "elemental spheres of the human body," their "relatively grouped samples" giving off "a constant friction heat of 98.6 degrees," was explaining scientific concepts with authority to the readers of *Fortune*. That is not the crank's vector, which points into deeper obscurity.

Bucky also understood that to simplify, clarify, you may have to complicate things a good deal first. The indivisible point of Euclid, much controverted in Greece, proved to be a fructive complication. Taken by itself, it could sustain weeks of discussion, but a whole system of thought could be drawn out of it. Newton, to write the gravitational equation, had to invent the calculus, and also had to introduce a grave complication, one he shrank from, *force acting at a distance*. He could not say how such a force might operate, and postulating it was a very bold step. The crank does not take such courageous steps: he follows the declivities of his mania downward. His energy is rhetorical, not conceptual. And Bucky Fuller, not content to burble of spheres, worked out the details of his Energetic Geometry, which led to his map and his domes.

Still, the rhetorical energy survives, and the sense of mission and the operational sweep. So does the faith that, like the parts of his whole-world map, all his concerns abut on one another, being after all each of them segments of the whole world. Many of his later discourses are like articulate and detailed expansions of one blurred hasty phrase or another in *Timelock*, which took all human problems as its province. His way of thinking has not really changed since then.

For synergy, a word he didn't know in 1928, puts sharply a principle he already sensed, that it is always unsafe to start from anything less than the best Whole-Systems grasp we can manage. ("Dig Wholes," reads a sign in the Menlo Park, California, Whole Earth Truck Store, and on the back cover of *The Last Whole Earth Catalog* we find a NASA photograph of the whole earth, captioned, "We can't put it together. It is together.") To put parts together is almost certainly to add up a sum that is not the answer —Professor Newcomb's mistake.

So Bucky starts with the biggest picture he can manage, the Universe itself. That is why he seldom answers questions briefly; questions pertain to details and subassemblies. "After dinner," an intelligent journalist recalls, "I began asking Fuller some questions. Did he think there was still time to rescue the earth from pollution? Did he put any store in the ecology movement? What could be done to end racism?" And, "Fuller did not avoid these questions, but he did not quite answer them, either."

What he has to say is not the sum of such answers, for the same reason that reality is not the sum of such questions. Even human problems are not the sum of such questions. That is the political fallacy. Draw up a list of problems; devise a list of solutions; implement them; and see where it gets you (besides elected). Decide that racial imbalance in schools is a problem; determine that bussing children to unbalanced schools is a solution; then worry about the next problem, massive resistance to bussing.

Let's see how Bucky Fuller approaches racism.

He notes that if you take his whole-earth map (be patient just a minute) and ask what determines human distribution, you come down chiefly to temperature gradients. This doesn't mean gradations of heat, because most places get as hot as most other places. It means gradations of cold. "The difference is, how cold does it get? And the colder it gets the more annual variation in temperature you have." That's what race is, adaptation to temperature swings.

Mark the map with bands of color which signify how cold it gets where—this is how the standard Dymaxion Map is marked; apply to it (Bucky once did this) little dots of Helena Rubenstein pigments that match local skin tones, and behold: "A simple thing. The colder it gets, the lighter, and the hotter, the darker." He can also say why.

He sweeps off into one of his time-lapse overviews of history. "You find the population of the United States going right along the freezing line until the Civil War, when it started going mildly northward as man became master of the cold and could exist north of the freezing line for the first time." This freezing line was where men could get ice to preserve food and yet be warm in the summer to harvest, and almost 95 percent of humanity has arranged itself to live within 1,000 miles of the freezing line.

What about races, then? "People came up on land from the water, and small tribes got isolated following their sheep. They could use the sheepskins to make themselves clothing, and that permitted them to go into cold places, under their tents, off into scattered little tribes, isolated from other tribes for thousands of years. What we call a nation is a group of human beings who have become isolated over thousands of years." And the most adaptable, who are also the most powerful, "tend to want to make babies with others of the same type. Grandfathers wind up marrying their granddaughters." So survival characteristics get inbred. Russia had 148 different nations, with their languages, their physiques: virtual subraces. "We find the same thing in Africa. And great inbreeding is still going on there in very tiny little groups."

Q.E.D. "I'm absolutely convinced that there's no such thing as race. We simply have groups isolated over long periods, highly inbred and making their differences from others into a virtue. Sad, but highly informative."

All right, skin types, this is news to no ethnologist. What about differences in racial temperament?

"The colder it gets, the more annual variation in temperature you have. And the more variation, the more differences of conditions you have to adjust to. Therefore, the more man invents to be able to persist in that area." To cross Lake Victoria in Africa (mean low, 68 degrees) men invented boats. To cross Lake Baikal in Siberia (mean low, far subzero) they invented boats for summer, sleds and skates for winter.

"Not that the Siberians were the more inventive, they simply had more occasion to do inventing. The northerly areas were the natural, necessary areas for industrialization to occur first. It masters the temperature so you can go into the cold, then develops air conditioning so you can endure the heat. Now that you can control the heat, industrialization is spreading southward."

Back to the nub: "Groups isolated over long periods, highly inbred and making their differences from others into a virtue." So racial imbalance in schools is not the problem. Making superficial difference into a virtue, that is the problem. As to how America came to contain those blacks compared to whom lighter folk feel virtuous, Bucky recalls the splendid buildings he saw, still standing, at Delos in the Aegean. It had been a rich place; Delos was that world's slave-trading headquarters. "And the slaves were always produced by warring, with the prisoners simply put into the slave market." (War ended Delos itself. One day Mithridates' admiral massacred all the inhabitants.)

"But gradually it became obvious that the ones who wore the least clothing were the least impeded, became the strongest, and made the most valuable slaves." Clothing, therefore temperature again, and the pigment that goes with temperature. "Gradually the black became the most valuable slave, better than the white. The black became the slave because he was superior."

Then the European exploitation of this, selling the slaves in North America. "And the slave gets to be *an inferior man, chosen for his physical superiority.*"

He reiterates: there is no such thing as race. "We simply have humanity aboard this space ship," with more important things to give time to than how many children of *this* color to ship across town to the enclaves of *that* color. He is confident that the synergetic view has identified a false problem.

Anyone involved in human misery here and now is apt to retort that a good deal of big-picture talk has accomplished nothing except the reassurance of (a) white supremacists, (b) people who for other reasons either prefer things to stay as they are, or else doubt that interventions can improve anything, really. A prescription for doing nothing?

Not at all. There is no one to whom Bucky Fuller offers less comfort than the man who wants things to stay as they are. Things have never stayed as they were, and nowadays especially nothing stays so for long. But the area of meaningful change needs specifying. "Making their difference from others into a virtue," that is what has to change. How? Through the recognition that "we simply have humanity aboard this space ship." How is that recognition to penetrate? In a thousand ways. (Don't leave yet.)

The Dymaxion Map, on which all this discourse was based, crystallized out of geometrical research. Bucky was expounding geometry before some sharp kids from the streets when one of them wanted to know what all this had to do with the rats in his bedroom. "Shut up," cut in a sharper voice, "he knows what he's talking about." So the Rat and the Synergetic View were never squared off. How would he have answered, Bucky was asked later. "I wouldn't have," he replied. "I never argue."

To argue is to get bogged down in special cases, where minds cannot move but can only Indian-wrestle. Rats, nevertheless, are confrontable, and may teach us that the problem is not the rat but the bedroom, a housing problem which means a design problem.

Tenements are a housing problem. The political way to get rid of tenements is to bulldoze them, and then find out that you cannot afford to build anything on the cleared sites that the former inhabitants can afford to live in, or want to. This is called urban renewal, a formula for bulldozing the poor out of sight. It profits contractors and land speculators, land minus slum being a brighter investment than land plus. Its apparent demonstration that we can't afford to do anything clashes with the fact that if the slum has a telephone it is quite as good a telephone as Nelson Rockefeller's, and probably cheaper per month (it has fewer pushbuttons).

So it seems conceivable that the slum might have housing as satisfactory as Nelson Rockefeller's too (and possibly better, the Governor of California may want to interpolate; the wealthiest state's Governor's Mansion is a firetrap). This entails, according to Bucky, putting housing on the same service basis as telephony. (Think of the cost, if your telephone had to be crafted to order, like your house!)

This means *design,* which means (1) the inventory of the world's resources; (2) rational design principles.

The role of a resources inventory is easy to illustrate. Take Western Electric's list of the twenty-seven raw materials in a desk telephone set; plot their sources on the world map; and ponder the fact that your telephone draws literally on the whole world. (Beryllium from the southern hemisphere; chromium from Turkey and South Africa; cobalt from Canada and the Congo . . . the list goes on. A quarter of the things on the phone company's shopping list must be obtained outside the United States.) So why think of houses as if they were log cabins, restricted to local trees?

As to design principles, the telephone helps us realize that these are physical principles. It conforms to them, it can't do otherwise. It also conforms to the anatomy of hand and ear, which likewise express physical principles. (Imagine the man who lives in the Biggest House demanding likewise the Biggest Telephone. Or imagine a local code to require that any telephone installed in this county shall contain as much brick as ingenuity can manage.) Design principles take us even further than to the Whole Earth; to the Universe, where Tension, Compression, Precession are majestically discoverable.

The telephone is a frequent example of Bucky's, exemplary not because IT&T's designers were men of peculiar altruism, but because they could find no other way to make it work. They had not even an incentive to cut the corners that lessen unit costs but shorten service life, because repair expense is borne by the company, and the most trouble-free instrument is the most profitable. Bucky has spent forty-five years trying to persuade people that there is no other way to make housing work either.

We get by with houses analogous to tin-can telephones because people are wonderfully adaptable. Chinese women even adapted to bound feet. And we've had no incentive to look at housing except in familiar ways. We can define very narrowly what a telephone ought to do, so the phone has had the specialist's advantage of being able to insist on its own perfection. The less specialized house has such intricacy of potential function that so long as it more or less fulfills just a few of them—notably keeping most of the rains off—we're persuaded to settle.

Here we are again, somewhere out in the Universe, a long way from that Brooklyn rat. The Universe works: that is Bucky Fuller's first principle. We are part of it: that is his second; we are not intruders. And—this is perhaps his third principle—we concentrate its themes most exquisitely around us when we valve its energies for our immediate service: controlling the flow of electrons, fluids, heat; warding off the winds, the fires and the rats. We call this, building a house. The Whole-Systems view—the synergetic view—brings our thoughts back repeatedly to shelters, which are energy controls. It will also explain how we may hope to pay for them.

In the Universe nothing is spent.

The quickest way to relate this to one's budget is to reflect on the consternation felt by millions when they learned what precious equipment the astronauts had abandoned on the moon. A five-million-dollar car! A million-dollar color TV camera! Wasted!

But stay a moment with the TV camera, for which $1,300,000 appears on NASA's account books. Where is that money now? On the moon? Not at all. It is somewhere on earth, subdivided and circulating from pocket to pocket. Then what is on the moon? Four lunar pounds—twenty-five earth pounds—of glass and metal and plastic. (But some of the metal was *gold!*) Ah, but the total loss to the inventory of Spaceship Earth was exactly a few pounds of minerals, now transferred to the account of Spaceship Moon. If no one ever retrieves it, still that is a small loss. The entire space program has extracted from Earth's inventory perhaps enough metal to make a day's output of Volkswagens.

Yet over a million dollars was "spent"? Not really. What was really spent, that will never be recovered? Time, simply human time, hours of brainstorming, of pumping slide rules and then making sketches and working drawings, of assembling, testing and modifying mock-ups, finally of diligent dust-free handicraft. A few dollars' worth of paper went into wastebaskets (and one trusts will be recycled; anyhow the trees will regrow at no expense), and for prototypes a few hundred dollars worth of metal, chiefly copper, remeltable. Of all the resources that lunar camera drew on, only the time is not reusable. Would we get any of that time back, if we could somehow, at no cost, recover the camera from the lunar plain? Not one second of it.

Time.

Time wasted? Here we need a measure of waste. At minimum-wage rates, several million dollars' time a day gets expended in New York City alone by people doing crossword puzzles. Think out the implications of forbidding *that,* and come back in twenty minutes with your estimate of how the suicide rate might rise, balanced against the additional widgets all those man-hours might be made to yield in a planned economy. If you are fanatical about waste you will soon have modeled a day in the life of Ivan Denisovich.

Nor need we simply equate the lunar camera with the daily crossword, for the million-plus dollars' worth of time that went into the camera was time spent on purposeful learning. (Doing crosswords is random learning.) Assuming all had been learned that later experience proved needful, we could now duplicate a twenty-five-pound color TV camera for the cost of hand assembly. Hand assembly comes high (time, again). NASA says $115,000. If we needed a hundred we could automate somewhat: make up jigs to help us duplicate many small parts. If we needed a thousand we could automate more. Automating means spending time over a process, in order to save it on products. More products will make more process design worth while, and any demand for ten million color TV cameras would justify such elaborate production processes that the cost would drop close to the cost per pound of materials, which is always a limit. (Detroit's current rule of thumb for cars is a dollar a pound.)

We have here a familiar principle, that first prototypes are always fantastically expensive. Spread over many items, the first cost trends toward negligibility, and if the prototype gets destroyed, or left on the moon, all we've lost is a museum piece. That high first cost is simply the cost of learning. Once we have learned, we start modeling what we know. A book is one kind of model, a speech is another, a machine still another. What you paid for this book is a tiny fraction of what learning to write it cost me, or of my cost to the communities that maintained the schools I went to. More spectacularly, the $20,000,000 an airline pays for a Jumbo Jet is a negligible fraction of the investment the jet represents, an investment the Boeing Company's accountants cannot begin to trace. The Jumbo Jet, by the time it was fully explained, would prove to model a large fraction of all human knowledge. Against a background like that, models are cheap.

This means: "things" are not expensive. Learning is. And what learning costs is *time*. Mere things, if there is reason to produce them in sufficient plenty, can sometimes come to so little it is feasible to give them away. I cannot remember when I last bought a ball-point pen. The one I am using to correct these pages bears the imprint of a restaurant in Maryland, whose owners gave it to me as a bit of goodwill. It uses a half-ounce or so of materials, and to have it duplicated by hand would cost perhaps $200. But learning how to render its principle feasible cost so much that the first specimens, twenty-five years ago, retailed for nearly $30. They skipped and smudged, not enough having been learned yet, and to get purchasers interested at all the ad agencies asserted that they would write under water.

If ball-point pens had been left on the moon no one would have fretted, yet hundreds of thousands of dollars' worth of learning went into them. How much we cannot ultimately tell. If we were to trace some of the relevant metallurgical and chemical techniques as far back as we possibly could, we should find that the pen business had been drawing on almost the whole heritage of Western technology. The first Iron-Age man whose fire alloyed copper and tin took an early step toward the brass ink-cartridge. Many things, such as learning how to make a sturdy plastic cylinder, never entered the pen-maker's costs because when he got started they were already part of his heritage. And it is as true of the lunar TV camera as of the ball-point pen and Bucky Fuller's glasses that the costs on the account books (enormous, in the case of the camera) were but a small fraction of the human investment the makers were drawing on.

Most of the costs of most of the things we buy were long ago amortized. They are simply available, as "general knowledge." Everyone, most of the time, is riding free on all that mankind has learned. We are all on welfare.

For no one "earns" even $5,000 a year. Even a ditch-digger's income is an incredible bonanza, quite unrelated to the muscle-power he sells. If we want to know what muscle-power is worth we may ask a company in the power business. They will quote us a figure, a few cents a kilowatt-hour. We may remember from the calculation about energy slaves that a man working eight hours a day, 250 days a year, generates thirty-seven-and-a-half million foot-pounds of energy. Each day, at that rate, he produces 0.13 kilowatt-hours. As an energy source, he is worth far less than coolie's wages. Back in 1940, Bucky calculated that in energy prices then current, a $50,000-a-year executive was being paid as though he developed 16,500,000 kilowatt-hours per annum. Neither he nor the worker is "earning" his pay. They are both drawing dividends at a fantastic rate.

Hardly anyone believes this. A counterculture delegation from the commune called "Drop City" staged a confrontation in the welfare office. "We sat down with the supervisor and laid our heaviest rap on him about what welfare *really* means. That we're *all* on welfare, absolutely dependent on every other human being, plant, animal, earth, air, fire, water for our welfare. . . .

"As we put it to him the supervisor's face got redder and redder. He started chomping and puffing his fat cigar faster and faster, and when we got up to leave, he was in a blind fit of rage. He began pounding on his desk with both fists, bouncing and clattering pencils, pens, paperclips and ashtrays with every blow, and screamed like a little girl having a tantrum, 'YOU HAVE NO RIGHT TO BE POOR!!!' "

As they hadn't. The bind is complex. The accounting system the supervisor was paid to administer prescribes that whatever is paid to Joe, nonworker, shall be carried on the books as a levy, via taxation, on Jim, worker. Jim's view is that he has "earned" his $10,000, of which various governments take $4,000, used in part to keep afloat the likes of Joe. Jim resents this, and the welfare supervisor is paid to represent Jim, and scream on Jim's behalf. As for Joe, he is very likely unwilling to distinguish the communal dividend from the rip-off. Life being short, he intends to take it *now,* even though as things now stand it comes off Jim's hide.

As things now stand. At present the books are kept on the assumption that certain people—most people?—"earn" their pay. This assumption, irradiating the psyche like gamma radiation, can generate unlovely tensions. "I scratched for what I have," the lady said, "and they can scratch for what they get." One would think she was demanding that the sewer pipes her generation laid should be dug up and laid over, but no, the young people in question were simply being educated without incurring sufficient debt to please her.

"But indeed I earn my pay," cries an honest machinist, "for I put in forty hours weekly at this machine." The machinist's claim may be dissociated into two parts. One is that he would be useless without the machine. It places at his fingertips two centuries of design science, a precision he could never hope to attain and solar energy more efficiently valved than his metabolism can manage. The other is that the convention whereby he receives his slice of abundance in return for 2,000 hours per annum at his machine is just that, a convention. Another man draws his share in exchange for 2,000 hours riding in a train pretending to be a brakeman. (The brakes were long ago automated, but there are unions.) Another draws his share in exchange for time setting type which as soon as he sets it will be melted down, since the advertisements in question will be printed from stereotype mats. Another meets classes and teaches them nothing at all (a film is shown). Another watches a machine make condoms. All are paid. All obey the convention that they are earning a living. Elsewhere a man whose psychic processes may be comparable with Thoreau's (though it would be foolish to assert so) is buying his groceries with food stamps. He is "on welfare," and a bad example.

Which is only to state the obvious, that "earning a living" need have no connection with doing work, useful work, even useless work. It has to do only with contracting to surrender a certain amount of time, say 2,000 hours annually. The reason for this is not that much of the populace consists of scamps and loafers. The reason is that no other mechanism so far devised for distributing purchasing power has ever gained the approbation of a public obsessed with what Bucky Fuller calls "the fallacy of 'earning.'" Any means of distributing purchasing power which does not entail the indenturing of a man's time is called "welfare," and carries a stigma.

Such norms are carried over from an era of agriculture and handicrafts, when real need menaced any community whose able-bodied men were idle. ("Able-bodied"! Capable of metabolizing solar energy at a rate barely sufficient to keep a flashlight glowing!) Under those conditions, it was just that whoever wouldn't work shouldn't eat. Dawn to dark, a nail-maker made nails, hammered out red hot one by one. Nails were needed. If he didn't make them there were none. The bargain was obvious: he worked, he was fed. Since that meant that in return for being fed he spent twelve hours a day with his mind on nothing but nails, he might well have rejoiced when a nail-making machine was invented. Society would gain cheap and abundant nails. He would gain freedom from his forge. Since his work was being done, it would have been equitable to go on paying him. But no, his meal ticket was lifted. He was "automated out," and if he was properly roused by the injustice of this development, he tried to smash the machine. (Weavers, also automated out, tried to jam the mechanical looms

with their wooden shoes, called sabots, giving us the word
sabotage.)

It seems sensible to think of automation as a freeing of
people from toil. We might even think that *one reasonable
objective of automation is to create unemployment,* the
more the better, and that a society optimally industrialized
should be blessed by nearly total unemployment. In 1919,
when the Industrial Revolution was about a century old,
C. H. Douglas calculated that three hours' work a day for
adults between eighteen and forty should supply all Eng-
lishmen's necessities. That was one measure of how far
England had come since Watt, and a half-century later one
might expect the figure to have been halved. Instead we
are doing everything we can think of to keep as many
people employed as possible, and call unemployment a
problem, not a benefit. If 7 percent of the potential work
force, defined as able-bodied men under sixty-five, count
as "unemployed," the industrial system is failing, to an
extent that verges on the catastrophic. That is how poorly
we understand the industrial system.

Whole industrial sequences are now performed without
the intervention of human muscle. One can imagine the
logic of present-day procedures leading to an ultimate
automated factory in which no one need do anything at all;
and every morning a work force marching in, each man
to be manacled for eight hours straight to a station beside
the Ultimate Machine, in return for which penal servi-
tude, once a week, he will be issued a pay envelope. He
will have "earned his living." Many jobs are already like
that: contracts to surrender a portion of one's time.

For over fifty years a continuous underground tradition
has advocated some such view of things. Since its advocates
have seldom been trained economists, they have been

brushed aside with relative ease. C. H. Douglas was an engineer; Frederick Soddy was a Nobel Prize chemist, discoverer of isotopes; Ezra Pound and Gorham Munson were men of letters. Each of them in mid-life became convinced that economic reality was about as we have outlined it. Encyclopedias do not give a line to their economic insights, beyond noting how Pound's got him into trouble.

Douglas ("I read him," Bucky says, "in the 1930's") said that wealth has two main sources in addition to brute labor. One is the accumulated sum of what men have learned, a knowledge concentrated in machines and processes. He called this "the cultural heritage." Some of it is perfectly weightless. The inventor of zero contributed to the cultural heritage, and the inventor of logarithms, and the discoverer of the periodic table of the elements. Our wealth and comfort today derive from such things.

The other prime source of wealth, on Douglas' showing, was men's ability to do in concert what they could not do singly. He called this "the increment of association," and Bucky can teach us to identify it as a form of synergy. Thus many men together can make and operate a sailing ship, which at no expense for power can proudly tack round the world, bringing back what we have not at home.

It seemed clear to Douglas that men deceived themselves when they ascribed their communal wealth to many million laborers, each paid for his work as though he alone had generated his fraction of the product. He proposed an early form of guaranteed annual income, a stated dividend drawn on what he called the community's social credit. Discussion of this, what there was of it, bogged down amid power struggles and hoots about "funny money," and his Social Credit Party went the way of all splinter movements.

Fifty years later such talk seems much less abstract.

Though no one yet knows how the common wealth might be monetized, Puerto Rico is considering a scheme to distribute industrial dividends to the workers. The planners may some day get around to the nonworkers. For some years Robert Theobald has been writing books on what he calls the Economics of Abundance, abundance being easier to recognize than it was in Douglas' time, and increasing unemployment—no one calls it increasing freedom —easier to identify as a characteristic built into industrialization. The necessary work force gets smaller and smaller. We keep children from working at all. We discourage adolescents from working by prolonging their school years (half American youth go to college, and even graduate schools now get crowded). We are ambivalent about married women working. We retire men as early as possible, and during their working years we are careful to specify that any work beyond, say, forty hours a week is "overtime" and abnormal. All these devices diminish the labor pool, and even so it is difficult to keep more than 90 percent of the labor pool occupied. Someone has calculated that in the United States less than 25 percent of even those who work are engaged in "primary production." The rest work for governments, or nonprofit employers, or in "people-service" occupations. And still we talk of people "earning a living."

As to the folk who say they earn theirs, "The trouble with them is," Bucky said one day, "that they don't think about how they got what they've got. Put them on a desert island and see how far they'd get." (They call themselves the enterprising ones.)

He has a simple model. Put a man down in a deserted tropical place, and in a couple of days he can spin a geodesic shelter over his head, using the local bamboo. He can only do this, however, if he has (1) the requisite mathematics and (2) a knife, which means bringing with him, in his head and in his pocket, a substantial portion of "the cultural heritage."

No one man's head or pocket contains more than a fraction of it. The cultural heritage—which is more than crude "know-how," embracing as it does every kind of intuition, including all the things artists have glimpsed before anyone else—belongs to the "world-around intercommunicating continuity of consciousness" which he calls "Continuous Man."

Continuous Man is ultimately weightless: he is our unfaltering knowledge of all that we know. The things you tell me, the things I tell you, all that the dead have told us, all we vicariously share—Columbus' voyages, Homer's measured pulsebeat—these and the idiosyncratic way each one of us metabolizes experience, these and the regenerative networks of consciousness in which all thought, all experience is new-formed, accelerated, shared—these are "humanity"—Continuous Man.

In "the rotation of night as a shadow around the earth," Bucky perceives an invisibility more important than anything astronomers imagine or astronauts see: the "rotating wave of shadow sleepers," consciousness disconnected for a third of anyone's time, and its converse, "two-thirds of all mankind at all times continuously awake." That rotating wave of consciousness is the most important phenomenon in our part of the Universe, more transformative than the interaction of chromosomes, more massive than the tides. It sweeps on, absorbing principle as the Earth absorbs sunlight. It lives by integral cycles as Earth-life lives by the water-vapor cycle and the carbon-dioxide cycle. Its cycles are in part as invisible as photosynthesis, in part as public as the growth of leaves. Ships and planes emerge,

satellites rise and circle, atoms are coaxed through syn-
chrotron tunnels, notebooks blossom with symbols, the
very void is patterned with new information. This book is
a tiny increment; there is nothing "new" in it and yet it
regenerates old knowledge a little, in a way new to me as
I write and I hope to you as you read. (At least you have
never read *this* sentence before.) My trust in you, yours in
me, on just this unique occasion, is yet one more novelty
in a cosmos where everything is new under the sun.

And yet we talk of "Work," as if it much mattered.

We should pay people *not* to work, Bucky has speculated, and pay them handsomely; then some work might
get done. In the depths of the 1930 Depression there were
still too many people working; their drag pulled millions
down into starvation. Continuous Man was working nevertheless, isolating the first trans-Uranium elements, devising
aluminum airplanes, writing *Finnegans Wake*. Man the
automaton was already obsolete. We still pay millions an
hourly dole to pretend to be working. We should pay them
to go to school, or go fishing. Minds can marvelously re-
pattern themselves while fishing. Fuller's quick answer to
anyone appalled by costs is to suggest that of every 100,000
set free, one would make some discovery sufficient to maintain the other 99,999.

A column by James J. Kilpatrick (*Los Angeles Times,*
March 15, 1972) cites instance after instance in Catonic
tones. Two men lay 100 blocks of masonry a day; in 1926
one man laid 600. A little gasoline-powered generator
must be watched (union rules) by an operating engineer,
an electrician and a pipefitter. The engineer draws nearly
$400 a week "for starting once or twice a day a gas engine
smaller than those on many home lawn mowers." The
electrician, similarly paid, puts a plug in a socket when-

ever the machine is moved. No one knows what the pipe-fitter does. "On a motel construction job in Philadelphia, electricians and carpenters quarreled over the installation of a chain-hung ceiling lamp. In the end each union got a piece of the action. The carpenter screwed two hooks in the ceiling and draped the chain; the electrician put the plug in a wall socket. Cost: $40 per installation."

Surveying such instances, Bucky Fuller does not deplore "the loss of the work ethic," not at all. A great truster of popular wisdom, he would remark that these men know very well that their "work" is obsolete. But if the game requires simulated work as the price of eating, why, they will simulate, shielded by union rules. A system that can support such a host of freeloaders clearly draws on wealth unrelated to their "work." It would cost nothing whatever to put them on affluent welfare.

Wealth is real, whether monetized or not. It has grown enormously since my parents' time, and my share in the increase is real, though heaven knows my bank balance doesn't show it. It exists as enhancement of access: five hours to cross the continent, not three days; tires that run 40,000 miles, not 8,000, and are almost never flat; a diet as diversified in winter as in fall. In my world it is normal for adolescents to summer in Europe. Paying adult fares, I have gone there eight or nine times myself. My parents visited Europe just once, and were more fortunate than most of their generation. I could lengthen this list indefinitely: not an inventory of possessions, nor a stock of money, but nonetheless a balance sheet of wealth.

What then is this wealth?

Bucky says it has two complementary parts: (1) the energy of the Universe, much of it radiant and gravita-

tional, the rest locked up in ninety-two elementary patterns; (2) all that we know. The first transforms. It cannot
be created or destroyed. The second grows, because "We
cannot learn less." So wealth can only grow.

Ah, but what of destruction of resources?

Not at all, he replies, they are not destroyed, though it
is true that we lock away appalling quantities where we
cannot easily get at them again. (Chess players do the same,
and learn better chess.) Entropy—energy randomized,
hence inaccessible—need not worry us while the sun pours
on more. Chemical transformations need more careful
watching. At present all the sulphur escaping from all
the world's smokestacks is exactly replaced by the sulphur
we mine each year. We can imagine a day when every
bit of it has been mined, and has been dissipated as sulphur dioxide "pollution." That would be "destruction
of a resource," and wanton deadening of the breathable
air, but not destruction of sulphur, every atom of which
Spaceship Earth would still carry on inventory. But such
dissipation is insanity. Those smokestacks ought to be our
sulphur mines. Reclaim it before it dissipates! And sell
the cost as sulphur stock, if you want. And do not suppose
there is some natural law that says whenever we handle an
element we must ruin it, and ourselves.

Locking gold away in vaults is in just this way a destruction of a resource. Complicated rules of bookkeeping (not
of physics) make it nearly impossible to get at it again. So
gold grows scarce, and yet there are sensible *uses* for gold,
the seventy-ninth element. Those bookkeeping customs
intimidate us like natural laws. Yet we have only to change
them ("Forget the gold standard"). In the same way no
natural law compels us to dissipate the resources we use.
We have only to apply Wealth Component #2, Knowl-

edge. Industrialists who say reclamation "costs too much" are not taking the synergetic view. They think that wealth is sulphur, or oil, or gold.

Totaling at today's costs the energy increments—ultimately solar—that slowly transformed fossil cells into oil, we can say that Nature invested one million dollars in every gallon of petroleum we harvest. That is not regenerated like trees and corn. It is short-term capital; Bucky compares it to the food deposited inside the egg, to nourish the chick till it breaks out of the shell and makes contact with the great Universe.

The chick was not designed to consume that deposit and then starve. Nor were we designed to consume our deposit of coal and oil and then starve. We were designed to start using our minds, eventually.

His glasses, as he talks, slip down his nose. He tugs them upward with an elbows-out gesture, like a diver adjusting his mask. That is a transient nuisance, like pollution. Most of his movements are a choreographic counterpoint, unconscious, functional. Watch him speak his 7,000 words per hour on the integrating function of the human intellect; keep an eye on the kinetics. At key occurrences of the theme-word *intellect* he is pointing to his head. A clutching and kneading movement of the left hand substantiates the shadowy word *integrate,* and *nature* in its countless manifestations, the impinging sunlight, the self-interfering knots, the lapse of pattern into the seemingly random, is elucidated by arm- and finger-work of Nijinski-like intricacy. In full communion with his theme he is weaving, tensing, leaning, straightening, to twist invisible valves and arrest split-second deterrences as though piloting a lunar lander amid strange new boulders.

(The pilot's license in his wallet rubs against the machinists' union card.)

No transcribed words correspond to any of this. It is a turning loose from New England decorums which Bucky ascribes to a remark of his daughter Allegra, who was twelve and already on her way to a dancer's career when she told him what he was repressing by standing immobile like a union electrician. "If you just dare to let yourself move . . ." He takes dares. "I decided she was right and I would try to do it. It was a reversal of all the training I'd had, the Naval Academy and everything else. But today I'm absolutely unaware of my motions. Sometimes when I see a film of my lectures I'm amazed to see that I'm all over the stage like a ballerina. Absolutely unaware of it."

"If you just dare to let yourself move." Watching him, we can believe in a transformational Universe, Bucky Fuller enacting man's role in it. When Allegra said that —if she said it: she doesn't remember—she spoke for Continuous Man, supplying a theme her father would multiply by as many thousand as the thousands who have watched him. That is, in essence, what he has to tell them: "If you just dare to let yourself move."

One man can be paradigmatic (none is an island). There were times when Bucky lived on a bowl of soup, bought every other day. There were times of great affluence, put out as fast as gathered. (His normal "bank balance" continues to hover near zero.) During the times of thin soup he harvested principle. During the times of affluence he made a car, a house, numerous domes, transforming principle into availability. That has been, more or less, the story of mankind.

SEVEN

Stillbirth of an Industry

What Fuller had conceived in 1928, with his eye on Ford, was an industry. He had seen, moreover, that it would alter the world, far more than the automobile had. Unlike Ford, whose mind was on producing a product, he set out to imagine the world his housing industry would create, and worked inward from that to the function of the house. When he came to the house itself he reversed this process; "designing from the inside out," he envisaged the maximum enhancement of human lives, tailored the innards to suit and hung around them a logical envelope. So one process ran in from macrocosmic man, newly placed in relation to his world, and another ran out from microcosmic men, newly placed in a new kind of intimate environment, and the two met in the house itself. It is misleading to isolate the house, though in the absence of either industry or inhabitants a tabletop model of the house was all there ever was to attend to.

The reason this industry would alter the world was that it implied total mobility. People would cease to be anchored to the houses they were scrimping to buy, the houses would cease to be anchored to the utilities grid, and everyone would cease to be anchored by tons of debt. He conceived a world full of houses like telephones: simple, functional, ubiquitous, mass-produced, components in a system and rented.

To indicate what such a world might be like, he had suggested houses deliverable by zeppelin. A tower-shaped structure 170 feet high could be slung beneath a 700-foot dirigible, and planted like a tree in the crater made by a bomb the zeppelin could drop. While cement was setting around the base to hold it, the crew could be drilling a well. Then the ten-story structure, with its own power generator and provision for recycling its inhabitants' wastes, would be independent of the network of "utilities" which today dictate where it is feasible to build. Men could populate the terrene outlaw sector, far from the vetoes of idiots like the police chief who once forebade the Stockade Building System in his community. He was the building inspector "because his father built the first privy in town." He scratched, smelled, even bit a Stockade Block, recalled a sad experience his father once had with concrete and turned the system down.

That tower was not only to be planted like a tree, it was shaped like a tree, ten decks suspended from the trunk-like central shaft. A year or so later the tower had been scaled down, for the time being, to the "4-D House," a one-family minimum model less unlikely to go into production. Bucky detailed it inside and out, and showed a beautiful dollhouse version with the parts demountable and a nude in the bedroom (to demonstrate the climate control). A central mast still bore the weight, and the floors were still hung on tension cables. Thus tension and compression were separated out, "compression diminishing directly as we recede from the vertical until the building finally flows downward in pure tension," hanging about the mast like a hoop-skirted dress. Bucky's rhetoric took

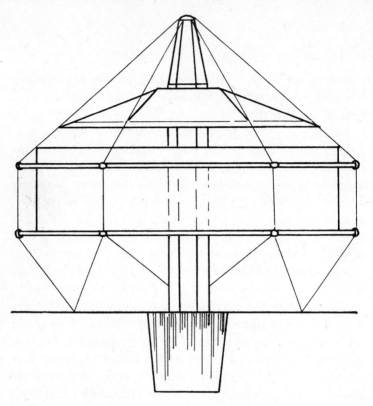

Dymaxion House

a characteristic flight: "Then may the exterior enveloping shell, completely freed of spiny skeleton, present a lithesome fullness and harmonic grace, not dissimilar to the sheer and lovely, though sufficiently austere lacy veils flowing from the hennins of the fifteenth-century French court ladies, so marvelously portrayed in Maurice Boutet de Monvel's Joan of Arc at the court of Chinon."

More pertinently, a house that was going to hang would be symmetrical all around the mast. Circular? No, suspension points for the cables suggested corners, in fact six of them, making the floor plan hexagonal, the rooms wedge-shaped. Since the floor deck and the ceiling deck were both suspended, the walls that joined their edges bore no weight whatever and could be wholly glassed. Atop the upper deck was sunbathing space, with a rain canopy above that. Below the bottom deck was car space or plane space. The house between the decks was to feature every manner of appliance, all machinery housed in the central mast: exactly, and in ways Le Corbusier never envisaged, "a machine for living."

As Reyner Banham tells us in *The Architecture of the Well-Tempered Environment,* Le Corbusier and the Bauhaus designers learned nothing from technology except a visual style. The simplest physical transactions were beyond them. Their lights glared, their corridors echoed. Bucky on the contrary started from real machines, to "valve the environment into preferred patterns."

Though most of the machines he talked about were still to be invented, Fuller understood quite clearly what he meant them to do. Decades before the key concepts were widely accessible, he was thinking of single-family homes as ecosystems, trapping sunlight, recycling wastes, taking a minimum toll of unreclaimable resources. What goes on in an ordinary house is *consumption;* its input is resources, its output trash. Bucky wanted to build not a trash factory but a valve, to deflect the circulating energies of the universe into serviceable patterns, taking thought for their next retransforming (on the premises if feasible). One could shower with a "fog gun," using just ounces of water; and that water could be reclaimed.

Nobody understood what he was talking about. Forty years later a substantial part of the world's engineering talent was working along such lines, though not to increase man's freedom on earth but to help him penetrate space. Fundamentally the space program is a shelter program. Take a man off Spaceship Earth, move him to Spaceship Moon, and both in transit and after he's on the moon he needs, if he's going to stay alive, a shelter more scrupulously thought out than any shelter has been in human history. The simplest spacecraft of the first Mercury program was not just a capsule but a Whole-System environment control, modeling at absolutely minimum weight as much as was needed of the ecosystem we all depend on at home. The longer people stay in spacecraft, the more elaborate the recyclings and the more of the ecosystem they must reproduce. We now envisage Skylabs for months-long habitation, and Bucky expects that some day everything we call "utilities," all that ties our homes to a network of buried wires and pipes and a graft-ridden trash-collecting system, and subjects us to the controlled scarcities that enrich subdividers, will be packaged into a 500-pound "black box" for which the space program will have done the research and development work. With a lightweight dome for envelope and a lightweight black box for resources, anybody would be able to live at whim anywhere.

The house was to do the laundry and the dishes. It was to warm and circulate its air, bearing smoke and odors away. At ideal temperatures, the pneumatic beds would need no "bedbug incubators" (covers). One would walk across a soundless pneumatic floor, supported on a tensional net. In the bathroom one might use the "vacuum tooth brush," also the chinning bar. The shelter would be erectable in one day, proof against "earthquake, flood, fire, gas attack, dirt, pestilence and cyclone," and complete with "sewage-disposal tanks, fuel oil tanks, diesel engine, electric generator, storage batteries, motors, artesian well, water pump, water softener, water heater . . ." A hand intercepting a light-beam would open doors.

The idea was not silly luxury, but the canceling of silly

toil. Bucky tabulated years later the rituals of a cleanliness that is next to godliness: dish-cleaning, clothes-cleaning, house-cleaning, food-cleaning, self-cleaning: "an eight-hour day devoted to yesterday's dirt," with "not one constructive act" accomplished. Thus it took a seventh day, "hallowed for resting, and considerable preaching, praying and psalm-singing, to keep a mother housekeeper in good humor."

These ideas were all developed during little Allegra's first months of life in that Chicago apartment. He was watching a child explore the universe, and his wife spending "ten hours a day keeping the baby from killing herself." Out a window, down an elevator shaft, into the street where cars maimed a million a year—the baby saw no reason not to head in any of these directions. Eliminate openable windows then; eliminate elevators; move the house away from traffic (abolish the jammed city).

The directness seems nearly insane. What is really unsettling about the Dymaxion House is that it doesn't perform the most important office of a house in most people's lives: it doesn't tell you what to do with yourself, doesn't give you so much as a hint. That's up to you.

A man who could *use* twenty-two hours a day needed no directives from the brickwork. Why should standardized housing generate standardized people? What an insult to people. No, they deserved "a home wherein the real individualism of man and his family may be developed, as a minimum of time is given to what he *has* to do, willy-nilly, eat, sleep and be clean." Real individualism means people doing what they want. The logic of architectural practice was to put people into "individualized" houses, whereupon they all found themselves doing just the same thing, i.e., looking after the house.

As he wrote, the majority of the houses Americans inhabited were "still without even bathrooms, toilets or sewage disposal." That was in 1927. They were "pasted, piled and tacked together," out of materials no maker of ocean liners would contemplate: brick, stone, wood, concrete, their structural virtue mindless Egyptian *weight*.

As to those who were affluent enough to consult an architect, he devoted to their plight the most memorable of his early flights of rhetoric, a 347-word sentence still sometimes reprinted:

> If today a man, let us say a resident of Chicago, wishing to acquire an automobile, were to visit one of 2,000 automobile designers in the city, equivalent to Chicago's 2,000 architects, and were to commence his retention of the designer by the limitation that he wanted the automobile to resemble in its outward appearance the Venetian gondola, a ginrickshaw of the Tang Dynasty, a French fiacre, or coronation coach of Great Britain, pictures of which he had obligingly brought with him, all final embellishment of course to be left to his wife; and they were together to pick and choose from the automobile accessory catalogues, advertisements, and auto accessory shows, motors, fly wheels, fenders, frame parts offered in concrete, brass, sugar-cane fibre, walnut, etc., and succeeded in designing an automobile somewhat after the style of some other fellow; and they were then to have the design bid upon by five local garages in Evanston, picking one of the bidders for his ability, or price; and the successful bidder were to insist on the use of some other wheels than those specified; and the local bank, in loaning the money to the prospective owner to help him finance, had some practical man to look over the plans and absolutely guess at the cost and base a loan thereon, incidentally insisting on the replacement of several parts and methods in which they were interested; and then the insur-

ance company were to condemn a number of units used, because they had not been paid for their "official approval" and other units were therefore substituted; and fifty material or accessory-manufacturers' salesmen were informed by a reporting agency whose business it was to ferret out this poor man's private plans, that he was going to build and hounded him with promises; and finally the local town council had to approve of the design and individual materials and give permit to build, sending around assertive inspectors while it was being built, it is certain that few of those desiring automobiles would have the temerity to go through with it.

He added that the car would cost $50,000 and perform ludicrously. Also, "It should have been mentioned that in the building of the automobile, not one but many mechanics from different trades would have to be employed, though many times there would be but room for one man to work. The contractor, who would also be building other cars in Lake Forest, Elgin, etc., would stop in for an hour a day to look over the work, outside of which it would receive no organization of method. There would likely be strikes by the plumbers or electricians, who would insist on most of the improvements in design being left out as they had no rule permitting them. To cap all, the car would take from six months to a year to build."

By such insanities were roofs gotten over heads. And still are.

Not a "house," then, an industry. The house did not even exist, and Bucky would not have known how to go about building one. The mechanisms did not exist—the automated washer-drier, the temperature-controlled ventilation, the dishwasher, for that matter the "radio-television receiver." Prototypes existed, in hotels, hospitals, ocean liners. What we know today was evident then, that they were all possible. But not off the shelf, not in domestic models, in 1928.

He was counting on the rapid research and development at a huge industry's command. Let someone of Ford's stature give the word, and battalions of engineers would bring what was possible into the domain of practice. We are as used to this idea now as we are to dishwashers. Men were on the moon nine years after the word was given, though when it was given not one of the requisite items of hardware existed. But in 1928 there was no such example of an intricate set of problems solved on command from scratch, and it's hard to know which to be more astonished by: Bucky's grasp of what industrial teams might do, or his belief that anyone else would believe it.

No one did, at least no one capable of giving the word. In 1927, Fuller estimated that perhaps a billion dollars would be needed for research, development, tool-up. Five years later much basic work on the all-important metals and alloys had been done; the investment was down 90 percent, to a mere hundred million. Still there were no takers.

But in 1945, the Dymaxion Dwelling Machine was almost produced. Two prototypes were actually assembled, with their furnishings and their mechanisms in place. The structure weighed just three tons, the parts would nest for shipping into one truckable cylinder, and no component a workman had to handle weighed more than he could lift with one hand. It would sell, erected, for the price of a Cadillac. The tooling cost was down to ten million dollars. Ten million was not forthcoming. Bucky never devised a complete working house again. His attention for the next twenty years was focused on the envelopes only, developed from the geodesic principles he was discovering. The innards could wait for NASA's power pack. There is still no housing industry.

Still, it is not quite true, as Fuller contends, that American building techniques remain where Egypt and Greece left off. About 1860, an American student of trends might have supposed a housing industry was coming. The need to roof a new continent in a hurry inaugurated a kind of spontaneous industrialization, seldom perceived because it stopped developing.

America's first innovation was to build houses wholly of wood, with clapboard outer walls attached to the frame, and a wooden frame has a certain structural integrity. You can jack a wooden house off its foundations and move it, something a brick box won't tolerate.

Moreover, wood can regenerate: forests grow back. One need not think of a house lasting forever. It would make ample sense if it lasted till nature had replaced its materials.

Most important, these houses were soon built in a new way. The craft method, used in New England as it had been used for centuries on European barns, was superseded by an industrial method which depended on railways, power saws, machine-made nails, and the geometry of the frame was altered accordingly.

Thoreau's cabin was built the medieval way. In *Walden* he describes the procedure. The main timbers, hewed from fresh pine with his borrowed axe, were six inches square and stood eight feet high. Each piece of the massive frame, and likewise each stud and rafter, was carefully mortised and tenoned—skilled work indeed—and as sections were fitted together neighbors helped him raise them. Once the frame stood by itself, he nailed on the clapboards and shingles. He is so proud of his thrifty shopping—$8.03½ for boards, $3.90 for nails, a thousand old bricks for the chimney at $4.00—that we do not notice the enormous investment of time that went into the framing. So much labor, anyhow, seemed a mode of virtue.

But when his cabin went up in 1845, Thoreau's way of framing was already obsolete. In Chicago, about 1833, George Washington Snow had devised what was soon called, in derision, the balloon frame—"the point," says Sigfried Giedion, "at which industrialization begins to penetrate housing."

The balloon frame dispensed with those heavy six-inch timbers and all that careful mortising. It was simply nailed together from 2-by-4's, like a box, the vertical members sixteen inches apart. It is still the normal American method of framing. It depended on mechanization: sawmill lumber and machine-made nails, cheap enough to be used lavishly. Handmade nails had run 25¢ a pound, which was high. By 1828, machine nails were down to 8¢, then 5¢, and by 1842, 3¢. (It is not clear why three years later the nails to make Thoreau's cabin cost $3.90. Did he really use 130 pounds of nails?)

The new frames looked so light it was clear they would fall down. Though they didn't, the "balloon" nickname stuck. Contemporary observers soon pointed with pride. By 1865, a man and a boy could "attain the same results, with ease, that twenty men could on an old-fashioned frame." The saving in cost was something like 40 percent, the saving in effort enormous. "If it had not been for the knowledge of the balloon frame," a man named Robinson wrote in 1855, "Chicago and San Francisco could never have arisen, as they did, from little villages to great cities in a single year."

Being wooden, they were both destroyed by fire, San

Francisco six times in a two-year span (1849–51), Chicago definitively in 1871. That was a drawback. Anyhow, they were quickly rebuilt.

When there were not even the local skills available to nail such a frame together, the nailing could be centralized. A survey called *Great Industries of the United States* did not miss this. "The western prairies are dotted all over with houses which have been *shipped there all made,* and the various pieces numbered." That was by 1872.

By a natural extension, there should soon have been production-line houses, but the evolutionary process terminated. American home-building practice did not stick, as Bucky would have it, in the Middle Ages; it stuck in 1833.

A related tradition didn't get stuck, it got deflected. That was the invasion of mechanical design into every detail of human surroundings. Sitting, especially, received ingenious attention. Toward 1860, and for thirty years thereafter, chairs were devised that moved as the body wished and supported it as it required to be supported. How people sat in trains was investigated, how a woman's posture at a sewing machine compressed her thighs if the seat did not slope forward. Backs reclined, seats tilted, chairs rocked on springs and moved on casters. There were metamorphoses too, for economizing space. Beds turned into sofas, a lounge turned into a swing, a tricycle was patented that would turn into a hammock. Living rooms, by a few touches, became bedrooms. On trains, beds came out of ceilings and compartment walls. Some of these devices were merely ingenious, some ludicrous. All of them indicated two principles: that imagination was playing over elements no longer taken for granted, and that leisure was being taken seriously enough for design to accommodate its postures.

Then in 1893, confronted at the Chicago World's Fair with sumptuous and tasteless European taste, this inventiveness suddenly felt ashamed of itself. "Patent furniture," Sigfried Giedion writes, "was banished from the house, and the countless attempts to create a truly nineteenth-century comfort went to waste." * It was banished to the office, where the typist sits on a chair someone gave thought to. That authority symbol the swivel chair her boss occupies was also thought out. It was designed in 1853 for the home, where instead we now make do with agglomerated cushions and springs.

The tradition that was stirring piecemeal into life might well have culminated in designed surroundings that understood the interplay of the body, the senses, the ambient mechanisms. Instead Bucky Fuller had to write at the top of his voice not about solutions but about the very principle, and got a reputation for being eccentric whenever he ventured a solution. His plug-in "Dymaxion Bathroom" of the 1930's is one man's attempt to achieve from scratch what the engineering genius of a society might have accomplished with authority had the principles of the Pullman roomette not been shut from home design by invisible barriers of taste and custom.

From the Dymaxion House he projected in Chicago, in 1927, to the Dymaxion Dwelling Machine he designed for production in Wichita, in 1945, Bucky was trying single-handed to do a tradition's work. It is not surprising that his detailed solutions sometimes seem thin and improvised. The 1927 house was a fantasy: a structural principle, plus a list of the amenities it should contain. The

* For more about patent furniture, see his *Mechanization Takes Command;* for the balloon frame, his *Space, Time and Architecture,* from which I have gleaned the nineteenth-century quotations.

Dymaxion Bathroom was in a way no less a fantasy: evidently designed by a stocky man not much more than five feet high, it had a tub three inches wider than standard tubs but not very long, the total floor area of the tub-shower-washbasin complex being only five feet by five. It carries on that lost nineteenth-century tradition, compacting the facilities and deleting petty annoyances. (The stream of mixed hot and cold water jetted away from the user of the basin, and couldn't shoot up his cuffs.) The principal annoyances it eliminated were great weight and great cost. The whole thing, shell, fixtures, heating, forced ventilation and all, weighed 420 pounds, assembled from just four stampings each of which two men could carry up narrow stairs. They bolted together, and a plumber could hook up the works in minutes. Twelve were built. It is said that fear of the plumbers' union underlay Phelps-Dodge's decision not to order quantity production.

The best fantasy of all was the Dymaxion Car, which Bucky insists was not a car at all. "I knew everybody would call it a car. It was the land-taxiing phase of a wingless, twin-orientable-jet-stilts flying device." The jet-stilts—he'd begun to conceive them in 1917—were inspired by the fact that a duck flies though it hasn't the wingspread for gliding. It fires sharp little spurts of air earthward from between wing and body. Maneuverable jet engines might do likewise, thrusting a vehicle both aloft and forward. Since no metals existed to contain the heat of those jets, he elected, he says, to concentrate on the "ground-contact maneuvering problems," where planes usually had trouble anyway. (Their pneumatic tires are "packaged sky-oceans to insulate earth and ship.")

Thus the Dymaxion Car, in the best American tradition of unlikely combinations, was really part of a jet plane, with a Ford V8 engine substituted for the jets. The whole was part of a still larger fantasy. Bucky was still propelled by his 1927 dream, developing the private air transport people would need to reach Dymaxion houses that had been air-delivered to mountain tops. Everything he did in the 1930's was a detail of something larger. In a sense, this is true of everything he has done.

The car, unlike the house, really got built. It looked like a bulbous wingless plane with two powered wheels up front, and was steered at the rear like a plane or a ship. The single rear wheel had a kingpin like a rudder post ("That was a beautiful casting") and airplane cables ran forward to the steersman through ball-bearing sheaves.

"She was the most stable car in history. Front-steered cars act like pushed wheelbarrows, always having to skid their turns. With my rear-steering car she's never skidding."

How did it behave when it did skid?

"She didn't skid. You couldn't skid her. I brought her from London, Canada, to New York during a big ice storm, when you had to be careful not to slide off the road just standing still. But she was so stable I learned to handle her on anything.

"In New York they used to have traffic cops at every corner. One would always stop me and say, 'What the hell have you got there?' And while he was talking to me, looking in, I'd put my wheel completely over to the left, and go completely around him, slowly, and he'd suddenly find himself facing the opposite way. I could describe a one-foot circle with the inboard wheel, bring it right around his feet."

What a fantasy! It was real. There is more.

"I practiced seeing how fast I could do that. Finally I got it to fifteen miles an hour. Any faster would pull the tire off the rim. You could hook it around 180 degrees, a turn no motorcycle could make. Like if the cops came after me, I could turn and go in the opposite direction. They could never catch me."

That happened often.

"It was lots of fun. They just wanted to rubberneck this thing, and take me to the station so they could show it off.

"At the Wings of the Century—the Chicago World's Fair—they had it as the last episode, after Indians going over trails, then the Pony Express, and so on. Then the Gray Rolls, then my car as the ultimate thing. And I used to go around the track, making my turn at fifteen."

This wonderful plaything was hand-built in a few months of 1933 on a gift of a few thousand dollars, by a crew of twenty-seven men under the direction of a yacht designer, Starling Burgess, who had some spare time between America's Cup defenses. Not surprisingly, she had one sailboat characteristic. She slid with so little turbulence through the air that crosswinds affected her as they do a boat; instead of yielding to them, she tried to nose into them. It wasn't steering play that permitted the swerve, it was the tires yielding. "So I had to practically fly her along the highway on a northwest gusty day. I wouldn't allow anyone else to do it."

Cars, like boats, move through weather. Buildings exist in weather. To hear Bucky talk of wind loads on a structure is to sense his sailor's respect for atmospheric movements. Like tensegrities, they do the opposite of what landlubbers expect. Everyone "knows" a crosswind pushes a car. Not the Dymaxion; her tail was sucked leeward.

Bucky's buildings fool us likewise. "Everybody knows that heated air rises. So I put a vent in the top of my dome, and they say, yes, the warm air goes up and out. But it's just the opposite. You have the sun beating down on the shiny dome, and a 'thermal' spirals up in that column of heat. You can see it carry birds up. And the air to supply that thermal rushes up the outside of the dome, and if you put little openings around the base, the stale air inside moves out to join the uprush. So the inside pressure drops. And that sucks a core of cold air down the center of the thermal, and through the hole at the top. Sun-powered air conditioning." He's demonstrated this on the equator, in Ghana.

The seemingly empty space within the dome is full of "invisible energy operations in your favor."

"Think of the structure as sailors think of their masts and spars: a mobile system for mounting local circuses of atmospheric and energetic events."

The first Dymaxion Car's energetic circus was terminated by a vacuum drag, human curiosity, which sucked in catastrophe. A man chasing it, which happened all the time, flicked its tail on a ten-lane highway and rolled it over. The Dymaxion driver—a racing driver—was killed. A distinguished passenger, a British aviation hero, was hospitalized for weeks. King George V telephoned about him, and newsrooms buzzed.

"The Associated Press called me, and I flew out from Bridgeport where I was working on the next car. I thought a steering cable must have broken, but I couldn't find a thing the matter with my car. Nobody knew what had happened. The man who caused it had simply disappeared. And the newspapers said, Freak Car Rolls Over, Driver Killed."

The man who caused it was a politician, with influence. By the time the British celebrity was fit to testify, thirty days had passed and the headlines had done their work.

"I felt I had a responsibility. I had demonstrated a principle that could be of advantage to man, and I didn't want it to suffer because of the falsehood. So I took all the money I had in the world to build the next two cars."

Impatient creditors closed in, and Bucky lost his share of Bear Island. (He was years getting it back.) The wrecked Dymaxion Car was restored and later lost in a garage fire. One exists somewhere. The third has been lost track of.

Broke again, he went to work for the Phelps-Dodge Copper Company, helping set up an R & D department. The twelve Dymaxion Bathrooms were one by-product. Two others were of more lasting significance. One was the discovery of a kind of quantum theory of discourse, which made Fuller for the first time continuously intelligible to anyone who would pay attention. The other was his inventory of human knowledge, arrayed along a time line, which led to the World Resources Inventory and the World Game of the 1960's.

What he learned about his own thinking was that despite its Whole-System continuity, it was conducted in small natural units, like aphorisms.

Something about working with one's hands conduces to aphorism: some correlation between the manipulable unit, grasped, lifted, and the mind's intermittent concentrations. Like tensegrity's islands of compression in a tensional sea, the quotabilities of a Franklin or a Thoreau are suspended amid connections they do not state, in the silent mental continuum of a man setting type, building a cabin, hoeing beans. Here's a contributor to *The Last Whole Earth Catalog* telling you how to build with stone:

"Stone walls and buildings. These are actually weaker than they look. It was the wood frame houses that survived the Alaskan earthquake."

That's the stuff of a moral parable—one can guess how

Emerson would have used it—or a place to start a discourse on tension vs. compression. But our man's mind is on conveying information, and he's soon explaining how "Strong beautiful wall is *laid up* rock by rock. No other way. . . . Knowing which rock to choose from your pile. Like a puzzle with no two parts the same. Choosing the wrong rock means that your work comes down on your feet. (So don't be barefoot! . . .) An old Maine stonemason told me that 'Even a round rock has a flat side if you can find it.' "

You can see this exposition weaving in and out of the zone where aphorisms are generated. You can also see the meditation emerging in discrete packets, time-structured, paced by the remembered movements of hands among stones. (It's been speculated that since dolphins have no hands, their famous language would distinguish event from event after principles we can barely make an effort to conceive. Is a "noun," in the first place, something you can pick up?)

Bucky thought this way, in increments, but tended to write differently. One man when he was putting lines into a drawing or parts into a car, he was another man entirely when he tried to graph trajectories of enlightenment on writing paper. At Phelps-Dodge midway through the 1930's, the Director of Research had to inform his Dymaxion deputy that a technical paper on "forward research strategies" was simply incomprehensible.

Bucky's response was to read it back aloud, "in spontaneously metered doses," watching for expressions of comprehension. "The Director pondered each verbal dose, and when his face signaled 'that is clear,' I would intuitively measure out the next portion." Retyped the way it had come clear it looked like poetry, which meant it couldn't possibly be submitted to the Board of Directors.

But, said Bucky, it is chopped-up prose.

No, said two poets, it is poetry. (Who were those poets? Where did the Research Director find them? The story glistens with wonders.)

When the report went to the Board it was chopped by dashes, commas, asterisks, everything but line-breaks. As long as they didn't see lines of irregular length the Directors weren't nervous: a fascinating conditioned reflex.

Thereafter, when there wasn't a Board to worry about, Bucky frequently let the compositor clarify a sentence like this:

> However, that motion is only measurable in dimensional limits of energy, time and space which are mostly infra or ultra to the dimensions which the personal faculties of man are accustomed to detecting by direct sensing and by conscious awareness of relative comparisons made by himself to previously established measures of any conscious experience with motion.

In "ventilated prose" it reads like this:

> However
> that motion
> is only measurable
> in dimensional units
> of energy, time and space
> which are mostly infra or ultra
> to the dimensions
> which the personal faculties of man
> are accustomed to detecting
> by direct sensing
> and by conscious awareness
> of relative comparisons
> made by himself to
> previously established measures of
> any conscious experience
> with motion.

Not that typography can ventilate just any prose. Bucky

had discovered something about the way of his own thought. Though he did not, like Thoreau, polish aphorisms till they resemble souvenirs, yet like the aphorist he thought in discrete energy packets, linear in sequence. The key to clarity was to make their boundaries somehow evident. From this time even the sentences he prints as ordinary prose have a new awareness of internal marking points.

He had discovered, in his own roundabout way, a mode of American poetry, the straightforward sentence collected out of energized units, and analyzed into them again by a visual aid. Marianne Moore, for one, understood this principle by 1921, the year of her first volume, *Poems*. ("What I write," she later said, "could only be called poetry because there is no other category in which to put it.") She had even discovered that the energized units need not be composed by the poet but could be borrowed from auction catalogues, magazine captions, technical leaflets—occasions when sincerity of perception (never mind whose) was engaged with some reality. (Bucky often quotes too, though mainly from himself.)

William Carlos Williams, who discovered the principles of his own mature poetic by brooding on her work, called a Marianne Moore poem "an anthology of transit," brilliantly aware that what the poet contributed was the tensional system between the compressive units. No audible words need correspond to that system, and the casual eye saw not an anthology of transit but an anthology of quotations.

Bucky's deliberate statements about poetry are fairly simple. "Emerson said the great poet put the most in the fewest words. By that test the greatest poem is Einstein's '$E = mc^2$', which says everything in six syllables." He also sees Henry Ford as the creator of America's epic, an orchestration of worldwide movement and transformation, ores from the ends of the earth converging on River Rouge, then evoluting as cars to putt-putt out again to the ends of the earth. Slowly and invisibly too the cars were transformed: steel after steel received special-purpose alloying, until by the time the Model T was discontinued it drew together 135 different alloys, folding in yet more and more knowledge, drawing with yet more exquisite differentiation on earth's resources of metal and man's of conceptioning. Ford's intentions were not aesthetic, by any stretch of the imagination. It was Bucky's response, as long as forty years ago, that exhibited the aesthetic imagination (and foresaw "conceptual art").

It is normal for him that Beauty should be transsensual, and look after itself. "Don't worry," he told some architectural students, "about making your work beautiful."

Too many architects, he insists, are willing to sit around drawing pictures.

"You don't ever have to worry about 'beautiful' or 'pretty,' because if you really understand your problem, if you solve it correctly, so life really goes on; if you do it so economically it is realizable: then it always comes out beautiful.

"That's why a rose is beautiful: as one part of the great regenerative process whereby the a priori design of the Universe is working. If you want to be part of that, you can't miss beauty."

Had Frank Lloyd Wright not been so exquisite a draftsman, would his imagination have expended itself in so many hundreds of special-case designs? Was the lovely paper in some sense his end product? His structures tended to solve local problems: how to build a house over a waterfall; how a skyscraper might look if it were a mile high. If your own life craved Wright's enhancing, you came in person to Wright. ("Frank," an architect said, "saw a client as an opportunity.") There was only one Wright, and the world's people were numbered in billions. His satisfactions were one-to-one. Bucky Fuller's satisfactions are conceptual: the domes, a general case, and the worldwide process he has envisaged for so long, a general case as well.

Similarly, the satisfaction he takes from writing (mostly verse now—the published prose comes from lecture transcripts)—is that of conveying with clarity the most accurately general statement he can manage. Beauty does not concern him. It is not banished, though, by those enjambed polysyllables. The 1956 poem he dedicated to Dr. Jonas Salk not only resembles Roman and Elizabethan attempts to versify advanced knowledge, it is the nearest thing we have to a Metaphysical poem.

The other Phelps-Dodge accomplishment was the Inventory of Scientific Events, done with six students he had at his disposal for a summer. They were listing key discoveries, "pretty well defined by scientists themselves. And the dates are very very sharp." As with his poems, he was following Max Planck's model, dissociating process into quanta. Every life consists of days, interrupted by sleep. Every day consists of experiences, separable. Every thought rearranges elements, recoverable. ("The sum of finite quantities is finite. Universe is finite.") And history has proceeded by increments, each irreversible. Each discovery divides the time line into two parts, a *before* and an *after*. One day vanadium had been isolated; thereafter machinists' hammers were possible. One day carbon steel was in production; thereafter the bicycle wheel was possible. One day the Wrights had flown. One day $E = mc^2$ had been written down.

"I made a long chart, a quarter-inch to the year. And

for each invention I would go up one increment in altitude, so the curve on the chart kept rising, discontinuously.
The earliest go back to things like irrigation systems in
India; then a 500-year lapse before the next item. As our
plot moves through time they get a little more frequent,
still more frequent, then fantastically frequent. The curve
picks itself up and tends to rise almost vertically."

Discovery augmenting discovery: synergy.

"I found I could grade them. A mathematical discovery
was weightless: pure principle. The chemical elements had
some weight. Bessemer steel—an engineering process—was
very heavy. So I gave them spectrum colors, the most
weightless concepts purple, the heavy mechanics red.

"So you saw patterns of precedence, purple constantly
preceding a related red. The mental discoveries, the abstract things, come long before the inventions. The abstract and mental set up an environment in which thinking
man invents applications rapidly. It was clear that the
metaphysical preceded the physical, and the greener type
of physical preceded the redder."

Later he devised a simpler chart, often reproduced,
which confines itself to the ninety-two chemical elements.
Man entered historical time with just nine of these at his
disposal. Each had been "discovered," we do not know
when, and isolated from Adam's environment by processes
men learned to repeat at will. These isolations transformed
life. From the Stone Age, men entered the Iron Age; then
(with copper and tin) the Bronze Age.

Arsenic followed in 1250 A.D.; antimony after two centuries, phosphorus after two centuries more. Then just
sixty years brought platinum and cobalt; then about the
1740's the curve starts to head upward. The work was
completed in the 1930's, and men had on the shelf the
regenerative components of everything that exists. In the

sixteenth century there would have been a poem about it.

In the 1960's, combining his principle of Inventory with the Dymaxion Map he'd developed by then, Bucky essayed a kind of Action Poem which he called the World Game. He was thinking of War Games, where someone, by Malthus' principles, ultimately loses everything, and he pointed out that in the World Game everyone would win. The idea was to pool every bit of available data about all the world's resources and all its technical knowledge, and let the players try "Moves"—collect this chemical element at this port, locate this industry here, join these two countries with electric wires—of which a computer could show them the consequences. The goal was to optimize consequences: to "make the world work." The Game would model the world's industrial ecology, and its results could then be tried out in the world. Since adequate computer resources were never obtained, nor the data, for that matter, adequately marshaled (what a staff that would take!), the World Game still exists chiefly as an idea, a sort of weightless model of a model.

Bucky's product even in the Phelps-Dodge days was tending toward weightlessness. By 1940 it was wholly so: explanations, clarifications. By then he had been for two years a Technological Consultant at *Fortune,* which guaranteed him readers and supplied editors.

Time, Inc., *Fortune*'s parent company, had a first-class research department, expert at turning up answers to odd questions. *Fortune* itself had a clear-cut purpose: to keep American executives aware of their work. Locked into the problems of his own corporation, the executive tends to specialize blindly, and Bucky, who had longed for ways of reaching such men when the 4-D house needed a backer, welcomed the chance to clarify for them their location in

Einstein's universe of change and Ford's world of coordinated process.

Forced by his editors to use very simple words and attach them to pictures, he mastered the techniques he uses before audiences today: the rope, the stacked balls, the wooden triangle, models so simple they need no longer even be shown. (In the 1940's he traveled with a trailer full of models; by the 1960's he was unencumbered.)

At *Fortune* they used little explanatory pictures. Pictures are discrete; their sequence structures the discourse into increments. Bucky's 1940 explanation of precession, in a story about the Sperry Corporation, is a small triumph of incremental enlightenment. Here is a man swinging a weight round and round on a chain. As he spins, the weight rises till its plane of rotation is parallel to the earth's surface, at 90 degrees to gravity. Here is the swinging weight replaced by a circle of orbiting balls, chasing one another round and round in near contact. Here is a finger pressing down on that whirling circle. Each ball is deflected, and the consequence of all those deflections is a new orbit, tilted at an axis we can visualize just where the finger interfered. The low point of the plane of spin is 90 degrees forward of where the finger was applied. That is precession, a resultant not at the point of applied force but somewhere else. And the gyrocompass, mysterious till you understand it, was precession enmetaled, disturbances receiving inexorable corrections, not instantaneously (nothing is instantaneous) but as fast as the spinning rotor's rim could move forward a quarter-turn.

His new habits coalesced into copious verse: typographer's increments. His notebooks were filling with odd dynamic facts:

—that the pipelines of the United States carried twice as much tonnage as all the motor trucks;

—that the interface "between which time and energy are masculated"—the total surface of all the bearings in the world—was about 1,000 square miles;

—that just in those 1,000 square miles (the battleground of humanity's one significant war) 94 percent of the national energy income was vanishing into heat.

Such matters, running down synergetic pages, became the *Untitled Epic Poem on the History of Industrialization* (not published until 1962), *Machine Tools* (partly written for *Fortune*), the famous *No More Secondhand God*. These all date from 1940, a bumper year. They were published twenty-two years later, which was more or less the usual industrial lag. Discoveries take about that long to get into the environment.

They offer swift startling glimpses: Lindbergh setting forth, "no hat and two sandwiches"; Lindbergh's antithesis, the ultragenteel pre-crash banker,

> a hot-house white-calla hybrid
> of the former wild tiger lily
> exuding soft negatives
> fertilized never
> with an imaginative "yes"

God, playing "shoot-the-works"; man, bemused by "super-whizzing atomic universes," dust-mote or elephant.

The *Epic Poem* has a page on mutual trust, its focal figure a man sorting mail on an express train,

> with unuttered faith that
> the engineer is competent
> that the switchmen are not asleep,
> that the track walkers are doing their job,
> that the technologists
> who designed the train and the rails
> knew their stuff,

that thousands of others
whom he may never know by face or name
are collecting tariffs,
paying for repairs,
and so handling assets
that he will be paid a week from today
and again the week after that,
and that all the time
his family is safe and in well-being
without his personal protection.

This man "constitutes a whole new era of evolution—the
first really 'new' since the beginning of the spoken word."
That was the new era Bucky had in mind when he wrote
the famous vision of trust going into action:

The revolution has come—
set on fire from the top.
Let it burn swiftly.
Neither the branches, trunk, nor roots will be endangered.
Only last year's leaves and
the parasite-bearded moss and orchids
will not be there
when the next spring brings fresh growth
and freestanding flowers.

Embellished, calligraphed and issued by a poster company,
this hangs now on thousands of walls. Its readers may not
all understand its indifference to the sacking of palaces.
It means to articulate the trust that sustains the railway
mail-sorter, and the jet passenger and the pedestrian, a web
of tensile trust that bypasses faith in "leaders."

Then the war, and war work, and much refinement of
what he was calling the Energetic Geometry, and among
much else, close experience with production lines, and the
realization that the auto lines had grown fat and static and

concerned with freezing design and taking out profits. Aircraft procedures stayed flexible—a million change orders as the B-29 evolved. Cars were made of steel, aircraft of aluminum. Aluminum could be processed with soft dies it was easy to shape and easier to remelt. Vividly, the diminishing weight of the product was correlated with facility of change. It was in an aircraft plant in Wichita that the Dymaxion Dwelling Machine (1946) almost went into production. One account of the fiasco has Bucky refining his designs till even aircraft executives ran out of patience.

Whatever happened, after so many years' concentration on that house, it seemed a major and irrevocable defeat. Instead of pounding other executives' doors, he returned to his geometry, and pursued something that had crossed his mind in wartime, while he was working out his one-world map: the fact that you could subdivide triangles with great circles, the sailor's straight lines, called geodesics. He had the idea that there might be a structure in this.

EIGHT

Domes

"But he didn't tell about domes." And it's true, he will talk for up to five hours without ever mentioning the one thing everybody associates him with. "Fuller? Oh yes— Geodesic Domes." "He wants to put everybody in domes." (He doesn't.) The dome is his emblem; there's a geodesic sphere on his private postmark. The dome was his break- through, his one solid commercial success; the validation, therefore, of his way of thinking, because success means your thinking coincides with a need. Securely locked up in U.S. Patent No. 2,682,235 (filed Dec. 12, 1951; issued June 29, 1954), it drew the royalties that set him free to buzz round the world evangelizing. Its fame, moreover, elicited the invitations to come and evangelize.

But it is not his obsession, and by no means his end product the way the car was Henry Ford's end product. It's a graceful, practical structure, incredibly light and strong; it's an intersection between materials and mind, mind di- minishing reliance on matter to such an extent that a fairly primitive example, forty-nine feet in diameter, supported seven pounds with each ounce of structure, could with- stand 150-mile gales, and be packed flat into a station wagon; it's a model, complex, delicate, mysterious yet in-

telligible, of the Fuller system of discourse, concentrating
so many principles that if you talked about a Geodesic
Dome long enough you would leave little of the known
universe untouched: not a fashionable shape for cabanas,
but something to think about. It would remain all that if
some breakthrough made every geodesic building obsolescent tomorrow. It repays acquaintance.

Where to start? Perhaps with their intuitive appeal.
Children love them. So do most grown-ups, even when
they serve no practical purpose whatever. In one California
health-food restaurant you sit with your Sesameburgers
on log benches outdoors beneath the spiderweb triangles
of a geodesic umbrella that isn't meant to deflect a drop of
rain, the frame, of gaily painted thin metal tubing, being
completely open. It gives you a sense of being somewhere
in particular, and it also models, down close, the dome of
the sky; and "Every vertex," smiled the hairy denizen, "is
a mandala."

It's simply a skinless dome framework, not saucer-flat
but five-eighths of a sphere: what Fuller calls a Geodesic
Skybreak. How much closer is the skybreak than the sky?
That uncertainty is part of its appeal. Since there's nothing
to compare the triangles with but each other, they could
be huge and distant or small and close. Their outlines etch
the blue-gray with webs of color. Directly overhead—some
thirty feet up—a white pentagon encloses five radials like
an X-rayed starfish. They triangulate it and meet at the
zenith point. Edge to edge with the sides of the pentagon
spring hexagons, likewise triangulated like abstract snow-
flakes. Four different colors, in perfect, elusive symmetry,
repeat, repeat, repeat the tri/hex theme. The eye picks up
five more pentagons, arrayed around the fishbowl part way
down. Whichever way you face, one is ahead, two are in
your peripheral vision. Hexagons spring from their sides,

surround them, abut. Fiveness interpenetrates sixness; still larger pentagons, uniformly colored, surround the six we've spotted, and each corner of a large pent is the center of a hex, and also the corner of yet a different hex. . . . It may one day wear a transparent skin, or whim or the fluctuating building codes may make twining vines preferable. There's even talk of removing the framework after vines take over: geodesic arboriculture, nature pursuing the co-ordinate system of nature as branch marries branch at hexagonal intersections and small stems twine toward the light.

It's strong enough for a dozen men to climb on, as a dozen men did when it was going up, inserting and tightening bolts. Hardware-store bolts, that's all, and bones of thin pipe, flattened at the ends and drilled. At the end of each pipe the structure changes direction by some 10 degrees, so the flattened ends have been bent a little inwards. That part wasn't critical. The dome as it goes together imposes and sustains its own angular accuracies. The critical part was the spacing of the holes, strut-end to strut-end, the more accurately measured the better. Hole to hole, that's the effective length of a strut, the effective side of a triangle. "A dome won't tolerate funk," say the authors of *The Domebook* out of extensive experience. "Accuracy in drilling the holes is *very* important unless you like lumpy domes assembled by beating them with a sledge-hammer." Those triangles, that look so alike, differ slightly; those slight differences curve the surface by the sum of numerous tucks, and when they're accurate they guarantee that everything will meet again on the other side, hole still coinciding with hole, generally six at a time, aligned precisely to receive the bolt. The four colors were functional when the dome went up, helping identify struts of four different lengths, symmetrically intermixed. Radomes on the DEW line were color-coded similarly for Eskimo assembly.

The Domebook, fifty-six big pages, sold out two printings (17,000 copies) in less than eight months of 1970 to gratify the proliferating dome freaks of the Pacific Coast and Southwest. How many habitable domes were built is anybody's guess, but *Domebook 2,* twice as thick, commanded a first printing of 20,000 copies, half of them on firm order before the ink was dry. Subsequent printings have reached 100,000. Lloyd Kahn, the guru of this enterprise, lives in a dome up north of San Francisco, generous with time and information but declining to sell, to preach, to do anything but meet a natural demand that seems to be running away without stimulation.

Domebook One was "put together in fourteen days in the *Whole Earth Catalog* production garage," and the appeal of a dome of one's own seems most magnetic to the commune-waterbed-neo-Thoreauvian lifestyle. "New life contained within new geometrical shapes and patterns. Shelters designed and built with beauty, efficiency and grace. A skin instead of a roof overhead, a light membrane protecting you from the rain. Symbols of quick escape from the cities. Economical and orderly use of materials. Minimum violation of land. A structural system so simple that anyone willing to exercise a reasonable amount of 'quality control' can build his own shelter."

"Quality control," a phrase on which Thoreau would have gagged, means what it means in Detroit, an eye kept on specifications during a production run of interchangeable parts. The dome folk are the first to understand that attacking infinite nature with your little hatchet won't yield anything geodesic, nor even habitable. They use radial arm saws, staple guns, synthetic extrusions, silicone caulks, polyurethane foam insulation, ultraviolet-resistant flexible vinyl: fallout, some of it, from the space program. Domes just weren't practical for individuals until tools and materials like these became available, along with "chord factor" tables generated in NASA computers. These domes spring from the intersection of the space age with *Walden*.

That was an intersection of Yankee vectors. At Walden, Thoreau began by building his cabin, and his acquaintance Margaret Fuller's great-nephew Buckminster both inspired the *Whole Earth Catalog* and devised the geodesic structures in consonance with the American theme, mass-production, whose principles Henry Ford, that crafty yokel, used to think out while sitting on a fence.

Bucky Fuller never expected his domes to be hand-crafted. When he came upon their principle in the 1940's, it seemed the most adequate fulfillment yet of his long-time dream: a rational system for enclosing living space, mass-producible, readily erected from standardized parts, maximally economical of materials (hence of weight), and moreover something you could take apart and move, or even move intact, slung from a helicopter. He had been seeking it since 1927, when he first dreamed of a posturban world in which people erected shelters where they chose.

The Dymaxion House of that dream encased much machinery, which was meant to be more important than the shell. The conventional house contains more machinery than you'd think: for instance terminals of the machines that move tons of water through tons of plumbing; machines to heat water and soften it; machines to chill food and machines to cook it; machines to heat and cool the house; machines to suck up dust; machines to toss clothes around in soapy water; machines to blast soil off dishes. All but the plumbing, these are bought separately. The Dymaxion idea was to make them all available at a time when most housewives couldn't dream of owning most of them, and treat them as one big interrelated machine installed in a vertical core. That core was where the Dymaxion thinking started. The house was just the enclosing weather-break.

So the visible house becomes, logically, an envelope. Perhaps with stressed skin, like an airplane fuselage? Exactly; and the stresses are patterned. Nearly all the strength of the usual house is compressive; posts like caryatids, bearing weight on their shoulders, and the weights bearing other weights: weight, weight. Tension members are light, and in 1927 Bucky had separated out a good deal of the stress as tensile: compression, in the central column; tension, down the outside. One way to imagine the domes is to think of the hollow central column growing larger and larger until it vanishes into the outer shell; and think of compressive stresses, residue of that column, still running along the inner surface of the shell, and tensile stresses enclosing its outer surface like a net. That is not the way Bucky in fact arrived at the domes, but it demonstrates a twenty years' continuity of principle. The hidden tension network around the domes is what defeats normal calculations of their strength. Its presence is unexpected: synergetic.

Normal stress analysis works part by part: what load does this part bear? Such an analysis of the great Expo bubble indicated that it would burst at the equator. The computer understood the top hemisphere to be *weight,* and the lower saucer *support,* and so much more weight than support would splay it outward fatally. Bucky understood his tension networks better than the men who instructed that computer, and the 600-ton bubble went up as designed.

As to how he did arrive at the domes, he arrived at them while working on his Dymaxion Map, and plotting great

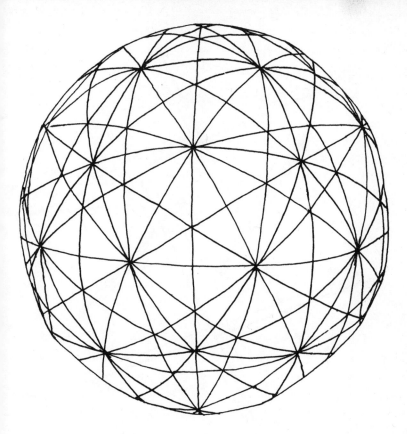

The thirty-one great circles

circles which crisscrossed triangular sectors. Thirty-one
great circles will crisscross a sphere symmetrically, dividing
it into triangles of various sizes. A great circle is called a
geodesic. Every great circle is an equator: a band of maximum length, running clear round the sphere, and shifting
local stresses as far from the point of impingement as possible. What if one simply constructed a network of great
circles? At Black Mountain College, in 1948, he and a class
tried a hemisphere of thin flexible metal strips, Venetian-
blind slats in fact. At every crisscross a fastener went in.
A small model was rigid. A much heavier forty-eight-foot
model gently folded as it neared completion. Additional

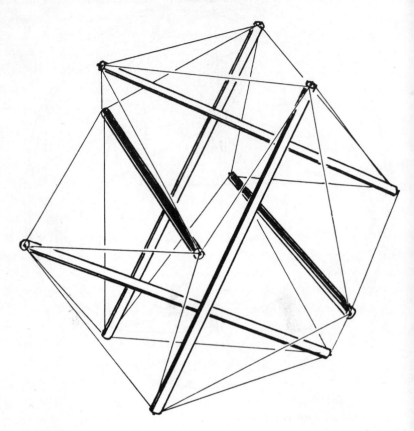

Tensegrity icosa

pieces of slatting—not stiff braces—restored its domical integrity. It weighed about a pound per foot of diameter.

Since a child could readily bend the thin metal strips,
this hemisphere was clearly relying more on tensional
than on compressive forces: it is tension that pulls things
straight. A year later Bucky was threading cables through
tubes, to make an intricate necklace that lay on the ground
until the cables were tightened. But when they were tensioned to draw the tubes tight together, the structure
erected itself into a dome shape. A photo shows nine men

hanging from it. Their weight tended to compress the tubes, which ran vertex to vertex. Their weight also stressed the tension network. Since slacking the cables would let the whole thing collapse, and omitting the tubes would leave only a structureless net, the demonstration of tensional and compressional interplay could scarcely have been neater.

Pause a moment and look at a brick wall. It has no *tensional* integrity whatever. Brick laid on brick, pressing down by sheer accumulated weight, that is compression purely*

Replace the brick wall with a wooden skeleton. The compressive strength of the wooden posts is still what holds up the roof. If two posts try to fall away from each other, they impose tensional stress on the cross-bracing, but they do not impose very much, and a good thing too. Wood is fibrous, gripping nails by friction, and really severe tension loads would part fibers and rip out nails.

Replace the wooden structure, piece by piece, with one of aluminum. You have the substance of a 1972 Alcoa advertisement, in which metal framing members have been substituted into a standard frame. Such a frame is fireproof, and good for the aluminum business, and misemploys materials ridiculously since the great tensional strength of metal is not being exploited at all. As for housing mankind that way, there isn't enough aluminum in the world.

Tension, tension. It was at Black Mountain College, about the same time as his thirty-one-great-circle domes, that Bucky did his most intensive work with the strange class of structures whose working principles he calls tenseg-

---

* Though not within a single brick, which coheres (unlike a cube of sand) by intermolecular tension. When you compress it you strain those tension bonds till at last it bursts. Which is just to say that a brick wall doesn't repeat the structural principle of its components.

rity, tensional integrity. Here the sculptural intuitions of his gifted student, Kenneth Snelson, helped him greatly.

In a Tensegrity the tensional and compressive forces are separated out so completely they appear in different parts of the structure: posts here, wires there. The word *integrity* points to their structural completeness. They differ from Calder's mobiles, which are also tensional, in not coming apart if you turn them upside down. The continuity is in the tensional network, a sort of stressed cage in which compressions float.

We've already looked at the Tensegrity Sphere, where tensional continuities run through the sticks, and leap from stick to stick. That was a late development. Bucky's starting-point seems to have been the bicycle wheel, in which some anonymous nineteenth-century genius exploited the tensile strength of carbon steel. It is a true tensegrity: a compressive hub, a compressive rim and a tension network between. Then Snelson, after a Fuller lecture at Black Mountain, devised the Tensegrity Mast, which we've also examined. The wheel is flat, the mast is elongated. Now the search was on for tensegrities that would occupy symmetrical volumes of space. It became a collective quest. Students and associates—Snelson, John Moehlman, Lee Hogden, Francesco della Sala, Ted Pope—were fertile with prototypes.

One of the curiosities Bucky developed was the *tensegrity icosahedron,* a toy no home should be without. It is as hard as anything else of Fuller's to draw on flat paper. You can easily make one by taping six sticks to a box, wiring the ends together systematically and then destroying the box.* Nothing else is destroyed. The six sticks float, in parallel pairs, pointing three ways, framing three-dimensional space, tautly suspended in a wire network

* For instructions which bypass the box, see page 321.

whose junction-points they hold apart. The pattern of wires sketches an icosahedron, one of the figures that fascinated Euclid, Archimedes and Plato.

Stranger still, one's intuitive sense of action and reaction is topsy-turvied. If you press two of the parallel sticks together, the others do not compensate by moving apart. No, they also come together, as far as the wire network will let them. This means that under pressure from outside, the whole structure tends to compress, rotating slightly as it does so. (It rotates because the eight* triangles' edges won't change, so there's nothing they can do but swing.) Under pressure from inside, which you can stimulate by trying to move two of the sticks apart, the whole structure expands symmetrically, also rotating a little. It is in short a Whole System, and synergetic.

Standing on a table, it trembles a little when jarred. Do some chemical bonds run like those tension wires? Jelly trembles just so. "That's a Tensegrity," said Bucky suddenly (1971), disturbing his Jell-O with the spoon. In 1959, Arthur Drexler had made the clearest statement yet of Bucky's criteria for things to build: "He builds very large diagrams of the lines of force by which atomic particles— matter itself—seem to adhere. . . . He believes that the designer's real responsibility no longer is the creation of individual buildings or objects, but the interrelating of physics, mathematics and the well-being of the race."

Let's play a little more with this large diagram. Imagine the six sticks no longer straight, but bowed outward till they run just inside the enclosing figure. The tensional integrity is undisturbed. You now have a model of some-

---

* Yes, yes, an icosahedron has twenty triangles. But in the tensegrity version we omit six wires as redundant, so twelve of the triangles merge into diamonds. If you want to be fussy, what we've got is a distorted vector equilibrium.

thing sort of spherical, and hollow, like a basketball not curved but with twelve corners. It does not dimple when it is squeezed, but contracts symmetrically, and does not bubble when it gets a bang from within, but expands symmetrically. You also have a model of how the domes work when something falls on them: a tree, Antarctic snow. They respond as Whole Systems, not bulging here in order to dimple there, but shrinking or stretching microscopically.

This was beautifully validated on Long Island in 1955, where a fifty-five-foot geodesic ping-pong ball was assembled from plastic panels thin enough to be translucent. The shell of a fifty-five-foot egg would have been 160 times as thick. An area round the summit was loaded till conventional theory said it ought to dimple down two feet. Instead the loaded segment contracted symmetrically, shrinking inward less than two inches. The rest did not bulge out, but contracted also. Later Walter O'Malley, the Brooklyn Dodgers' president, threw rocks at it in lieu of baseballs. There were resonant bongs but no damage, and O'Malley commissioned a model of a 750-foot umbrella for his ballpark. He was pleased when he saw it, but the wonder was never built, and the Dodgers moved to Los Angeles.

Well before his dealings with Mr. O'Malley, Bucky had taken a step that was to determine the geometry of all his future domes. He abandoned the great circles as explicit structural members, and moved them to a plane of pure principle where they were not always easy to notice. (The name, Geodesic, was kept.)

He had gotten his pattern of thirty-one great circles by systematically rotating an icosahedron in every possible way, and noting the equators it sketched. Now instead of weaving networks of circles, he took to subdividing the faces of icosahedra, and noting that great circles and portions of great circles always turned up. The resulting structure was a three-way grid of triangles, through every member of which ran the synergetic tension-compression interplay.

On December 12, 1951, he filed a patent application on "a framework for enclosing space" derived from the subdivided icosahedron. The pattern on its surface is far more symmetrical than the thirty-one-great-circle domes he had begun with in 1948, in which as many as twelve struts met at certain vertices and as few as four at others. The icosahedral derivatives use sixes and fives exclusively, and the numerous triangles look to the casual eye exactly alike and moreover equilateral (they aren't quite). That's the key patent for Geodesic Domes. The Patent Office is said to have hung a framed copy.

One can get to find the icosahedron quite friendly. It's another structure children intuitively love. Its twelve vertices are connected by thirty struts, which divide its surface into twenty precisely similar triangles. Any way is up. It is omnisymmetrical, one of only five omnisymmetrical objects that can be constructed in space.

It seems odd at first that only five should be possible, but the Pythagoreans knew that this was so, and Euclid gives a proof. They were called the Five Regular Solids, or sometimes Platonic Solids, and so entranced Greek geometers that Euclid's *Elements* has even been diagnosed as a somewhat long-winded treatise on their properties, all the early propositions—the ones we studied in school—being groundwork merely. Euclid's methods are so cumbersome it takes him twelve books even to get to the solids. This is partly because they are difficult to analyze on flat paper, which may explain why things so elegant and simple are still comparatively unknown. The most schematic diagram is apt to get baffling.

One of them, the cube, most of us understand pretty well, since its 90-degree angles rise off the paper in a way that seems oddly natural. And everyone can draw a cube in perspective, chiefly because when the back surface lies squarely on the paper the front surface is another square parallel to the paper, and we have only to connect their corners with slanty lines. But without those right angles, paper stops being helpful.

It's easier with models, and the easiest way to make models is to buy some star-shaped flexible connectors and push sticks into them. (Or you can use the dried peas and toothpicks they gave Bucky in kindergarten.) The flexible connectors are very enlightening because they give no rigidity to the corners and we soon discover which geometries are stable. The cube's is not. If its corners are not rigid the cube collapses. So does an ill-built henhouse, and for the same reason: it contains no triangles, and a principle of the universe seems to be that there is no stability except in triangles. Run a diagonal across one of the square sides, and that side is triangulated and grows rigid. Do this for all six sides, and you have a rigid cube at last.

Now walk down the street to where they are building a house, and note that the cubic frame has diagonal braces. Those braces—in a small house, one per wall—hold the frame erect. Without them, as the nails pulled, it could sag like that hasty chicken-coop. One diagonal per wall is doing the *holding;* all the rest is *held.* Walk back home, pick up your braced cube and take away the cubical edges, leaving behind only the system of braces. The system of braces holds up by itself. It is omnitriangulated, and its

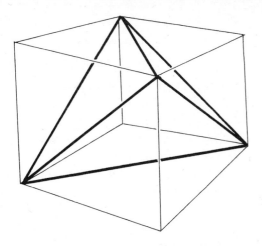

Tetrahedron in cube

corners are perfectly rigid despite the flexible joints. It is a *tetrahedron*.

This may lead us to think that it would make more structural sense to leave the braces and remove the house. So it would, and we should have a tetrahedronal house. Indians were content with this general shape, but modern man, having moved a great many activities indoors, would find it over-confining.

The *tetrahedron* (four triangles) is the simplest of the Five Regular Solids. The others are the *octahedron* (eight triangles), the *cube* (six squares), the *dodecahedron* (a dozen pentagons fitted edge to edge), and the twenty-triangled *icosahedron*. Like the cube, the dodecahedron is utterly unstable, so we are left with three stable systems and only three. Of these three, the icosahedron has obviously the most space in it (nearly nineteen times that of a tetrahedron with the same edge-lengths) and makes the most sensible starting-point for domes.

So we've learned that the Geodesic Dome, even before any Fulleresque geometrizing, has a stable configuration underlying it. The Empire State Building has not, being a pile of hollow cubes, nor has Madison Square Garden; and when large floor spaces are wanted a cubical building needs a great deal of bracing and trussing, and internal columns as well. (Check the next hockey rink you visit.) None of this bracing and trussing keeps the rain off, it simply keeps the cube from collapsing. And none of the cubical structure contributes stability, it simply keeps the weather out. Such buildings accumulate enormous redundancy, and one can see why they eat up thousands of tons of materials. One can also see why disruption of a few braces, for instance by an earthquake, brings them down like megaton cardhouses. I was writing this page when a forklift struck a single post in Los Angeles, and brought down 2500 square feet of warehouse roof ($40,000).

We can slice an icosahedron near the bottom and stand it on the ground. It is stable. (Once we take off that bottom cap the lower pentagon is deformable, but we'll spike it to earth and lend it earth's rigidity.) With eight-foot edges, say, this makes a cozy little cabana. The Ananda Meditation Retreat in the Sierra Foothills uses them for guest cabins. Longer edge-beams would give trouble, sagging of their own weight. So we subdivide the triangles. And we subdivide them the way we did when we were finding out how to make a triangle twist-proof: not with equal members but with members of slightly varying lengths, longer ones toward the centers of the triangles, shorter ones toward the outsides. Then the triangles will curve, and if we do the geometry properly the curves will match to make a smooth spherical surface. Six-way vertices appear where the members meet, everywhere except at the junction-points of the large icosahedral triangles we started with. Just at those points five members will come together, exactly as they do in the parent icosahedron. In a whole sphere there will always be twelve of these, the twelve icosahedral vertices; in a dome, fewer.

So that's it, except for a catch you may have noticed: "If we do the geometry properly." Doing the geometry

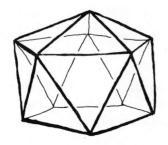

Sliced icosa

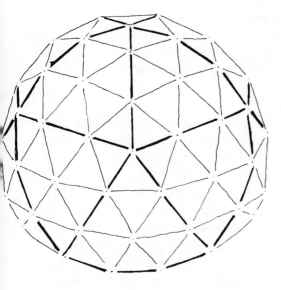

Icosa subdivided

properly is very laborious. Bucky and a young engineer named Don Richter were two years doing it for his first large practical structure, the ninety-three-foot dome he installed atop the Ford Motor Company's Rotunda in 1953. They had no computer, not even an electric multiplier, just an adding machine. They used seven-place tables of trigonometric functions which they hoped were free of typographical errors.

Fortunately this misery needn't be repeated. Once the calculations are done they can be used for any sized dome of the same configuration, and a few years ago a man named Joe Clinton wrote a computer program to generate tables from which you can retrieve all the geodesic data you are likely to want. He was under contract to NASA, which published his tables in a report called "Structural Design Concepts for Future Space Missions." The most useful parts are reprinted in *Domebook 2*.

NASA were the logical folk to be interested. The enormous cost of lifting each pound off the earth haunts NASA engineers, and the domes' ratio of weight to space enclosed suggests that the first lunar structures are almost sure to be geodesic.

Performance per pound, an old shipbuilders' concept, has been on Bucky's mind since Bear Island days. For various reasons it's not a housebuilder's concept. The Washington Monument principle that weight means strength has dominated builders' intuitions since the days of the Pyramids, and anyway what was the need of frugality? There were always more forests, there was always more brick. Nothing makes builders think except a shortage.

Sometimes manpower is short, and then careful figuring commences. Thomas Jefferson covered the margins of his architectural drawings with calculations of the number of bricks, and rethought structures to get the number down. Bricks were made like nails, one by one, with human time, and Virginia hadn't human resources to squander. For his University of Virginia grounds he devised serpentine garden walls, curving to and fro, because a curve stood on edge is stable though it's only one brick thick; straight walls needed a double thickness. Performance per brick, that's a form of performance per pound. But later designers have lacked that frugality, and Bucky Fuller has never yet encountered an architect who could tell him, even within 50 percent, what his newest brainchild might weigh. He knew just what the Dymaxion House would weigh: three tons. A conventional dwelling for five weighed fifty times that. Ephemeralizing weight by a factor of fifty might in long production runs ephemeralize cost by something comparable. The price of materials per pound is the lower limit, not to be lowered by just tinkering with assembly techniques. So research into low-cost housing is mostly misdirected, since it never begins by asking what a house weighs. Once you start lifting your components to the moon—an extravagant fulfillment of his old dream that housing might be air-deliverable—you suddenly need to know their weight to the ounce, and Bucky grins at the notion that rational housing may yet come about as fallout from the moon. Mankind, he likes to say, backs into its future.

He got the Ford Motor Company commission because his domes were so light. For the company's fiftieth anniversary, Henry Ford II wanted to fulfill his grandfather's dream of a dome above the Rotunda Building Court. The best domed roof in the textbooks weighed 160 tons, far more than the old walls would support. Someone had heard of Bucky. Could he do something? Indeed he could, with a design "off the shelf," the one that embodied those two years' figuring. He could predict its weight, furthermore: just eight and a half tons. So the contract was signed. Bucky was fifty-seven. He had been orbiting through the building world for twenty-five years, and this was the first time anyone had come to him to buy anything. The *Archi-*

tectural Forum headlined the occasion: "Bucky Fuller Finds a Client." Bucky had his own slogan: the patron who had finally come to him was "Mr. Industry himself."

For once everything went with the zip of a blackboard demonstration. The two years' math had dictated a framework using 19,680 struts, each about a yard long. In aluminum, they weighed five ounces each. The suppliers who mass-produced them couldn't believe the delivery schedules asked for, nor could anyone but Bucky believe, really, in the tolerance to which the holes at the ends were to be spaced: five one-thousandths of an inch. He had reasons for this accuracy. If you are less accurate you will make the holes a little large, to be sure the rivets will go through. When the holes are a little large the parts will slide, and tend to chew at one another. You cope with that by making them more massive, and end up with twice the weight you originally calculated. So by making up special punches on indexing lathes, to accuracies no human eye could effect, and punching five-ounce struts with these, you get two buildings for the weight of one. So one source of the Ford dome's strength was subvisible dimensioning, folded into the metal like vanilla into a cake. Very few pieces in a standard house are fitted closer than one-eighth of an inch to one-fourth of an inch, or need to be.

It was Bucky's old dream, a factory-generated shelter, and necessarily so because its accuracies defeated workmen. What was left for the workmen to do was relatively simple: stamp out the struts, using those accurate punches; rivet them into triangles, marked with bits of colored tape; assemble the triangles by matching colors; join larger triangles into a domical shape, starting at the apex and jacking the structure up as its circumference grew, ring by ring.

Though somewhat overdesigned by his later standards,

with a good deal of Octet-Truss infill, the ninety-three-foot span, at just eight and a half tons all skinned, weighed a mere two and a half pounds for each square foot it roofed. Eight years later he made Ford a portable dome for a tractor exhibit pavilion. Spanning twice the area, it had made an eightfold gain in performance per pound: only five *ounces* per square foot covered.

The dome of St. Peter's in Rome, spanning 137½ feet, weighs 10,000 tons. That's 1,350 pounds per square foot of floor. Ever since the sixteenth century it has been trying to collapse of its own weight, and is prevented by a primitive tension ring in the form of a huge iron chain laid all round the base.

St. Peter's has a dome because there were Roman domes, notably the dome of the Pantheon, a massive temple that has endured wonderfully for nearly nineteen centuries. (Domes are spectacularly durable.) Since time has not dissected it, we are still unsure what system of vaulting lies between the inner and outer concrete walls we can see. The most expert guess is that eight huge brick arches lean in to touch a vertexial ring with their keystones. Each arch would fall in save for the mass of the other seven. Mass is the inevitable theme. Moving as the day moves, a long finger of sunlight descends through that ring at the vertex: the only light in the building. Otherwise the Pantheon is blank and blind: piled tons of deadweight, to sustain such an impending of brick and concrete. The dome does not even rise free. To contain the immense outward thrusts, the piled mass of a cylindrical outer wall rises round it like a brick canister. It is a stupendous feat, its 141-foot span unsurpassed till the nineteenth century. All that free space! One cannot begin to guess at its weight.

St. Peter's dome has sixteen upcurving ribs, to sustain a brickwork shell and themselves be sustained by that chain. A century later (1675) St. Paul's dome in London used wood. The Capitol dome in Washington (1855) uses iron sheets. Always, worn like a hat by a building not otherwise domical, the dome is a monumental stunt, justified by the classical idiom it quotes and by the vast space it vaults within. After the Pantheon, to dome over your most sacred space was one European tradition.

Space, unbroken space, was what the architects of the Pantheon were after, space in which to collect the cults of all the gods. Great crowds of people thronged it: Rome's was a *busy* religiousness. Communal space is a dome theme.

Earlier, in Greece and in Egypt, sacred places had been kept dark and constrained. Worshippers did not enter the Parthenon, where the monumental image of the goddess dwelt. So the Parthenon is a building to appreciate from outside: a compact becolumned crystal, its detailing of vertical shadows emphatic enough to hold attention afar off. (Ever since, men have thought of exterior appearance as the measure of an architect's accomplishment.) Within the rectangle of columns stood an inner stone box, to contain the divine privacies. (So much inner structure meant that holding up the roof was no trick.)

And as these rectangular dark shrines developed, far older ways of doming over space were forgotten: the beehive-shaped Mycenean "Treasury of Atreus," over forty feet high, nearly fifty feet in diameter, all of cunningly crafted stones, underground and sustaining tons of earth; other stone beehives rising from Cretan plains; Mesopotamian domes from the fifth millennium. Circular ground plans are very primitive. Men's oldest ceremonial structures—as at Stonehenge—are circular, men's oldest dwellings were circular, and domical. Rome's resurrection of the dome seems to have been derived from Etruscan cupolas and the simple domical huts of shepherds. The oldest intuitions of space we can recover appear to discern special virtue in the circle: a concentering of meeting people, an homage to the encircling universe.

Bucky Fuller discerns virtue in roundness too, and derives it, like the first men, from conceptions religious in nature. It is out of homage to the Universe, he suggests, that we should refrain from squandering its energies, and likewise from making arbitrary rectangular cuts. Nature does not chop and slice; rivers are sinuous, eggs and skulls are vaulted, Einsteinian space is curved. As for the perpendicularity that Egypt made a central theme of building (the obelisk, the column)—it would express the nature of Nature very well if the earth were flat, but reality has no parallel perpendiculars. There is no "up," only "out." Verticalities on a round earth radiate, explode. The true way for walls of buildings to trend is "in."

Again and again, the newest experiences men can devise correspond to the oldest they can recover. Picasso's sense of space is like a cave painter's. George Chapman's sense of Homer and of his time's modern poetry coincided. And Bucky's mathematics, with its mystique of the triangle and the tetrahedron, feels as Pythagorean as the domes he has derived from it look modern. The map he was working on when he discovered domes affirms a concept of the world Odysseus would have recognized, earth-island engirdled by Ocean. And archaeologists find no human habitation older than the domes men made of clay or of woven sticks when they first came together in communities and a tribe could suppose it was the whole family of man.

In August, 1951, four months before the patent application was filed, an *Architectural Forum* headline made the

phrase *Geodesic Dome* public currency. The lavishly illustrated eight-page story described for the building world
"Bucky Fuller's spidery new framing system," and hinted
at imminent developments. Up to now, said the *Forum,*
Fuller's innovations "have not been timed right for a
hammer-and-nail building technology," but this one had
irresistible advantages. "One of the *things-to-come* has
come," and the only problem, it seemed, was to keep the
lines of potential customers orderly.

There were model numbers and prices. An 8C270
Weatherbreak (forty-six feet) would be $7,000 delivered
and erected. A twenty-seven-foot vacation house, called
Skybreak, sold for $700 f.o.b. Montreal, where aluminum
and steel were not under Korean War restrictions. Airplane hangars seemed a beckoning market: "We can do it
for one-third the cost." Shelters would be leased like telephones, and replaced with improved models when pertinent, at a monthly rate per square foot. Manufacturing
rights would be licensed. At MIT an "autonomous house"
within a geodesic envelope was in late stages of design.
Tomorrow the world would alter.

This becomes a familiar theme, as we turn through the
Fuller stories in building magazines. As of press time the
world is just on the point of altering. Designs are updated.
Licenses are being negotiated. And tomorrow . . . Tomorrow, domes everywhere.

In mid-1971, when the fundamental patent had run its
seventeen-year course and expired, most people had still
never seen a Geodesic Dome, unless at fairs.

What happened? It's a complex theme.

Remember, to start with, Bucky's old intuition of the
need to get shelter clear of existing cities, where streets
are straight and building lots rectangular, ready for boxes.
A dome on an arrowlike street, between strip fences, looks
oddly withdrawn. It also looks small. That is one peculi-

arity of spherical shapes: from the outside they look much smaller than they are, in part because they present no wall for the eye to estimate. The Montreal Bubble looks perhaps six stories high; it is twenty. So long as shelter is tied to prestige, the psychology of this fact will remain to be reckoned with.

From inside domes seem larger than they are, and people feel freed up (Bucky says, "decompressed"). The Montreal Bubble encloses six million cubic feet. The immensity of that space, blowing the visitor's mind as he passes in and looks around him, may make him wonder how the frame was put up. Mohawk Indians, skilled in high places, did the steelwork; at the top they were working 200 feet aloft. That was a special project, entailing great altitudes. Special projects are not too difficult to arrange. But what of something on a gentler scale, in real quantity production: the 1927 dream of the 4-D single-family house, industrially realized at last?

That would be down near the ground where the home-building industry works, and it would threaten to obsolesce most of that industry.

The building industry first confronted geodesics in 1956, when a dome of aluminum tubes with stretched vinyl skin was to be erected for the St. Louis Golden Jubilee Fair. It had been designed in the first place for rapid erection by native labor (matching colors, putting nuts on bolts). In Kabul, Afghanistan, that had taken forty-eight hours. In St. Louis it would take longer, on account of unions. To the first question, Which union?, the answer turned out to be the boilermakers' union. Something bolted together and with a thin skin is obviously a big boiler. But boilermakers do not manage scaffolds. That was the province of a different union, which also pushed the towers around and handed up small parts. Atop the scaffolds "the boilermakers sat in chairs under sunshades in conversational pairs, putting the nuts on the bolts," and the forty-eight-hour job took a month and a half. (In the United States, says Fuller, "we erroneously assume that the building erector must be a skilled artisan.") In 1959, the whole silly story was repeated, when skilled tradesmen in New York managed to consume one month assembling for exhibit a plastic radome which Eskimo labor had routinely assembled along the DEW line in one fourteen-hour Arctic day.

And these were still special projects, as much so as the Montreal Bubble. What if battalions of carpenters had sensed invasion of their territory? And bricklayers and plasterers and pipe fitters? In San Francisco a powerful plumbers' local kept plastic pipe out of building codes for years.

Bucky is proud to be a card-carrying machinist, and furthermore is convinced that labor's gains, during the decades of unionization, made mass production possible by financing mass purchasing power. (That was a synergetic benefit of Ford's famous five dollars a day.) Still, he feels constrained to observe that when a structure that takes fourteen hours to go up in the Arctic takes a month in New York City, "clearly there has been an inordinate shunting of social wealth in a direction in which legitimate value is not added to the product." (When he is most aroused he sounds most like Henry James.)

It is a brilliant example of the principle that "jobs," the only present means for getting pay into anyone's pocket, are apt to be parasitic upon production. "That is an indirect, illogical and therefore indefensible way of distributing wealth for it hides the new advantages and therefore retards the growth of those advantages as wealth generators of commonwealth." He can say that again. He has, over and over.

It's a knotlike self-interference. No dome homes without mass production; no mass production without mass consumption; no mass consumption without mass demand, on the existence of which any company that financed the tool-up would be taking a truly enormous gamble. For the domes would work against people's intuitive resistance to having their life-styles changed. Perhaps the changed life-style would somehow have to come first, to make people want the domes. Then once they wanted them they'd need to pay for them, amid a full-sized depression emanating from the building industry, all its plasterers and plumbers obsolesced overnight. In the kind of world Bucky foresees, of lightweight housing units by the millions that need only some bolting together at the site, or may even be air-delivered, the relationship between *incomes* and *jobs* would have shifted to a degree we can barely conceive. So long as jobs mean incomes the fight against joblessness tends to make such housing too expensive to afford. It's a Whole-System impasse.

Or so it seems, Bucky will tell us, because we do envisage a large enough system. Like the bricklayer, the dinosaur once seemed here to stay. Think of the Universe, that scenario of "nonsimultaneous, only partially overlapping, transformational events." Consult evolution. Think how many big pictures have been changed beyond recognition by an inconspicuous novelty.

If about 1860 some design genius had planned an eighty-story office building, he would have been wide open to the objection that in housing the businesses he had wholly overlooked the customers. How would they get in? Eighty city blocks' worth of offices, say close to a thousand firms, with only the doors around one block for access! And then think of the stampeding elevator traffic; it would overload any system for which there was space. But faith in evolution would have been well placed. Within a lifetime his problem would be solved by the telephone, which was quite literally what made the skyscraper feasible.

No one in 1860 could have foreseen that traffic through business offices would be cut to a trickle, because few of the day's business contacts would any longer be made face to face. Some analogous revolution may lie ahead of us, synergetic and therefore surprising, and instead of designing a Geodesic Dymaxion House, Bucky seems to have decided he might as well wait for it. Meanwhile he devoted his unflagging energies to "academic to-and-froing," dropping in on design schools to give crash courses in the Universe which always culminated in a group of students working out the nuts and bolts of yet one more geodesic variant. He also gave time to military customers, who had uses for the geodesic envelope minus dishwashers and sun parlors. In the course of a series of tests for the Marine Corps, several very large domes were airlifted fully assembled, fulfilling one dream of 1927. The frustration some of his young associates felt is a different story. They found themselves swept into an alternate trip whose goals weren't the ones they envisaged, and a number dropped away in bitterness.

One might argue that Bucky Fuller and human nature were at last on a collision course, that they grazed like two knitting needles, and are now on paths of what he calls "tangential avoidance." Had he actually, all these years, been telling people what they ought to want because it was efficient? Had there been, at last, a tacit decision not to want it?

His friend and admirer the anthropologist Edward T. Hall develops in *The Hidden Dimension* (with a handsome acknowledgment to Bucky) a contrary view of what housing is for. Noting that Germans, Frenchmen, Arabs,

Americans, have totally different notions of intimacy and
of privacy, Dr. Hall argues that a house expresses such
habits. Arabs find American ceilings too low and rooms
too small, since they like to intermingle without the en-
croachment of *things*. Le Corbusier's balconies in Chan-
digarh were unacceptable to the hierarchic Hindus, who
walled them up. German doors are substantial and German
yards well-fenced, because in Germany you have intruded
upon a man if he can hear you, or if you can see him.
Man's extensions, therefore—houses and cities, for instance
—need more anthropological than engineering attention.

"I have found it somewhat difficult to talk to Bucky
about these things," Dr. Hall says, "because they are not
technological problems. But if technicians are going to
serve mankind, they must start with man and learn how
men behave. With rare exceptions they start with technology, and expect man to adapt as best he can."

Bucky's belief is that environment creates such patterns
and can also alter them. It is like his answer to questions
about race: "We have only humanity aboard this spaceship."

He has a point. People can change without resisting it,
without knowing it. When the telephone separated *access*
from *traffic,* it changed everyone's idea of what it means
to live through a day. We no longer write notes to decline
invitations for lunch. The people who invite us need not
plan on post-office schedules; they can call up at whim.
We compose our thoughts en route to an appointment far
less often than we pick up a phone and improvise. First
thoughts surface first, which tends to change what is meant
by taking thought. And since the caller can't see that we're
busy, our notion of privacy is irrevocably altered. All that
amounts to a social revolution. Yet had anyone announced
it in advance, it would have seemed like a proposal to alter
human nature.

It's worth noticing that such agents of social mutation all started unobtrusively. The telephone was once an office appliance. The automobile was once a toy for the rich. The airplane was a plaything for daredevils, civil and military. Only later, slowly, did phones come into houses, and autos into working people's garages, and planes into public airports to be boarded as casually as streetcars. (Half the adults in the U.S. have now boarded one.)

Bucky's domes, similarly, have been playthings for governments and rich corporations, turning up in festive places like World's Fairs, and exotic places like the South Pole and the DEW line and Hollywood (where the Cinerama Theater is geodesic). But they haven't yet created a Geodesic Environment, the way the telephone created a Telephone Environment that made it seem indispensable to everyone.

This may be because in 1900 the man with the first phone in the neighborhood saw no need to confront the psychic restructurings of the Telephone Age. But the purchaser of a radically different house may feel he has gone into free fall. Just to move across town, from one cube to another cube, is to pull up and put down roots. (Roots? "Man is no plant," Bucky cries, "man is mobile." Yet men's souls grow attached to places.) And to desert squareness altogether, and corners, and move one's rectangular furniture into a hemisphere, no longer even able to say which is the backyard—that takes much preparation, much fantasy.

One might ask a cultural anthropologist's kind of questions about Bucky's preoccupation with symmetry and with spherical segments: that circular ground plan, that part-circular roof-line, alike from every angle. Imagine such a neighborhood, and—no, the point isn't sameness. Most neighborhoods are almost insanely same. The point is that domes don't reach toward one another. They withdraw from one another, almost primly, like Puritan moralists. (Puritan; is that part of an answer?) Rarely, to defeat the circle, a few have been clustered and merged, as at the Placer County Administrative Center in California. As rarely, ovaloid and free-form shapes have come from Fuller drawing boards, and in theory it is possible to geodesicize any compound-curved surface that can be mathematically described, but such possibilities have been little explored. One can't help feeling Bucky resists them. He wasn't pleased by the ellipsoidal designs a young mathematician named Peter Calthorpe offered readers of *Domebook 2*. Did patents worry him? Credit? More profoundly, perhaps, a sense of insult to the omnisymmetrical modules on which his intuitions keep converging.

Bucky Fuller, the Last Puritan? Not absurd when you remember the modestly impeccable black suit, or that glimpse, in San Francisco, of the counterculture being rapped with by a man like a trim little clergyman. His domes yield him, as their deepest satisfaction, their conformities with Nature's economies, energetic but seclusive as peach-pits. *Things* clutter them; and that's a point of intersection with counterculture Puritanism.

"The effect of an empty dome," writes one *Domebook* contributor, "is to concentrate your attention on the other people in the room instead of on things as in a museum." Another concurs: "Our conversations are more centered because we sit in a circle and stay in closer touch with each other." That is the power of the sphere. The sphere "makes us wholer people. We feel more whole and have our whole trip around us." And straight lines, observes the Swami Kriyananda, attract stiff minds; firm heavy buildings are for people hung up on solid matter. "Boxed houses belong to an age when men stood in opposition to the world around them," while "The dome is expressive of our new approach to the universe."

That's a vibe-centered Puritanism, orthodox in its dislike of clutter, novel in its reach toward other persons (though local decorums are meant to be observed). Its approach to the universe isn't all that novel. Cotton Mather was rapt by the "Wonders of the Invisible World" (though his "wonders" exacted fear; they weren't Bucky's pure principles), and Salem's descendants in the nineteenth century were welcoming Oriental lore—Confucius, Buddha—as the counterculture welcomes its swamis. It's hardly an accident that the counterculture has fashioned the first real prototype geodesic domiciles.

These are unofficial domes. Of official domes, by 1972 estimate, there are some 50,000 world-round, though many of these are little playground climbing-gyms. How many of the unofficial ones there are nobody knows, but certainly more than Building Inspectors guess. One outlaw hides his son's nursery dome from street viewing with bamboo, which he waters faithfully so it'll close overhead before the Inspectors take to helicopters. He's one of the *Domebook's* clientele. They aren't all paranoid, but they're all outsiders, at least fantasy-outsiders.

Lloyd Kahn remembers his own transformation by Fuller. He was helping build a huge house from bridge timbers, no balloon frame but with massive members to be hoisted in place with a tractor and boom. Then "On a stormy weekend at Big Sur Hot Springs, Fuller talked about spinning a dome framework of light members. When I went back to work on Monday, I looked at the ponderous beams we were struggling with, thinking in terms of cutting them up into dome struts—soon I quit the job." His dome, by comparison, "felt like the spinning of a spider web."

Big Sur is an old outlaw hangout—Henry Miller's long-time address—and the thoughts of Lloyd's friend Stewart Brand on outlawry are apropos: "Reasonable laws made by reasonable men in reasonable times proscribe trying everything. For a good reason: people get hurt trying stuff. If you're bound to try stuff anyway, then either you're working directly for City Hall, or you're an outlaw, or both. One thing we need is better outlaws."

That might have been a Bear Island motto. Stewart Brand's form of outlawry was *The Whole Earth Catalog*—inspired, he says, by Bucky Fuller's insights—which began as an outlaws' information exchange and ended leaving him pondering what to do with profits so colossal it was immoral to spend them casually. Lloyd Kahn's was domery, leading to *The Domebook*.

A year removed from Big Sur, he was into domework with a subgroup of outlaws, building an experimental high school community in the hills above Los Gatos. Handcrafting one dome is a bit like handcrafting one Volkswagen, using wood where possible. Wood swells and shrinks, pulling joints, augmenting leakage problems. Glass panes are impractical. Plastic panes turn brittle in the sun, all but plastics too expensive for most outlaws to contemplate. Lloyd slowly came to feel there were better ways of working with wood. Eventually the lifestyle for which he had left insurance brokering came to seem incompatible with the Fuller gospel.

The lifestyle runs deep in his being. "I know my hand," he says, flexing its sturdy fingers. "It's not a machine." And he now feels that you violate long timbers when you cut them into little angled struts. And the earth is violated by plastics chemistry, the more so, apparently, the better the plastic. Drawn back to the solo worker's traditional crafts, he affirms a disenchantment that often seems to supersede involvement with the Fuller theme.

Fuller professes no surprise at word of defectors. Such people never saw the whole picture, and the details aren't self-sustaining. Domes, for instance, are meaningless apart from machine-tooled Industry, and Industry apart from "making the world work."

The whole picture, another ex-disciple feels, exists only in Bucky's rhetoric. "When he dies it'll all come apart."

Meanwhile handcrafted domes, however anomalous, continue to go up, all over the country, one at a time, often hidden away on back lots or down slopes. A day's *Domebook* mail for Lloyd may come from twenty states. Here and there maverick contractors specialize in wooden domes. Some of their artifacts, though not spectacular, are perfectly public. More than one private school has gone into wooden domes.

There may be dome-kits, some day, in the Sears catalog, but Big Industry, on the scale of Ford or Boeing, has been paying no noticeable heed. Big Industry, peering short distances ahead, sees signs that its fiscal sands are running out, and even hears influential talk about the folly of "growth." Growth, of the spectacular kind, is exceeding the limits of private capital. Only government funds could finance the SST (and the government reneged). Bucky, according to his architectural partner Shoji Sadao, still dreams of that mass-produced housing industry he envisaged nearly half a century ago. Economic crises do not impress him. His own work was twenty-five, thirty years bearing fruit; crises, he thinks, are illusions produced by the myth of the fiscal year, which expects an annual return like a cotton crop. His sights are elevated to exciting levels of abstraction. His talk, as never before, is concentrated on vast evolutionary patterns: on man's role in the regenerative functions of the Universe: on making the World work. He seldom speaks of Industry now.

NINE

Dialogue with a Skeptic

"So we have an impasse," said the Skeptic. "He has lived long enough to see that nothing is going to work out as he expected. Certainly not the Shelter industry in which he invested the greater part of his life. To accept this would be to throw a lifetime away. So he keeps very busy jetting about, and talking. That Universe he expounds is not ours. He's spun it out of his impulses, and spun it so cunningly a fact can no more dent it than Walter O'Malley's stones could dent that plastic globe. Or perhaps the Tensegrity Sphere is a better image: the pieces are tautly connected and arrest attention by the way they float, but they present little surface to objections. An inconvenient missile will pass clean through, and he can remark that there has been no collision. As for the rest of us meanwhile, perhaps we muddle on toward doomsday, or perhaps only through a long tunnel, but Fuller is no longer relevant to our muddling. We may guess that there will be no domesday. Domes, that is what his life now comes to, domes and verbiage. I'll return to the verbiage. Let us talk more of the domes. You did not mention that they often leak."

"Someone always says that," I replied, "and never thinks

to add that conventional houses leak too. Leakage plagued Frank Lloyd Wright, who once advised a client with water dripping on his head to move his chair. It still plagued homeowners within living memory. I can remember pans catching drip in leaky attics. If few houses built today leak, that is because they inherit some centuries' concentration on the problem."

"You talk like a book," said the Skeptic, "and since I am in a book I shall talk like one too. May I point out that the maligned cube has advantages? It segregates functions, walls for one job, roof for another. Builders can apply special techniques to the roof: lapped shingles, covering one another's joints, over sheets of tar paper to stop what gets past the shingles. No leakage. But every part of a dome is both walls and roof, and moreover you cannot lay tar paper on a compound-curved surface."

"This grows trivial," I answered. "Why worry about fitting tar paper? There is design, integral gutters along the joints. There are space-age sealants. The great Expo structure is watertight except where a few of the 1900 plexiglass panels had their fit disrupted by ice the day they went in. Sealants are very versatile. The *Domebook* folk, who can't manage precision fit and whose plywood sheathing expands and contracts alarmingly, went mad with leaks for a while but have lately been finding a leakproof answer in sealants."

The Skeptic said he was glad to hear it. "I bring up leakage," he pursued, "not because I suppose it cannot be defeated, but because it has concerned Bucky so little. It is typical of what does not concern him. He is happy in his geometry's abstract rightness. His second cousin John P. Marquand once remarked that the Dymaxion Laundry was to give back your shirt in three minutes washed and dried, but not ironed. Bucky said it was silly to have an ironed shirt. 'This is illustrative,' said Marquand, 'of my cousin's entire mental process. The trouble is the shirts never come out pressed.' It's worth thinking about. When Bucky tells us we are silly to want shirts pressed, he is telling us we must adopt his priorities, and dispense with anything he thinks silly."

"And yet he is the least coercive of men."

"Ah," said the Skeptic, "but how those environments of his would coerce. 'Don't reform the person,' he says, 're-form the environment.' In the 4-D specifications, the re-formed environment included a 'vacuum toothbrush,' also a chinning bar. The 'vacuum toothbrush' is probably something he saw at a dentist's. I don't want its hose round my neck like Laocoon's first snake. On the other hand I want a hot bath, in a tub."

"There was a tub in the Dymaxion Bathroom."

"A short tub, yes. But his next speculations were ephemeralizing that away. See what comes of reforming people's environments. He stated the bath's objective, cleanliness. (How fanatical he is about cleanliness, by the way. The reason he wanted photo-cell door openers was to break the microbe chain.) Then superior 'external skin cleansing,' as he calls it, will be obtained from the Fog Gun he developed after noticing that fog removes grime from sailors' faces. This would cut to a fraction what he calls 'the quantities of water involved in the older bathing,' and bring him one step closer to his goal of cutting the water-lines that immobilize homes. But a phrase like 'external skin cleansing' is one of his hypnotics. It mesmerizes us into forgetting the satisfactions of lying in a hot tub. The Romans understood those satisfactions. Sigfried Giedion calls their baths places of 'regeneration.' "

"Habit, habit," I replied. "You might also regenerate in some other fashion, and let the bath be an external skin cleanser only. After all the bath is not a human constant. Eskimos have not your passion for baths."

"Nor I for the Eskimos' snow domes. But do not evade the principle. As Professor Hall said, he is apt to identify selected functions, and drive straight toward them. I gather that was Professor Hall's point, that he doesn't ask us what we want. Or he takes advantage of the fact that we cannot quite say what we want. We simply do it, when we can. And while we are fumbling for words he is drawing up his Cartesian checklists of bloodless categories. We might modify any of these categories—we might insert a bathtub, or delete a vacuum toothbrush. But their whole spirit is inimical to human satisfaction."

"What categories?"

"Well, look at the *Universal Requirements of a Dwelling Advantage,* its 1963 updating, and consult section II.A. Here it is:

II.A. *Provision for* (unself-conscious) (spontaneous) *mechanical performance* of *inevitable organic routines* of the dwelling and its occupants with minimum of invested attention or effort.
1. Fueling of
   A. house
   B. occupant (eating) (metabolism)
2. Realignment of house or occupants in sleep by allowing muscular, nerve and cellular realignment accomplished by designed elimination of known restrictive factors
3. Refusing of house or occupants
   A. internal, i.e., intestinal, etc.
   B. external, i.e., bathing or pore-cleansing
   C. mental, i.e., elimination by empirical dynamics
   D. circulatory: external—atmospheric control; internal—as respiratory functions

'Pore cleansing,' and that lovely word 'realignment,' by which he means 'sleep.' And 'Fueling of A. house; B. occupant.' That is priceless."

"It is also witty," I said. "And don't think he doesn't know it. He will speak of birds patrolling 'areas of maximum anticipated metabolic advantage,' and pause and add, 'Worms.' I admire the nimbleness of mind that can withdraw at will from worms to so grand a pattern. It is like the great description in *Nine Chains* of the phantom captain's courtship, with a view to 'suitable hook-up conditions' for 'the manufacture of an improved model replica.' You remember the explanation of the lover's word 'Beautiful!' It meant that Murphy had noted in Julia 'a mechanism that was highly uniform, i.e., not deformed, and therefore favorable for plant hook-up.' If that is playfully satiric, it is also poetic. The poet's trade, in part, is finding unexpected reasons for unexpected categories. Donne called his lady 'O more than Moon' in part for the sake of fine sound, but he also supplied the logical reason that her weeping made a tide of tears. That is not your romantic Moon, as Fuller's is not the romantic Julia. Minds take pleasure in such witty accuracies. They are also heuristic. We can never break out of habits till we see them recategorized. Buggy-makers went under for not grasping that they were in the transportation business."

"Very well, very well, witty. But it is also in the fashion of the 1930's, from which that passage dates. Thinking of people as machines was a nineteenth-century highbrow habit. Like everything highbrow, it was a couple of generations becoming part of the unchallenged environment. But at last it was everyone's habit, and needed to be challenged, not indulged. Chaplin was challenging it in *Modern Times,* not long after Fuller designed the Dymaxion House, and not long before he wrote that courtship passage. No one forgets Charlie at lunchtime, being 'refueled' by a machine that moved a corncob past his teeth like a typewriter carriage. When Bucky surrounded the Dymaxion dweller with a plenitude of gadgetry to free him from labor, he was unconsciously fitting a mechanical man to a mechanical house. Beware of whoever mechanizes your body. Beware of glib efforts to separate *you* from *it*. Whether Bucky Fuller, calling it a machine to be fulfilled by mechanical extensions, or Mrs. Eddy ephemeralizing it away to be discounted in a limbo of dream, such speculators are provincial: not bold at all, not innovative at all, but naive recursors to that oldest and most insidious of simplifications, the gospel of the Gnostics, of the Manichaeans, for whom salvation was enlightenment, and the cure for a toothache or a leaky roof was to deem them beneath notice. Lloyd Kahn's 'I know my hand' is as profound as any remark you have quoted. The Phantom Captain is not apart from the hand. He is a Synergy, one of whose subsystems is a living hand.''

"Emphasis, emphasis," I said. "I distrust dualism as much as you. But like you I wear glasses, and like Bucky I hear with mechanical help. In certain respects the body has functions we can augment, and we may as well call them mechanical functions. Nor does Bucky discount body-knowledge, not all the time. Remember his love of athletics, and his 'intuitive dynamic sense.' No, the point of his talk is to undercut the real robot-mongers, the Skinners for whom we are nothing but machines, for whom all passion is a surge from the endocrines, all behavior habit shaped by stimuli, all thought a traffic-pattern through synapses. Mind is not Brain, he keeps telling them. He is right. Have respect for Mind, and gadgets need not enslave. They are partly conveniences, and partly toys."

"But," said the Skeptic, "gadgets, like toys, preoccupy. They impose *their* routine. Also—he seems to have forgotten—they keep breaking down, and their owners are soon working for them. That house is as much a caricature of a home as the courtship passage in *Nine Chains* is a caricature of love. The difference is that the house is an unconscious caricature. Which is only to say that his wittiness, like anyone else's, comes and goes. And when it goes, we find him elaborating an unexamined stereotype of man, and with truly Messianic fervor."

"Not so fast," I said. "A minute ago you used the word 'home.' 'Home' is a romance word, and Bucky is right to see romance as the great emulsifier of habit. Thirty years ago, after remarking that when you have seen your first one hundred low-cost wartime houses you have seen one hundred too many, he went on to explain why people put up with them. Human beings, he said, will 'engulf these drab items with a foolhardy romanticism that will turn Umpty-umpty Panel Boards into a "home." ' As for machinery, it can indeed tyrranize. But the relation between man and machine he has in mind is ideally like your relation with a refrigerator. Nothing is so trouble-free, nothing so durable, nothing so indispensable. It does its job far better than the icebox it replaced. And it relieves you of a great burden. If you did not have one in your house you would be able to buy no more fresh food than you could consume within hours. Refrigeration warps nobody's life-style, unless he goes in for such nonsense as TV dinners. Bucky's vacuum toothbrush is a bizarre detail, long behind him. It was special-case. The machine he dreams on now is as general-purpose as the refrigerator: the Space-Age power pack, the black box that will serve your metabolic needs anywhere."

"Ah, but serving my metabolic needs means recycling

my food and water. Do you never see something alarming in that ruthless simplicity of mind of his? It still envisages 'Fueling B. occupant.' Is not frugality his pattern of virtue? Not a drab necessitous frugality, but spick and span like a ship's galley. Plain living and high thinking."

"We are coming full circle," I said. "You began by talking of leaky domes, by which you meant that his environments may not work. Now you are arguing that they may work too well."

"It is not a circle," the Skeptic said. "It is a pair of approaches to the same principle. The principle is that reality and his reasonings do not coincide. For instance, he reasoned that the great Montreal Bubble need not get hot if mechanically operated shades covered triangles as the sun moved, to cut off its direct rays. Too few were installed—not his fault, I agree: there was a budget. More to the point, motorized window-blinds need service, and some of these were 200 feet off the ground. The Montreal Director of Public Works writes me that access was so difficult repairs and maintenance were almost nil."

"Remember," I admonished, "that it was an Expo structure, designed for six months' service, then dismantling. No one expected it to be there five years later."

"Quite. But then the general problem of maintaining a huge Geodesic remains unsolved. Yet in principle it can be made to sound like no problem at all. A far more complex theme, human behavior, also sounds like no problem at all as he discusses it. But he oversimplifies with quite stunning blandness. It is always the technologist talking."

"Technologist," I said. "An easy term of abuse."

"Let me specify carefully," said the Skeptic. "I do not paraphrase for the $n + 1^{th}$ time the 'humanist' indictment of a barbarous scientist. Much 'humanist' baggage is carried about sentimentally, and many men who felt no one was watching would be happy to bury it. No, I claim that Bucky is himself sentimental. His conception of man sounds generous. It is utterly naive. It is the old Romantic conception: Rousseau's embarrassing baby, bottle-fed for two centuries and never growing up nor moving away: the conception of the child born good, in fact perfect, in fact a 'comprehensivist,' a genius, until his environment corrupts him. Hence the obsession with environments."

"Wait," I said.

"Listen," he said. "It is as consistent a theme as we shall find in Fuller's utterances. Here he is arguing in 1928 that children, born truthful, only learn untruthful habits 'from the selfish prohibition of truth by their elders.' Much of this in turn stems from 'great unconscious selfishness of parents, due to drudgery,' for which we are to blame unsuitable houses. Solve the housing problem, he says, and other problem areas—politics, education, unemployment, crime—'will practically solve themselves.' There will ensue 'a glorified system of spontaneous education of choice, similar to the Montessori system,' to make life ever 'cleaner and happier, more rhythmical and artistic.' "

"A young man's rhetoric," I said, "long outgrown like the vacuum toothbrush."

"The rhetoric is outgrown," said the Skeptic, "but not the dream. After forty years we may discover that the 'house' of 1928 was really a facilitating metaphor for the child's whole intellectual environment. Yet he still supposes that to optimize that environment is to leave no adult problems whatsoever. In a man who has seen life for seventy-six years, I can only call that a nearly pathetic naivete. Imagine those liberated millions and millions, mostly idle. Can you not see them smashing things in sheer boredom?"

"His reply would be that the Universe cannot bore."

"My reply would be that the Universe is only accessible to an intensity of interest that is quite exceptional. Your average sensual youth is soon looking for something to *do*. How often he smashes a window."

"That is not exactly boredom," I protested. "He will smash a schoolhouse window, or a pawnshop window, which he takes to be a symbol of futile oppression. By definition, in a rational world such oppression would be absent. Still, I agree that experience tells against Bucky. We have no instance of a functioning Utopia, and the advocate of 'work' will always point out that it keeps folk out of mischief. The old cliché about Heaven being boring suggests some inherent human lack, some inability to fill up the time if much unwelcome bother does not fill it up. Fuller of course might rejoin that all our experience is irrelevant, because it pertains to people whose imaginations have been crippled since childhood by exactly the kind of environment he hopes to renovate. World Man in his leisure, having known nothing but freedom, would in fact be a new kind of man."

"That is not a new idea," said the Skeptic. "The great revolutions of 1776, of 1789, of 1917, all promised a new human birth. The American Revolution was to have set free the American Adam, and the story (ironically for Fuller) is that the Machine ruined his Garden. Flaubert devoted a career to inventorying the anguish and absurdity which the promise of the French Revolution left behind. Journalists after the Russian Revolution told us fairy tales about happy workers, free from anxiety, all spontaneously studying integral calculus. Our newest fairy tales pertain to Mao's China, a sanitary state erected upon millions of corpses. Yet Fuller's faith in the Industrial Revolution does not falter. At least one order of human experience seems unable to teach him."

"But again," I put in, "those were all *political* revolutions. There is nothing, he says, that politics can do but rearrange the patterns of scarcity, move the deprivation—often bloodily—to a different sector. Only industrialization can increase the supply. You mentioned Flaubert. His Emma Bovary was not liberated from scarcity—far from it. Her suicide was not only her final Romantic gesture, it was also an escape from converging debts. And his Bouvard and Pécuchet, those ninnies whose endless studies seem to discredit study itself, came too late to the life of the mind. A legacy brought them freedom when they were fifty."

"We are not going to resolve this," said the Skeptic. "If there has been no possibility of evidence for human sweetness, then what Fuller must ask is blind faith. Primarily, these days, he is a religious leader. The fact does make him uneasy. He has spoken of the dangers of a cult. Unhappily he has no option but to ask for faith alone."

"True," I said. "And it is an endearing faith. How many men act on their faith as he does? How many are confident that you are both able and willing to understand the most complicated patterns they can lay before you?"

"Few, I agree. What most men know, they guard as a monopoly. A textbook has been described as a device to prevent the student from learning *too much,* and curricula seem designed to prevent him from learning too fast. It is also true that children want to learn nearly everything—in his language, they are not specialists—and that somehow this universality of theirs gets disconnected. I remember that Fuller calls himself a 'low-average' individual, not a 'genius' at all, but fortunate in having escaped too many disconnects. We may grant him this much: our schools are so incredibly wasteful they diminish the potential of every child who passes through. (It was Maria Montessori, by

the way, who first used the 'house'—*La Casa dei Bambini*—
as a name for a learning environment.) Nevertheless,
Fuller remains self-deceived—by his own character, as it
happens. For he is exceptional in one important way. He
does not waste time. He never suspects that people freed
from toil might slump in front of TV popping tranquilizers, because he himself, even when Dymaxion Sleep gave
him twenty-two-hour days, had more he wanted to do
than he could fit in. That talent for self-disciplined work
is as much a New England heritage as his tidiness. It is
the ethic pertinent to scarcity in a harsh climate. I find
that ironic."

"It is true," I agreed, "that there are many inconsisten-
cies in his talk. When he is lecturing on how to make the
world work, all is environment; but his Myth of the
Water People seems genetic. Do you remember that version of prehistory? In Indo-China, it seems, in mankind's
dawn, men divided spontaneously into two groups: those
who drifted with the prevailing winds, those who sailed
into them. The former floated across the Pacific, peopling
such places as Tahiti. The latter, pursuing what he calls
the North-easterly Spiral, progressively mastered the forces
they confronted, turned into mind-over-matterists, peopled
Europe, crossed to America, sired the Yankee achievers
and permitted Bucky Fuller to suppose that people given
time will use it to advantage."

"A charming story," said the Skeptic, "and I am sure
impervious to anything an anthropologist might say. Bucky
has a gift for overriding troublesome facts. Thus it suits
him to make Einstein's universe of motion supersede Newton's universe of rest as a consequence of the discovery
that light takes time to travel. He gives the impression
that this fact was discovered about 1900. He is thinking of
Michelson's measurements. But Newton knew that light

has a velocity. Olaus Römer calculated it in 1676, and his figure was only 3 percent too high."

"Though often," I said, "he is right in principle when his facts are wrong. Newton may have known the velocity of light, but he knew it as a complication merely. Jupiter's satellites were eclipsed sooner or later than predicted, according as Jupiter was nearer or farther from the Earth. This was a nuisance which Römer explained away by assigning light a velocity. Men went on thinking the satellites were 'really' eclipsed at the calculated times. Einstein in effect said that the word 'really' in that sentence was meaningless, and it was with Einstein that the time light takes was brought into a comprehensive structure of thought. In that sense at least, it was discovered when Bucky says it was."

"How do you mean that 'really' was meaningless?"

"I mean that the difference between the static and the energetic universes is one of Bucky's profoundest insights. It is on record that he grasped its implications more fully than Einstein himself. In 1938, Einstein found the exposition in *Nine Chains* acceptable, but was astonished to be told that there were practical consequences. Bucky had written, '$E = mc^2 = $ Mrs. Murphy's Horsepower,' and calculated the retail price of light as one and a half billion dollars a pound. What he had grasped was the difference Einstein made to our notions of Theory and Practice.

"In the all-at-once Universe, where the norm is Rest (as at Harvard), things 'really' happen as though our knowledge of them did not depend on light's timing. When they are seen to happen later, we correct for the time it has taken us to see them. In this way, the 'real' is always theoretical, and there is always a gap between theory and practice. Bodies fall *in vacuo;* we correct for air resistance. Wheels spin forever: we correct for friction.

These are all lags of *time*. Time is the domain of inconvenient error. Weight, friction, resistance, shift phenomena into time, where imperfection presides.

"Buildings, in the same way, theoretically lasted forever. It was only in an imperfect world that they fell apart.

"Bucky grasped that change was no imperfection, but
a principle. 'Nature,' he says 'never fails.' And he had the
wit to attach this to Einstein at one end, and to the duration of artifacts at the other. Going one way, we get his
Energetic Geometry. Going the other way, we arrive at
calculated life-spans and recycling. Einstein and ecology
are continuous. Duration is a normal fact about any phenomenon, a lightning-flash or an automobile. That is why
'ownership,' which implies permanence, seems to him obsolete. He now rents cars. I am told when he 'owned' them
he used to forget them at airports."

"It is a beautiful pattern," said the Skeptic, "the kind
of pattern at which he excels. Cranks too excel at such
patterns, of comparable simplicity if not of equal beauty.
You surprised me, by the way, in supposing the crank to
be indigenous to America, and still more in being so ready
to distinguish Fullerism from crankery. Have you forgotten the long history of infatuated minds, for whom precisely Bucky's primary patterns, the five Platonic solids,
were paradigms of God's way? Plato himself, who was
something of a crank, set the example when he identified
the dodecahedron with the all-embracing ether, within
which were four kinds of molecules: tetrahedral fire, octahedral air, icosahedral water, cubical earth. And since
you've mentioned Kepler in your book, let me remind you
that Kepler's lifework consisted in nestling the planetary
spheres into and around those same five solids, in the faith
that he could make their fit agree with what observers of
the sky reported. The Three Laws for which he is immor-
tal were by-products, trial balances which it seems he

never took seriously. They did fit, he noticed, but they used the wrong shapes and numbers, and Arthur Koestler, whom you've also cited, remarks that it took Newton's genius to dig them out of the jargon–jungle Kepler left. And here is Bucky, playing that ancient game, but not struggling with details in Kepler's way. He simply disregards details.

"Look at *Utopia or Oblivion*. On page 101, we find pictures of linked tetrahedra, labeled 'Chemical Bonding.' We are told that point-to-point tetrahedra—single bonded —resemble a gas. Hinged edge to edge, they are like water. Face to face, they are rigid, like crystals. Interpenetrating, they have the hardness of diamonds. Alas, Linus Pauling, who is mentioned on that very page, tells us (*The Nature of the Chemical Bond*, page 559) that 'The presence of shared edges and especially of shared faces in a coordinated structure decreases its stability,' since the positive ions the tetrahedra enclose dislike coming so close together. Pauling's pictures of tetrahedra touching only at corners depict crystals, not gases. Bucky's is a pretty intuitive model, but it is not chemistry."

"I will concede," I said, "a large problem area, in which three different things tend to get mixed up: a coordinate system, a set of quick analogies, and the actual modeling of natural structures. All a coordinate system needs to claim is that it is close enough to actuality to give an economical accounting. You remember our analogy of the bathroom tiles. They were hexagons, and their area was *always* irrational, inescapably so, if we computed in squares, because $\sqrt{3}$ is irrational. If we use a three-way grid the area need not be a whole number, but it can be. In that sense, the grid follows the grain of reality. Using it, though, is not the same as asserting that all reality is neatly, symmetrically triangular or hexagonal."

"I could wish," said the Skeptic, "that his expositions

observed that distinction a little more carefully. There are times when one might wonder if he understands the import of his own words, and he is not always scrupulous about that of other people's. Look at page 107 of *Utopia or Oblivion,* where Dr. Benjamin Bloom's *Stability and Change in Human Characteristics* is misrepresented by the amazing statement that 'If you can give Dr. Bloom an adequate report of environmental factors governing a given young life from birth to seventeen years of age—such as description of the home—private bathroom or no —drunken parents—play only in streets—etc., he can give you the IQ of that life within 1 percent.' I can find no such claim in the book, which is for the most part a sober study of how various sorts of statistics correlate. Bucky's eye was caught by a summarizing paragraph which showed the effect of environment on IQ tapering off till at age seventeen it seemed inoperative. But the sentence he gives us, with its odd implication that middle-class children from homes with play space and private bathrooms will have uniformly high IQ's, cannot be ascribed to Dr. Bloom of Chicago. It has the stamp of a Boston Brahmin."

"I am afraid," I said, "that *Utopia or Oblivion* contains many more such creative misrememberings. Everything in it was talked out before audiences, and the editing has not been tidy."

"Still, it reflects what he said, and yet another departure from reality, in this case another man's book's reality. He is very vivid. He can make whatever he is promoting at the moment seem reasonable and acceptable. But out in the real world we sometimes discover we have been misinformed, and we always discover the reasonableness vanishing. Barry Farrell, in his excellent article in *Life* (Feb. 26, 1971), reproduced the effect very well. Leaving behind the entrancement of Bear Island talk, he drove toward

New York, a 'mounting disaster' where 'the smog and din seemed lethal.' Surrounded by noise, pollution, violence and rot, he felt the vision fade. 'I couldn't maintain my grasp on the belief that human welfare was a function of technological advance.' "

" 'Noise, pollution, violence, and rot,' " I repeated. "Now let us note that in 1928, Fuller would have told him that this would be the reality of a modern city, and would not have been believed. Back then, he spent countless hours trying to persuade men that the world they had built was not only less than perfect, it was doomed to crumble of its irremediable imperfections. What Farrell perceived in the fall of 1970 was the fulfillment of a forty-two-year-old prediction."

"Ah," said the Skeptic, "I wondered when you would get around to his record as a prophet. I grant he was diagnosing rot in 1928. But he was also announcing the birth of a new era, to be inaugurated by industrially reproducible housing."

"Exactly," I said, "and of course it was not born. And we have about us the alternative he foretold. Moreover he did not think it would be born overnight. Twenty-five years was to be the research-and-development lag; the Ford Dome, in 1953, came just on schedule."

"A favorite instance," said the Skeptic. "But (1) we do not find him saying in 1928 that it would take twenty-five years. In *Timelock* we are teased with the notion that it is imminent, and even hoaxed by talk of a Syndicate that did not exist, ready with designs for which the very materials—by his own later admission—did not exist either. And (2) the Ford Dome was a one-shot; it started no massive trend."

"You are right to say that the Ford Dome was not the first snowball of a domical avalanche. As to why Domes are not all around us, I have suggested some reasons. As to the bluff in *Timelock,* clearly he was fishing for an industrial commitment, to inaugurate the research. He was not as self-deceived as we may think. He knew that the Dymaxion House needed heat-treated aluminum alloys, and that the aluminum industry thought of their product only as a soft metal. Those alloys did come, after five years, and the aircraft industry was born."

"Very well, we will set aside his show of conviction that the 4-D house could be realized tomorrow. Though that did not prevent his writing in 1932 that the Bath Iron Works and Starling Burgess were about to 'take over design and fabrication responsibility for the first Dymaxion House, which a syndicate, now forming, will underwrite.' There was to be a kind of designers' commune, apparently, up on the Maine coast. Note the habit again: something announced as imminent, which never eventuates."

"Note the date: 1932. The financial flux of that era surely explains what happened to the prospects of the commune. And he received a gift of money, and turned his attention, with Burgess, to the car."

"We are drifting from my point, which is simply that for a man with a prophet's reputation he has a poor record of prophecy. How many of the people who acclaim his foresight have seen a first edition of *Nine Chains to the Moon?* In the front matter, dated 1938, we find a list of prophecies, twenty-two of them. They were to happen by July 12, 1948. Almost none of them did. They included 'Beamed radio transmission of power employing gold as the reflecting surface,' and 'Substitution of a man-hour for a metallic monetary base,' and 'Conquest of cancer.' "

"What did happen was war. It disrupted all short-term trends."

"And he did not foresee the war, of all things? It is like not having noticed an onrushing elephant."

"He was hardly alone, in the United States, in not fore-seeing it."

"But his business, he tells us, is foresight."

"His special-case foresight has been no better than any-one's. That is always a risk. There are too many random elements. He is better at reading trends. He saw airplanes replacing railroads as passenger carriers when railroads still enjoyed thirty times the passenger-mileage of planes. He foresaw impressive scrap recirculation. He foresaw children learning from TV."

"Special cases and trends," said the Skeptic, "a delicate distinction; it is futile to compute his scores. It is true that he now specializes in trends, whereas in the 1930's, like *Popular Mechanics,* he saw all manner of marvels just ahead. That was the decade when 'the future' was popularized. The Dymaxion Car at the Chicago Century of Progress makes a fitting symbol. In those days every fall fair had its robot, a tin man who would stand or sit on spoken command. Little boys paid their dimes to mar-vel at him, and their parents expected a servant like that some day. Bucky's guesses were far better informed; still, they were part of the history of that decade. Robotry with-out problems. But these trends of his: they have also their effect, which is sedative. Henry Luce once accused him of thinking man was determined, whereas he, Luce, believed in man's capacity to shape his future. Luce could not have been more wrong. If anyone believes the human future lies in human hands, it is Bucky. Still, it is an interesting error. What Luce was responding to was the curious fact that Bucky does not tell *you* what to do next. Certain things will happen, he tells you, whether you participate or not. One can see why it sounds like determinism."

"It does. But a trend is made of innumerable decisions. It is a logical direction mankind may well take. Mankind may not, though Bucky trusts they will. Your way of participating is up to you. At least you need not suppose that everything inevitably gets worse."

"Ah," said the Skeptic, "but if you are close to Bucky your way of participating seems not to be up to you. It is astonishing how many disaffected disciples one hears of, who were once participants but found they could not participate. He's not a good master, one of them said; not like the Zen master, who understands that the pupil will impart a personal inflection."

I said, "I've no experience of his mastery. It's quite possible—and would be quite understandable—that a condition of intimate discipleship would be willingness to hook into Bucky's trip of the moment. He always knows what needs doing in his own vicinity, which is not necessarily the same thing as what a disciple is really able to do for humanity. The tension between these two things might strain anyone's psyche, if he thought that by being near Bucky he would learn what his own vocation was. Not that everyone who has come near him, nor even everyone who has split off again, wanted to be told what to do, but it's inevitable that he should attract people who do want that. He has remarked how easy it would be to build an organization of weaklings. The World Game, for example: it was to be man's next hope: the computerized interplay of world resources, world strategies. Yet where it was tried it tended to turn into encounter groups, and Bucky finally issued an encyclical disqualifying participants who had not been properly trained."

"Which appears to mean," said the Skeptic, "participants who had not gone through his curriculum to the extent that their thoughts were indistinguishable from his. The World Game is a good case to examine. Like everything else he's envisaged, it needed funding on a dangerously large scale: I mean dangerous in the sense that any

source of so much money—think of the computer time!—
would feel entitled to control of the enterprise. Yet its
whole point was that no one should control it. It was to
be as impersonal as Nature, and if the data showed that
Alaska and Siberia ought to share a power grid, that decision would come with compelling inevitability, regardless
of the wishes of any sponsor. Now Bucky had already suggested such an international electric network, based on
the principle that the peak demand for power travels
around the earth with daylight. In New York, without a
computer, they attempted a World Game Workshop, and
sure enough, one of its announced conclusions was the
need for that power grid. What the participants learned
was invaluable to the participants. What the world learned
was what Bucky had already told it. The output was the
input, translated, and had they had their multi-million-
dollar endowment, its true function would have been to
hang wreaths of greenbacks around bright ideas of Bucky's.
Has any World Game session ever discovered anything it
had not been told to start with?"

"One thing, as a matter of fact," I replied. "The exact
balance between the sulphur we mine and the sulphur we
discharge from smokestacks. But before you decide that
the World Game is nothing but an amplifying device connected to Bucky Fuller, remember that it has not really
been tried. The programs and the computer time have not
been available."

"Once more," said the Skeptic, "the idea has a splendid
plausibility. But once again, we come to hard reality. Can
you imagine America and Russia depending on each other
for power? He may be right to call politics obsolete, but
political realities are realities. He may be right to say that
statesmen who cannot yield to one another can gracefully
yield to a computer. But the minute they did they would

be ousted from office, and they surely know it. No one really trusts a computer. The public's working experience of computers is that they mess up the records of charge accounts."

"Everyone who has flown has trusted his life to a computer."

"No one knows that half as well as he knows about the computer errors that get him dunned over and over for bills he has long since paid. My point is, Bucky is relying on the psychological prestige of computers, and ignoring the plain fact that it is low. My other point about the World Game, though, has to do with its illusion of impersonality. It may yield many novel details, like that one about sulphur. But the large answers seem predictable. They will be Fulleresque answers, in response to Fulleresque questions. In the 1950's, when Bucky was zooming from campus to campus, group after group began by hearing about the vast patterns of humanity, and ended by finding themselves designing a dome that Bucky wanted designed."

"But what they wanted to do was design a dome," I responded. "Many of them chafed through the part about the vast patterns. Moreover, he knew quite well that student designers would have to ride piggyback on his experience. He had two choices. One was just to tell them how to build the dome. The other was to let them share the design process the only way they could share it, which was by seeing its logic at that moment in history. This involved, he was frank to admit, a certain artificiality. What could be done in two weeks? So he set up his exposition in such a way that a dome project was its logical outcome."

"I have also heard," said the Skeptic, "that he was fussing about licenses and patent rights, and requiring signed waivers. There is a certain anomaly, you must admit, in someone holding a patent on what he tells you is a law of nature. That may have been part of the stress disciples felt. These things are so simple many of them have been invented before. Alexander Graham Bell made Octet Truss structures. Some German in the 1920's made what looks in a photograph very much like a geodesic structure. Kenneth Snelson made the first Tensegrity Mast. Bucky enjoys the credit for all three."

"That reminds me of James Joyce's question," I said. "If someone hacking in fury at a block of wood should produce an image of a cow, would that cow be a work of art? Joyce answered no; the art lay not in the artifact but in the consciousness. Bucky understands those structures. It has always been possible for people to make them without understanding them. Triangulating a sphere, and understanding the virtues of the structure you get by triangulating a sphere, are quite different things. The German planetarium-designer seems not to have known what he stumbled on, since his Geodesic Dome had no successor, and was attended by no explanations. Can a man have invented a thing, if he cannot explain it? The Patent Office avoids such metaphysics; all you can patent is a special-case realization. A patent lawyer would probably tell you that the Octet Truss patent covers only the systems of joinery it enumerates. A principle is nonpatentable. So is one's insight into principle. The patent gives you a kind of ownership over ways of fastening pieces of metal together. But the virtue of the structure is not in those fastenings. It is synergetic, invisible and only your mind can get at it. And it is what you are giving away when you explain."

"Nonsense. The virtue is in the thing itself, standing there."

"Tell that to a building inspector. Years ago someone used the Octet Truss to support floors in the Fine Arts Building at Yale. The structural engineers, knowing nothing of synergy, demanded that any one of the three sets of beams should be heavy enough for the job. Enormous redundancy, therefore; aesthetic nonsense."

"Why did they demand that?"

"Because the textbooks say that two beams intersecting in midair have the strength of the stronger only. The stronger acts as a fulcrum over which the weaker bends, like a stick snapped across one's knee. So you figure loads as though only the stronger were there. The second is redundant. And three, they said, would be even more redundant. Bucky was rightly annoyed, because that architect had used a system he did not understand well enough to defend. Every such incident fritters away people's confidence in anything but good old tried-and-true Strength through Weight. And Bucky's real interest is in altering our consciousness of reality. Every synergetic structure cleanly employed is a teaching machine to alter consciousness. Hence his long insistence on keeping control of their use. Hence his tight rein on students. People who wanted to fool with geodesics met a wall of discouragement when they tried to get data. He wanted to indoctrinate them first. Geodesic orange-juice stands were proposed, and he might have gotten rich on the franchise. He scorned such trivialization. To some associates it seemed maddening behavior, especially in a man who had long scorned the monopolies created by patents."

"That," said the Skeptic, "would be Fuller's version of many skirmishes and many aborts. There is a sense in which everything he has touched has aborted, leaving him to expound an ever more detailed vision of the Universe. There are many more themes I might raise. I shall raise just one more, the most general one I can. It has to do with his habitual way of expounding, which is to commence with the largest intelligible system and work inward by subdivision. He has always insisted that a local achievement must be the special case of a larger solution. That is why he is not a millionaire today; he would never stick to some invention and develop it as best it could be developed in an imperfect world. It was always necessary to change the whole world first, and never possible. Now just as he will not permit us to build special-case buildings, he will not permit us to think in special cases either. Thinking of what is nearest to hand, that is comparable to a Geodesic orange-juice stand. But observe the analogy with Twenty Questions."

"What analogy?"

"Progress by subdivision. Better still, observe how efficiently I can direct you to a single word in a book of 400 pages. I can tell you it is in the first half of the book. I can tell you it is in the second half of that half. My first statement has excluded 200 pages. My second has excluded 100 of those. Nine such decisions will exclude all the pages but one. Eight or nine more will exclude all the words on that page except the target word. Fewer than twenty questions—seventeen or eighteen—and we have zeroed in. We zero in by throwing out irrelevancies, and in early stages throwing them out in great handfuls."

"So?"

"So the crucial decisions are the earliest ones, the ones made at the greatest remove from the target. You remember when Bucky was asked a question about race, he brought out his map on which you can see the whole world—that passion for wholes!—and in effect played

Twenty Questions. What reality coerces naked men? Temperature. What skin withstands warm temperatures? Dark skin. What of men who wander where it is not warm? There is no reason their skins should not be light. . . . Eventually isolation and interbreeding have given us men with skins of different shades; a further sequence of factors has produced the European custom of enslaving black men; and anyone who follows the argument can see that the black man's inferiority is a white man's self-serving illusion. People have only to understand this, and a nasty problem will simply go away. But the psychic response of races to one another, and the economic trap in which certain races are caught, is far more complex than any misunderstanding about pigments. The heart of another, said Turgenev, is a dark forest. In that dimness dark fears, inaccessible to reason, can be triggered by the sight of an alien face. Bucky excludes that whole territory, I grant not out of insensitivity but because his habits of thinking cannot get at it. What he might one day say about racial problems was very nearly determined the day he decided, decades ago, that the colors on his map should zone off temperatures. That meant we should no longer be able to see, as we see on earlier maps, the line across which Frenchmen glare at Germans. Such distrusts are quite as 'real' as temperatures. Habit may erode them away, or may not; whereas the effects of temperature can be engineered away. He chose for his key realities the factors an engineer can get at, and only those."

"You are saying, I gather, that his major decisions, the ones most remote from some immediate question, after all reflect his biases. But what would you expect?"

"Nothing," said the Skeptic. "I merely wished to get it said. But observe, as with the World Game, how the system shapes its own output. Take maps again. They show obstacles to travel. Mountain ranges are obstacles; so are deserts. Political boundaries may be serious obstacles. If you are sailing, America is an obstacle to traffic between Spain and China. For sailormen the Arctic and Antarctic seas are such consummate obstacles the Mercator chart ignores them completely. Bucky's map omits all such obstacles, because it is a flying map. Its realities are those of the air age. It also shows you how cold it gets where, a factor which shapes air currents and also the distribution of peoples. It does not show the Ural Mountains, nor the Sahara, nor the Sino-Soviet frontier. These realities have not gone away. He has simply declared them irrelevant to an air-ocean World. The map shows you many things no previous map made clear. My point is, the things it omits are none the less real. Yet any decisions it shapes will omit those things. And yet all our talk will have the look of rigor, of having started from the Whole World that map shows."

"I see," I said. "You have talked much of his disregarding reality. Now you are showing that he sets aside certain aspects of reality—highly publicized ones, it may be added—to emphasize the coherence of other aspects. That coherence, and its novelties, continue to fascinate. It is a feat of conceptual art. It helps free the mind. 'Can Buckminster Fuller Save Us?' was the heading *The New York Times Book Review* once put over a piece they commissioned from me. They had me answering 'Yes,' which is untrue. I do not expect him to "save" us or me or anyone. As for what I value in his activities, it will take one more chapter to try to summarize."

The Skeptic said he would read it.

TEN

Incoming

Beirut on Sunday (day's work with a mathematical collab-
orator), Cyprus on Monday (inspection of World Man
Center site), Athens on Tuesday (confer with city-planner
Constantine Doxiadis), London Wednesday through Friday (nothing specified, which permits anything), Boston
by Monday (commencement speaker), Connecticut Tuesday (address on "We and the Cosmos"), a blank on
Wednesday, Israel Thursday and Friday. . . . Long ago
he commenced wearing three watches, time here, time in
Carbondale, time at the place after here. He resets two of
them almost daily, and has trouble getting his hair cut
because he's never free when a barbershop is handy and
open. Each year he sleeps in 200 different beds and aboard
some hundred planes, which leaves about sixty-five nights
for three familiar environments (Bear Island, his Carbondale base,* his daughter's home at Pacific Palisades). Mild
versions of such a routine have murdered poets, but Bucky
seems in better shape than ever. He stopped drinking years
ago, having found that people were ascribing the things he

---

* A tidy Geodesic Dome made to his specifications by a resourceful local
contractor. It has two bathrooms, two bedrooms, and an upper floor with
a circumferential library round which he zips on a low castored chair.

was saying to the glass in his hand. His digestion thrives on his minimally varied fare, steak and Jell-O and fruit and tea. ("The cattle metabolize the vitamins for me.") He can will himself to sleep whenever he chooses, for instance a reviving fifteen minutes in the car from reception to auditorium. The minute he touches ground he's thinking out loud, and when mike cables anchor him before an audience the collective trip commences one more time.

"The century's biggest ego trip," someone said. Fair enough. He may as well thrive on its satisfactions. Most lecturers are sick to death of themselves.

Vectors radiate from where he stands. (There'd be twelve of them.) Bucky's minute self streams out, finite, self-regenerating. No more sleeping on friends' spare pallets, no more soup bought every other day. As to what happens out where the vectors terminate, where the hearers sit, it's by no means all one-way. He says there's an equilibrium. The sphere pulsates. Thoughts come back to his center, thoughts beamed by all those eyes, all those other ego-trippers, elated by the reinforcement of what they hardly dare believe: that (as Stewart Brand put it) "We are as gods and may as well get on with it."

What people long to believe isn't necessarily not so. We'll never believe what we don't want to believe. Educators sometimes forget that.

What do they take away really, all those hearers, emerging into dark streets much later than they'd scheduled? A kind of bewildered euphoria, very often. Reviewing notes won't help: there are generally none to review. "Specialization," a confident girl wrote atop a blank page, then waited for subheadings; three and a half hours later that was all she had written. Sheer information overload, unannounced shifts from the "local" mode to the "express," radiating instead of linear patterns, make him rather an experience than a list of enlightenments.

It's not a canned lecture; that's part of the appeal. It's a remarkable mind thinking out loud, remarkable most evidently for its eager presence. Who else cares so much about the next thing he will tell you? It's like that bright memory, father's undivided attention, when you were seven and the Universe was strutting its stuff. The two of you dropped sticks into the swift eddies below a bridge, and you stood on the lower rung of a black iron railing to watch the current catch them. Nothing failed, not his vigilance, nor gravity, nor those eddies.

Did the last man you talked with care what his next sentence would be? Does the President care? For that matter does the President think in sentences, taut between concentration and concentration? Does most discourse not shred into phrases, like a crumbling wall? But real sentences are tensile, extended discourse a Tensegrity. And Fuller keeps it up three, four hours unbroken, spinning his weave, departing on great hexagonal circuits from the juncture to which he will suddenly return, six struts meanwhile laced tight.

And there's the unfailing readiness to clarify, amplify, one mode of generosity. And always the elation of triumphant fit, as the great circle closes with six holes aligned for the final bolt. Those are the aphoristic moments:

—Principles do not begin and end.
—Nature always works in the most economical way.
—Nature never fails, it is we who invent failure.
—We have a function in the Universe.
—You do not need to prove your right to survive.
—Man is meant to be a success.

He means these things literally. Who doesn't want to

believe them, while the taxman cometh? Isolated, they seem vacuously optimistic, axiomata of hophead raps. Tied into his large system of discourse, they twang like articles of faith. Bucky preaches the building of the new city here on earth, harmonized with the beneficence of the Grand Designer whose waves and oak trees, radiant spheres and pulsating energy knots, do the very most always with the very least.

As for us, we do not tamper, he says, no more than the honeybee tampers. Like the bee, we shunt energy circuits into leveraging patterns. Unlike the bee, which settled down long ago, we blunder about, trying stuff. But also unlike the bee, we can select among memories of what we've tried, and gradually discern our own large-scale patterns. We've just now come to that stage. Always, we've altered the Universe, unwittingly. Now we commence to see how.

The first man who built a fire altered the Universe. That day some wood was oxidized, some carbon was airborne; those things had happened before, for instance after lightning struck a forest. But thenceforward our part of the Universe contained a novelty: fire was apt to occur independent of lightning; was apt to occur inside caves, or on hearths. It could occur, as we say, "at will." Our will was a new operative principle. Soon a million fires glowed at once in a single city.

People building those little fires did not reckon their interaction with Spaceship Earth, nor even with their local patch of its workings. Yet they accommodated to such interactions, not quite knowing that that was what they were doing. For instance the West End became the preferred quarter of London, as prevailing winds carried thousands of smoke plumes eastward. A large-scale pattern arranged itself unwittingly, zoning the less affluent toward the city's east. That was a kind of ecological decision, and a working-class district grew. (Marx acquired his constituency.)

Then fires were contained in Bessemer converters, and two bicycle mechanics flew. Meanwhile the atmosphere aboard the spaceship was changing. People learned to call the change *pollution,* and at last to think of large-scale patterns activated by simple activities. So the Total Thinker emerges from the egg. Just when he is capable of doing irreversible damage, bringing himself to "chemical process irretrievability" (i.e., species death), he has also learned enough not to. True, a precarious plight, the knowledge just capable of containing the power, but the vector equilibrium *is* precarious. We can fold it into an octahedron now, and the unreflective will call our escape miraculous.

But there are no miracles, outside of the fact that the Universe is a miracle, the Universe in which a set of weightless generalized principles—"the wellspring of reality"—transform and intertransform. Principles are never shy, never shrink away. They manifest themselves: that's part of being a principle. They were manifesting themselves before we came—from another star, Bucky even speculates—and whenever we learn one, acquiring pure weightless knowledge, we have hold of an imperative to rethink our actions. This is called putting principles to use; it is also called technology. Mind discerns order from the Universe, and subsequently injects new modes of order into its environment. Why be scared of the word *technology?* The word *automation?* (Automation is principle left to run by itself.)

Running by itself, it shapes bones, covers them with flesh, strings neural networks, pushes hairs through scalps. All that dimension of life is automated, and by Darwin's account the very species were shaped by long-term automation. Alter some parameter: that beast is favored, dominates; that other one becomes extinct. In that way Neanderthal Man might have emerged, the dominant ape of a time when conditions favored apehood.

But Mind, discerning order, impressing on matter the order it discerns: that is never automatic, never a function of principles running by themselves, and Bucky is not the first speculator to doubt that Mind simply evolved. So Mind, he supposes, came from elsewhere, as it were from the domain of the Great Mind that informs the Universe, and since Mind came here the only evolution that has really mattered has been weightless Mind's evolving understanding of the weightless principles Mind alone can encompass. A dog can experience tension and compression. So far as we know, he cannot conceptualize them. We can, because we share the Cosmic Mind in which alone they are real.

Myth, or History? It is hard to say. A myth is a story, told as if it were history, with the intent of transcending time to help us understand. We have seen Bucky extracting myth from his own past. In bringing Mind inward to Spaceship Earth from the stars, he seems to be mythologizing the past of humanity, of which he knows no more than anyone else, by way of emphasizing his cardinal theme, that Mind is not Brain (brains are automated), that Mind is not local, not trivial, not constrained, but integral, whenever it entertains principle, with the weightless integrity that sustains the nebulae and light and photosynthesis and grass.

Bucky tells us, then, that we are so designed that we can harmonize our decisions with the rest of the Universe, accelerating its evolution in directions that will yield a minimum of disconnects and irretrievabilities. We may not achieve this; we may become extinct. But—he slams the lectern—we *can* achieve it.

Mystical faith, groans the scientist, reaching for his hat.

He is apt to forget his own equally mystical faith that neat laws await a discoverer. No physicist contains so little of the mystic that a cumbersome equation will do. Millions of cats, all different, all specified by heredity, would seem to imply a rain of variables no one can keep track of, but when a double helix was said to accommodate them all the model was not rejected as over-simple. It seemed right. We are Pythagoreans all. Pythagoras had hold of a great principle, that the greatest principles are simple. Bucky simply extends this simplicity to the doings and the welfare of the law-discoverer. We already expect that what we know shall be neat and modelable. What we do, he is telling us, can also be neat: as diverse as the rest of the Universe, but as orderly. "No generalization ever contradicts another generalization in any respect. They are all inter-accommodating." It is Bucky's faith that human actions might present a comparable interaccommodative simplicity.

Audiences pick up the throb of this, and go away euphoric. Yet barely a detail is invulnerable to someone's carping. Names are wrong, or dates.* Paraphrases are hasty. When Bucky commences a sentence "Einstein said . . .", you can be sure that an Einstein specialist would take half an hour persuading you that what Einstein had in mind was a good deal more intricate. As for his irrefutable assertions, a committee would tell you that they were fervent platitudes, scraps from some specialist's alphabet. His science is "superficial." His mathematics is "trivial."

We'd better look into this. "Trivial" is a technical term. Mathematicians use it to denote a rather slight advance

---

* Improvising without notes, calling on memory for hundreds of facts, he'd be superhuman if he didn't fumble a few. Why the printed versions contain glitches is a different story. At *Fortune,* he says, he fell into the Luce-writers' habit of setting down approximate data for researchers to tidy, but he's never since had a research staff of that quality.

on what they know already, some bit of housekeeping, not a new wing for the house. Once we know that $3 + 4 = 7$, the deduction that $3 = 7 - 4$ is trivial. Much Fuller math follows that pattern. Descartes showed long ago that when you fold a flat surface into a polyhedron, the "tucks" you gather together will always total 720 degrees. It's easy to figure out that the sum of the angles round a tetrahedron's four vertices is also 720 degrees. By combining these facts, we can say, as Bucky does, that the difference between *flat* and *closed* is one tetrahedron, and as we look up we'll catch the mathematician's lips forming the word "trivial." True enough: that's not "deep" mathematics, not a breakthrough like the great theorem in thanksgiving for which Pythagoras sacrificed an ox.

Still, we may be arrested by the reflection that between a straight string and a minimum knot—remember?—the difference is also 720 degrees, as though that were a key number that presides over the birth of a system. (A system? Well, something to arrest attention. The mere string is featureless.) If your theme is attention, sit in the dust, like Job, or by a pond, like Thoreau, and reflect that all you can ever think springs from relationships between points of attention. They are finite in number. Compute, if the mood of Ecclesiastes is on you, the sum of all the relationships of all the days since you were born, each new day rearranging the Gestalt. When you have the number, send for that many oranges, and stack them into a neat tetrahedron. There will be none left over, a result so neat you may feel like sacrificing an epistemologist. Octet Truss patterns will permeate that stack. Their unit, the vector equilibrium, models uniform growth outward from a nucleus, and the tetrahedra it generates configure all carbon molecules and therefore every trace of living tissue. And if you shrink the center orange in a cluster of thirteen the others shift to make an icosahedron, which generates the geodesic structures which also give us the configurations of many viruses. . . .

Guided by Pythagoras' ghost, you have moved a long way from certain bleak insistences, as (1) that the vector equilibrium has been known for twenty-two centuries under a less glamorous name, and (2) that the strictly mathematical facts about it are neither numerous nor especially profound. Nor are the chemical facts we have touched on profound, nor the biological, nor the architectural. Each science has its own meaning for "profundity." Yet a theme of stubborn persistence runs through such chains of instances: that by way of pattern, every part of knowledge is accessible from every other part. The study of pattern is a new discipline, still forming. Whether patterns are simply mental conveniences, or real, and if so what order of reality they own, is still in lively dispute. Yet artists, in this zone, confer with historians of science, and design departments sponsor symposia to which metallurgists as well as draftsmen are invited. Scientific knowledge itself, we sometimes hear, is built less out of facts than out of master patterns, invented in moments of insight and for decades refined and filled in. The Periodic Table of the Elements was divined when just over half of them had been isolated. It predicted the niches into which the rest would fit.

Mendelejeff, who divined the Periodic Table, was right in principle on grossly insufficient facts. Newton, moreover, was right on faulty facts. His solar system fitted the observations he had. When more accurate observations spoiled the fit, it turned out that the system wasn't faulty; it was responding to more planets than Newton knew of. Science advances by synergetic leaps, achieving whole systems before all the facts are in. The great scientific innovators have often been right only in principle.

The principle is a model, to marshal later facts by. After a while, enquiry changes direction, and questions arise that the model will not accommodate. Then the pressure of nagging problems is responded to by the sudden formation of a new model—in *The Structure of Scientific Revolutions* Thomas S. Kuhn calls it a paradigm—and this Whole System (a Newton's *Principia,* a Darwin's *Origin of Species*, a Lyell's *Geology*) tells us what details are henceforth to be followed up. "Other problems," Mr. Kuhn writes, "including many that had hitherto been standard, are rejected as metaphysical, as the concern of another discipline, or sometimes as just too problematic to be worth the time." That is why science generally seems to be succeeding; it pursues questions the paradigm says have answers. Men engaged in that pursuit, once the paradigm is there, have the right to be very fussy about facts. (Lord, how they brandish that right!) The man who invented the paradigm was right only in principle.

Being right in principle is a common human experience. Some cases are spectacular. Working on *Cathay* in 1914, Ezra Pound misconstrued detail after detail of Chinese poems he knew only through the Tokyo classnotes of a Harvard-educated half-Spaniard; yet grasping the poem's Whole System, he made translations before which scholarship is helpless. Pythagoras and Heraclitus were right in principle about things they had no business understanding at all (how little they knew; how naive were their methods!). Homer was right in principle about geography, when he thought of the whole earth engirdled by Ocean.

Dig Wholes, then, as the Whole Earth folk put it.

Bucky's work, seen part by part, is a story of crisis and failure, buildings that don't get built, industries that don't get financed, theories that don't get heard. Seen whole, it is an effort to develop a vast new paradigm, the synergetic vision. Scientists have evinced no special eagerness for it, because their response is to scientific crises, in between which they feel no need at all for new models of the Universe. No, the crisis to which synergetics is pertinent is a crisis of popular enlightenment, popular faith.

The spectacle we've glimpsed, of specialists passing him from hand to hand, not quite venturing to dismiss him but hoping somebody else will worry about him, expresses a truth, that he's centered in no specialty: not mathematics, nor chemistry, nor ecology, nor architecture, nor even engineering. His concern is for all the onetime "Comprehensivists" who grew up to get locked into specialties or "livings," and see little sense around them. His subject is *large-scale dynamic patterns*, of a very generalized order: so general any special case, passing through them, will find itself on speaking terms with any other.

He made houses, made cars, made bathrooms, made domes, always with a view to demonstrating some larger pattern. One reason they never made him rich was his lack of entrepreneural fanaticism about the end product; they were not end products, but instances. In his sixth decade the large pattern finally worked itself clear. His mission, he has come to believe, has always been single: to supply folk no more than normally curious with a coherence for the experience they are likely to have. Bucky says with a "model." Commoner jargon says, "frame of reference." He rejects that phrase because frames are two-dimensional.

Frames of Reference are what we use now, and we find we need several. The girl who tried to make notes and

found she couldn't was employing one: the tacit conviction that anything comprehensible will fit a piece of paper.
("A clear outline," her composition teacher had said. But
try that for *Finnegans Wake,* in which, nonetheless, anyone who has dabbled has discerned a vast order.)

So *paper* is one of our tacit paradigms, its flatness, its
90-degree angles, its "top" and "bottom." You should be
able to put the first item at the top, and work down to the
last item, at the bottom, and that means the thoughts you
have set down are in order. This mimics the arraying of a
brick wall (remove a brick: things are weakened). Dryden
found English brick and left it marble, said Dr. Johnson,
remembering what Augustus had done with the buildings
of Rome: a neat instance of a transferred paradigm.

You are grasping Bucky Fuller's challenge to such a
paradigm when you have tried to *draw* one of his structures, and found it nearly impossible, and perceived that
this tells you something about what you expect of flat
paper. Structural integrity—whether of ideas or of artifacts
—is tested (we all suppose) by paper's willingness to receive
it. (We can all draw cubes. Quick!—can you draw an icosahedron?) This means we can draw a skyscraper's cubical
grid, and hence suppose it's stable, though it isn't till
workmen put little triangular gussets at every joint. No
one can really draw an Octet Truss. One meaning of
Bucky's 60-degree space grid is that it rejects the paper
paradigm.

Geodesic Domes aren't assembled from blueprints, not
like houses. House blueprints are instructive. One view is
as though the flat outside wall had been laid against the
flat paper, letting the facade register. Another view is as
though the paper sliced the house downward through the
middle, end to end. Everything it shows is on the plane of

the paper: walls, doorways, rooftree. From another, the floor plan, we are to imagine partitions rising toward us at 90-degrees from the drawing. The paper plane is intimate with a 90-degree structural system, and the carpenter, picking his measurements right off the drawing, translates what he sees on it into wood.

But press paper flat against a Geodesic Dome, and at most you pick up one triangle. Draw a section, and it looks like a jerky half-circle. A floor plan is a big uninformative polygon. There's no useful information here, nothing to copy, though a Building Inspector may insist on having it to file away. You can make a perspective rendering if you want to, taking infinite trouble to catch all those little subtle changes of angle in a grid system to which they do not comply. You can do a lot of useless things if you really want to.

Years ago the Chicago Institute of Design retained Bucky to give a crash course, and made a roomful of drawing tables ready. He began by announcing that drawings were obsolescent. What his students were going to learn to envisage would not take form at a pencil's end. The tabletops ended up against the walls, where they did for bulletin boards. The design work went forward with language, later with three-dimensional stick models, centered on the vector equilibrium's twelve 60-degree radii. Building instructions consisted of tables of figures, to index machine tools. Nowadays the route would go from concept straight to computer.

For the great Montreal Bubble there were no assembly drawings, except a few hub details. Assembly procedure for the Wichita House of 1946 called for color-coded bolts, carried in the color-coded pockets of special workmen's aprons. They would pass through color-coded holes, and no one would look at a picture.

These aren't just contractors' field tricks. They tell us something about our working sense of order: that it clings to notions of flatness, 90-degree turns, 180-degree returns and gravity pulling straight down through a piled stack. Mercator's map fills a paper rectangle to its edges and corners. The Dymaxion map depended on the realization that a world map needn't fit a rectangle. It has no special shape, and its system radiates from twelve gathering-points. You can diagram each sentence of Milton's, however intricate, but only some of Joyce's. To read Joyce is to spot the local radiating centers. The Miltonic flat page is a sample of a flat plane extending in all directions to infinity. But nothing real extends there. The real has always natural limits, incurving.

Then there is politics, an affair of 180-degree encounters, *left* meeting *right*: action, reaction. The party system, creation of the post-Newtonian century, seemed a natural way to order opposed forces, which intuition said had a natural existence. Today we increasingly suspect that the model may *create* the forces, as the blueprint creates the house.

The man at the post office asked for 6¢ stamps. The ones he was offered bore Franklin D. Roosevelt's image. He refused to buy them. Years ago the license plates issued to a thousand Californians bore the three-letter combination IKE. Despite stiffish fees in the event of lost plates, an unknown number were promptly, indignantly, "lost." Of such are political passions.

The party system presupposes that parties are functionally equivalent, otherwise one would be slowly squeezed out of existence. In the long view, either it doesn't matter which party governs, or else we project "good" and "evil" onto their surfaces, in which case our polity is Manichaean.

Many voters simply adopt the pragmatic view that power corrupts. The rascals must be periodically turned out, amid thanks for a system that provides a replacement team —of potential rascals.

These models fit short-term facts, but afford strange paradigms for major decision-making. Bucky will urge us to imagine two cases: (1) all the politicians on earth peeled off for encapsulation in a secondary spaceship for their own trip around the sun, and affairs on Spaceship Earth not a bit impaired; or (2) the power-station attendants, flight controllers, telephone repairmen packed off on such a trip, and on Spaceship Earth mounting misery and imminent starvation. (Imagine the day the refrigerators stop!) It's an over-simple model—men would hastily breed new politicians—and yet it underlines a truth: politics may answer many human needs, but politics is not where it's at.

He downplays politics to a sometimes alarming degree. He refuses to compare the human cost of systems, preferring instead to fix attention on the real gains which occur regardless of system (though system tries to theologize them), and are really to be ascribed to industrialization. After a time of hoping that Dymaxion ideas might be inserted into the five-year plans, he came to see that Russia never pioneered any completely new industry, that its adherence to capitalist prototypes was "slavish," but he doesn't dwell on this, and the patterns that hold his attention continue to transcend politics. In the same breath he will ascribe American drugs and insurgency to Mainland Chinese connivings, and find this "quite understandable" since the Chinese after all wanted to industrialize undisturbed. It's his faith that that's what they've been doing.

Still, he's right to observe that no politician, no political arrangement, can remedy scarcity. They can redistribute it, amid announcements that scarcity is caused by profits. If injustice is simply imbalance, then Robin Hood's way will redress it. But if its root is net scarcity, then Robin Hood's ministrations are cosmetic merely. (They may get him elected sheriff.) *More* wealth is not his to create, and when he allocates money—often for "feasibility studies"— he is "sprinkling greenbacks on the conflagration."

Then does Bucky think of the withering away of the state? No, but simply of reserving its role to "housekeeping functions." Don't waste time, he says, inciting governments to save us. It is not in their power. (If you can see how to keep them from destroying us, there may be some point in that.)

These days, such talk coincides with a deepening mood. It grows normal to trust nobody—nobody—who aspires to office, unless, like some of Eugene McCarthy's supporters in 1968, you sense that there's really no hope of his getting there. So we get symbolic campaigns, token candidates, metatheater.

At this moment a syndicated column comes to hand. Its author's commitment to politics is lifelong, to ways of fine-tuning the machinery of power. Yet he calmly notes, not expecting to be challenged, that there is no seeker after the Presidency, not one, whose campaign rhetoric an undereducated mule would take seriously. This moves our attention to a third paradigm, mental shrinkage. Talkers talk down, talk down: no eggs are thrown. Teachers teach down: no one fires them. Interviewers coddle: viewers stay tuned. We rehearse the rituals of failure. The great sphere of public discourse, political, educational, even interpersonal, becomes a Stupidity Factory.

That schools are such factories is by now an open secret. Each season brings a new spate of books to testify that the most education-minded people on earth are high-mindedly doing irreversible damage in every cubical classroom in the land. Teaching brings paradigms, formulated by the teacher, into contact with whatever experience the student has in his head. The fit is poor, but the system says it is perfect. Caught in the system, the student has a simple recourse: he "fails."

Since nature always pursues paths of least effort, there is always a short-term gain in appearing stupider than you are. The easiest way to evade the thrust of an order is not to understand it. This strategy has a hundred rituals: "I could never do math." "Art is beyond me." "You cannot expect our readers to understand that." There's the talk-show host's strategy: deputize for a million viewers, and either act lovably dumber than the guests, or by mugging adroitness make the guests seem deficient in the savvy that really counts.

With one remarkable exception, the network showing of Robert Snyder's film *Buckminster Fuller on Spaceship Earth,* that is how TV has preferred to deal with Fuller. He can hold a thousand people's attention for hours, but he has never been able to crack an interviewer's professional ignorance. On a Sunday afternoon late in 1971, NBC put him on public display for an hour. The talk, for some reason, was conducted outdoors, by a lake where water-skiers were performing. Since the whine of motors made every third sentence inaudible, viewers were able to concentrate on the grimaces. Bucky, as usual not noticing negatives, launched into his exposition of the nonexistence of straight lines. He used a rope and a blackboard. At one point, glimpsing obtrusive condescension, he said sharply, "Pay attention. This is important." After he had finished being clear step by step for ten minutes, the he-host agreed with the she-host that they hadn't, either of them, understood a word. This constituted their oblique directive to the audience, which after all spent many years in school, learning chiefly that its normal grade was C.

There have come to be just three kinds of diagnostic books about schools. Some are really political—schools are middle-class, they exacerbate the ghettoization of the ghettoes. Some anatomize the ever-bleaker facts about an environment in which children normally fail, and learn to camouflage failure or to accept it without going mad. Some simply promote "higher standards," i.e., more failures.

On the other hand the "positive" books, the what-do-we-do-about-it books, work from a political paradigm since what they promote is chiefly a restructuring of classroom communities. (Have two teachers. Have no teachers. Move to Vermont.) That reflects a conviction as old as America, that communities are *designed* (Oneida, Brook Farm, Levittown, the Company Town, the Retirement Haven). Emerson, we may remember, thought differently. He thought of communities that would simply express the way energy centers interact: the vector equilibria of properly confident, interaccommodative individuals.

Bucky Fuller, similarly, ignores classroom communities the way he ignores politics. He would ask whether classroom troubles are not arising from the wrong paradigms: the 180-degree traffic between teacher and pupil, its ideal model the pipeline, and the whole array of paradigms that pass for "subjects," increasingly divergent from anyone's real experience. We use seapower maps in an air-ocean world. We make arithmetic a rite of mysterious rules ("Here you put down seven and carry two." "Why?"). We model history as linear causes between unreal situation reports. We allude to the "structure" of just about everything, from a Shakespeare song to Jefferson's foreign policy, heedless of the intuitions bottled up in the word *structure*. And having raised these cardhouses of knowledge, we expect a roomful of plodders at exam time to massage them back onto the flat paper whence they arose (and Neatness Counts). Naturally failure is normal.

"How's school these days?" John Holt asked a friend's daughter. He describes the conversation in *How Children Fail*.

"OK."

"What sort of stuff do they teach you?"

"Oh, stuff like the difference between 'gone' and 'went.'"

"I see. By the way, can you tell me which is right, 'I have gone to the movies' or 'I have went to the movies.'"

Long thoughtful pause. Then, "I don't know. I can't tell when it isn't written on the board."

You can see that "the board" = "paper." No doubt the child's speech was expert. Think of it as a transfer of speech to a rectilinear coordinate system in space, where peculiar rules apply since normal experience does not survive the transfer. Think about it that way; think of "subjects" in general that way, as transfers of experience to an alien system, and you glimpse one thing a tireless world-traveler means when he walks off his plane talking of Nature's coordinate system, one we elect not to use.

In *How Children Learn* Mr. Holt tells of making some cardboard boxes, open-topped, folded from a single sheet of cardboard he had accurately cut. First-graders watched him. Then they wanted to try it. "By watching me, or each other, or by thinking, or by trial and error, they all figured out that to make a rectangular box with an open top you had to cut out a piece in the shape of a heavy cross." First they did it badly. Later they did it well. ("Nobody asked me for advice.") Later still, a boy figured out how to vary the cross so the box would have a closable top. Then he wondered about a house with a peaked roof. "I didn't see him work on the problem, and don't know by what steps he managed it, but within a few days his teacher showed me a cardboard house, with peaked roof, that he had cut out in one piece. It was well made, too; the sides and roof fit together quite well. And he had cut out, not drawn, the doors and the windows, before folding the house together. A most extraordinary piece of work." He had been a troublesome boy.

Models, you see. Something real. For first grade, the mathematics it entails is most advanced. Mr. Holt is careful to specify that to substitute *Model Building I* for *Arithmetic I,* "with the same old business of assignments, homework, drill, and tests," will leave us where we started. The "curriculum" is one more transfer of coordinates, from the vectorial outthrust of felt needs to the rectilinear "What Teacher Wants." The latter, by two-dimensional definition, stretches out to infinity. That is dismaying.

Not that any problems, any solutions, are simple. But Bucky's large-scale dynamic patterns gratify precisely because in touching on so many problems they leave his audiences with at least the feeling that a mind can move about reality freely, that strategies exist that don't entail vertigo. All real problems go finitely outward from centers. Grasp that, he wants us to intuit, and any reality you encounter has at least the prospect of making sense. We seldom reflect how deep runs the conviction that most problems are really insoluble, most reality unassimilable. Hence tranquilizers, and situation comedies, where the perennially insoluble at least yields laughs.

*   *   *

So what do *I* do? He's not going to tell me. An *Architectural Forum* article preserves his emphatic words to one young man:

> I realize you have this very big love and you want to do some very fine things with it. But I'm afraid you won't be able to do anything beneficial until you really start to think and get inside what's *causing* this love. You are going to have to think very clearly about basics and about what moves *you* can make to bring about changes in the things you see wrong. It doesn't do any good to get angry. And it doesn't do any good for you to sit here with me unless you can find in all this something of your *own* to say.

Thoreau also said something like that: don't bother looking for a lake and building a cabin. That will express nothing but your dropout's conviction that nothing makes sense.

A familiar plaint: nothing makes sense. (Parts predict no Whole System.) We go by nonsynergetic paradigms for "sense." Custom, language, paper, politics, the omnipresent Stupidity Factory, all teach us that sense, could we have it, would be static. ("People want single-frame answers.")

But the world changes. For single-framers, change seems unnatural. You cannot argue with a jet plane, but you can spend your life feeling it is a little unnatural. There are many things like that to find unnatural: *Finnegans Wake,* and *Hair,* and traffic lights hung above a Venetian canal, and a museum that can assimilate Rauschenberg's stuffed goat with a tire around its middle, and forks you throw away and young Italians strolling through Catullus' ruined villa on the tip of Sirmio with transistor sets clapped to their ears.

These are all technology: step-by-step implementations of some principle not widely understood. Writing *Finnegans Wake* was a technological feat. Joyce slogged at it for seventeen years, and one time even supposed he could retire and deputize another man to finish it. His innovative genius consisted in glimpsing the *possibility* of such a book—nonsimultaneous, readable only in weeks, structured only by patterns—and then working out its principles. Afterwards he was quite calm about it, as calm as a jet pilot. It is precisely the participants' calm that identifies a technology: the innovative frontier is safely passed. The stop-and-go light hung over waters in Venice is something to be calm about once you have made the great leap, which is seeing that the boat traffic at a certain blind corner is modeled after car traffic in a Roman street.

But it is hard to be calm about all those folk being calm. As technology goes on proving its own possibility, and people live with this or that manifestation, some with snowmobiles, an affront to silent woods, some with telephones, an affront to privacy, some with Tensegrity Spheres, an affront to common sense, a subliminal fear begins to insinuate itself, to the effect that society is breaking up, or going mad or marching toward some Tarpeian cliff. People fling off their clothes, or revert to sandals, or join societies for shouting Stop, or perceive in the political insanity of the moment an index to some radical insanity that only return to the woods will expiate. Some regress to bead-stringing, denying technology while tape-players blare. Others league to prevent people from being born, and hope the next generation will swell their ranks.

Bucky Fuller, in such a juncture, seems heaven-sent. (If you take a long view, the forces that produced the crisis helped produce him too.) When his words do no more than soothe, that is probably beneficent, though it infuriates stirrers-up of causes. But a commoner experience is that he invigorates. He lets us hope that the world in which all these changes occur can still make sense: that it has one Coordinate System.

There is a peculiar aptness in the story of his long life, which has consisted of successive fantasies being elaborated: suspended houses, air-delivered dwellings, even a three-wheeled car, actually built and faster than anyone else's car. (What a potent fantasy!) Which fantasies were fully realized, which ones remained talk, is oddly immaterial. Thoreau gave America one of its most fructive fantasies in going through the motions of a retreat to nature which in fact he didn't fully realize. ("On many evenings," Quentin Anderson writes, "he stepped off the scene of his demonstration and went home to his mother's boarding-house for supper.") We forgive the fiction. He was quite clear about the status of his famous gesture: not a panacea, that retreat to that handmade cabin by that pond, but one man's fantasy become a metaphor. He tells us not to emulate; certainly not to emulate *him*. (What if all 200,000,000 Americans headed for pond shores?) But because one man did it, out of his deepest private need, and wrote a book, the whole population has been freed a little.

Geodesic Domes, if they never go into production, still free us a little too. They are metaphors: Whole Systems, first of all. They draw together functional shelter, elusively simple laws of Nature's structuring, symmetry, medium-high math, countercultural community (or solitude, as you wish), Eskimo simplicity, utter up-to-dateness. It is much to have developed a metaphor like that, and the *Domebook* folk, whom Bucky never envisaged, have constructed what may be the most coherent fantasy of outlawry since Robinson Crusoe. Not content with dreaming, they hew timbers. Others read their building manual for escape literature, and read the *Whole Earth Catalog,* that Space-Age *Walden.*

It is also symbolically right that Thoreau's cabin used a framing system that was already obsolete. Important phases of his thought were obsolete too. The *Whole Earth Catalog* has sensible words on "the blanket rejection of technology that is trapping many people in an alternate life-style of shabby creativity." These people, such is the force of paradigms, repeat Thoreau's fundamental error, which was to suppose that invention merely complicates the simple. He thought you could walk to Boston in the time it would take you to earn the price of a railway ticket. That is to say, he did not think there was such a thing as synergy, and a naked Hindu at a spinning wheel was his paradigmatic disciple: Gandhi, who got the British out of India—a political triumph—but had no remedy for Indian starvation.

Bucky Fuller is here to tell us that synergy is nothing exotic, is in fact the most common of all human experiences. Every sentence exemplifies it, every child. Systems *always* yield more than goes into them. We can't predict what. Invention, systematized, makes available resources of knowledge the whole human community has accumulated. Thus a man building his own dome in the woods—unforeseen by Fuller—taps Fuller's insights, and NASA's chord-factor tables (reprinted from a study on "Advanced Structural Design for Future Space Missions"), and computers therefore, and the electric company (via a radial saw—how else make 300 identical struts?)—wooing simplicity only in zones of his choice.

That man, however numerous his tribe, is a metaphor, not a general-case solution. So is Fuller's synergetics. So

Apollo 16 splashdown (*NASA*)

is Fuller's life. Metaphors, paradigms, these are our deepest needs, irradiating minds with heuristic images: points of departure, not solutions; encouragements to Dig Wholes.

*   *   *

I stopped to watch Apollo 16 descend. A tensile thread invisible except to mind had reeled it in from the moon: one little compressive island rushing to rejoin another. As Spaceship Casper neared the liquid cushion spread out aboard Spaceship Earth, a vast tension-compression structure of minimum weight was erected in a split second: the three parachutes below which the conical capsule dangled, the system an indrifting dynamic tetrahedron. Casper had carried only the tensile part, neatly folded. Spaceship Earth carried the compressive part, air, which filled domical cloth cups at hurricane violence. Over the triple domes an unseen low-pressure cone formed, whose "tensile draft on the inertia of the atmosphere"—the phrasing is Bucky Fuller's—"can be satisfed at a rate so slow as to ease the paratrooper down." That was thirty years ago; now he would say "in." And three decades' evolution had transformed the paratrooper into a spacecraft and a trio of lunar explorers. Nothing was spent, not even energy. Energy parted the ocean, lifted its great mass, which subsided infolding huge gulps of salt-tanged air, to spray outward in many million spherical bubbles, each a short-lived equilibrium, molecule-thick, unique, instantly patterned, almost as instantly gone. On that sea, change is normal: on any sea.

In the forty-five years since Bucky Fuller had speculated that a modest shelter properly designed might be delivered by air, governments had gone on studying the "housing problem." Only this spring (March 26, 1972) the Office of Economic Opportunity proposed to devote yet another four million dollars to an experimental design program, "to find out," said a spokesman, "if it's possible to construct a low-income home on a massive scale." Those designers can be counted on—Bucky talking—to stay "settled upon the real estaters' sewers like hens on glass eggs." And they'll use simple cubes—cheaper, aren't they? It's expensive running-in-place.

Meanwhile a fully habitable environment, utterly self-sufficient for ten days, complete with three tenants, their mechanical shavers, their pressurized ballpoint pens and their foods and fluids and their sewerage system, cameras and films and computers and radios, even their 4-wheel-drive car, had been airlifted clear out of earth's domain and part way across the solar system to a base where the men did work. They discarded part of their subsystem and flew the rest home again.

Home? To the Whole Earth, with only humanity aboard: an earth blue and white, growing larger in the incoming spacecraft window. People in wooden cubical boxes, termite-eaten, crushingly mortgaged, linked by tons of buried plumbing, saw on their colored viewscreens the Whole Earth the astronauts saw. Meanwhile Spaceman Fuller traced geodesics through the air-ocean, touched down, talked, soared out, touched down again. His baggage is mostly weightless now: models of the dynamic universe, verbal strings from which to spin the tension systems we must fill with our local compressives to use them at all.

APPENDIX 1

Glossary

None of these definitions is rigorous, let alone exhaustive. The wording is mine, incorporating bits of Fuller's.

BEAUTY: Unredundant appropriateness, perceived by taste. (See *Taste*).

CIRCLE: A closed string of events more or less equidistant from a central event: in practice, a polygon with a large number of sides. The ideal circle to which *pi* pertains is eventless, since there is no point at which it can be said to change direction.

COMPRESSION: Pushing together, tending toward arcs of decreasing radius. A post or brick is a compressive element in a structure.

COORDINATE SYSTEM: An ideal grid from which you take measurements, most useful when its structure is similar to what you are measuring.

DYMAXION: Yielding maximum performance from available technology.

ECOLOGY: The interdependence of events in a regenerative system.

ECONOMICS: (1) Properly, the management of the household. (2) Commonly, the manipulation of public accounts.

ECONOMIST: An apologist for manipulated account books.

ENERGY: The agent of change, neither expendable nor augmentable.

317

EPHEMERALIZATION: The trend toward doing more with less.

EVENT: A unit of attention, characterized by the biblical "It came to pass."

GEODESIC: (1) The most economical relationship between two energy events. (2) The shortest distance between two points on a sphere; it is part of a circle whose center is that of the sphere.

GEODESIC SYSTEM: A construction, roughly spherical, whose lines of support are geodesic. A geodesic dome is sliced from such a sphere.

ICOSAHEDRON: A closed system of twelve events, each joined to five others by thirty vectors that frame twenty triangular faces.

IRRATIONAL NUMBER: A number, such as *pi,* that cannot be expressed as a finite fraction. Though it cannot denote a census of events, such a number is often useful for rapid calculation.

IRRELEVANT: What I don't want to think about just now.

KNOWLEDGE: The indestructible residuum of the mind's functioning.

LINE: A path traced between two events. Even the most economical path (see *Geodesic*) is never really "straight."

MASS: A locally self-regenerative pattern of energy.

METAPHYSICAL: Pertaining to weightless reality. (Remember that even light has weight.) $2 + 2 = 4$ is a metaphysical proposition.

MODEL: The physical embodiment of a set of principles, with minimum irrelevance or redundance.

OCTAHEDRON: A closed system of six events, called vertices. The twelve vectors that join them frame eight triangular faces.

OCTET TRUSS: A structure of alternating octahedra and tetrahedra, capable of filling space in all directions.

PATTERN: A recognizable set of relationships. If its elements sustain one another under stress it is said to be *self-interfering.* (Example: an overhand knot.)

PI: A rapid-calculating device which assumes an ideal circle and states what its circumference/diameter ratio would be, i.e., about 22 / 7.

POINT: An unresolved cluster of events.

POLITICS: The art of accommodating men's wishes to real or fancied scarcity.

POLLUTION: A nuisance created by an unharvested resource.

REGENERATIVE: Characterized by self-renewal. A forest regenerates at low frequency, the life-span of trees being measured in decades or centuries. A copper penny regenerates at high frequency, the time-scale of atomic events being exquisitely brief.

RELEVANT: Opposite of *irrelevant,* which see.

SIMULTANEOUS: Aha, nothing is, because light takes time to travel. The eye of God is perhaps independent of light, but none of us is God.

SPACE: What a change in your angle of vision subtends.

SPHERE: A plurality of energy events more or less equidistant from a central event.

STRUCTURE: (1) A shape that maintains itself, i.e., uniquely the triangle. (2) "Concentration of a complex of individual events in a self-stabilizing complex relationship."

SYNERGY: Behavior of whole systems, unpredicted by knowledge of the parts or of any subassembly of parts.

SYSTEM: A configuration that divides the Universe into (1) everything outside the system; (2) the system itself; (3) everything inside the system. The tetrahedron is the minimum system, since nothing simpler can have an inside and an outside. Your house is a system. So is your body. So is this book.

TASTE: Comparison performed with the certainty of habit.

TENSEGRITY: Tensional integrity, as in the earth-moon tug or a spider web amid branches. A *tensegrity structure* is a continuous tension network with compressional stiffeners. It is independent of outside anchorage, and stable in any position.

TENSION: Pulling apart, toward arcs of increasing radius. A wire or rope is a tensile element in a structure.

TETRAHEDRON: A system comprising four events, called vertices. The six vectors that join them frame four triangular faces.

TIME: What you wait in.

TOPOLOGY: The science of connectedness.

TRIANGLE: The minimum structure: three compressive sides, three tensile angles.

UNIVERSE: (1) The sum total of everybody's physical and metaphysical experiences: toads, stars, dreams, *Hamlet*. (2) "The aggregate of nonsimultaneous, only partially overlapping, discrete events." (3) "The minimum perpetual motion machine."

VECTOR: A direction with a definite length, which usually represents the product of mass and velocity; hence a model of an action that goes on for a finite time.

VECTOR EQUILIBRIUM: The cuboctahedron: a system of twelve events, each joined to four others by twenty-four vectors that frame six quadrangular and eight triangular faces. The vertices are exactly as far from the center as they are from their immediate neighbors.

WASTE: Escape of energies from a preferred pattern.

WEALTH: Energy directed by knowledge.

APPENDIX II

Model Making

Tensegrity Icosa (See drawing, page 236)

You need some ¼″ dowel, a dozen little picture-framers' screw eyes, wire no finer than #28. Cut six sticks, each 9″ long; put a screw eye at each end. Cut twenty-four pieces of wire, each 10″ long. With a pencil, number the two ends of the first stick, 1 and 2, the next 3 and 4, and so on on up to 11 and 12.

When you wire it up, each wire runs 5⅞″, screw eye to screw eye. Cut a strip of cardboard this length to measure with. Connect as follows, referring to your penciled numbers. When you finish, there will be *four* wires at every screw eye.

1 to 11, 1 to 12; 3 to 11, 3 to 12. Let sticks 1–2 and 3–4 lie parallel, with stick 11–12 sandwiched crosswise between them.

2 to 9, 2 to 10; 4 to 9, 4 to 10. Stick 9–10 also lies crosswise between stick 1–2 and stick 3–4.

5 to 1, 5 to 2, 5 to 11, 5 to 9.

6 to 3, 6 to 4, 6 to 11, 6 to 9.

7 to 1, 7 to 2, 7 to 10, 7 to 12.

8 to 3, 8 to 4, 8 to 10, 8 to 12.

Now go around it and tighten wires as much as you can. When you're satisfied, twist all joints securely.

Tensegrity Sphere (See illustration, page 90)

Materials as for Tensegrity Icosa, but more of everything. You cut thirty sticks, each 9″ long, and put a screw eye at each end.

Cut thirty wires, each 5″ long. Have five crayons ready, for color-coding as you go.

Drill a small hole straight through the midpoint of each stick, pass a wire through the hole, loop around and pass it through again, leave equal lengths hanging.

When you join two sticks, you always use the wire that passes through the center of a third. Call the crosswise stick in the middle of a joint the dangler. Length of wire, dangler to screw eye, should be about 1¼″. Twist surplus to fasten.

Make a pentagon— five sticks, five danglers—and hang it from a shower-curtain rod with its top stick horizontal. Put a green mark on each of the five sticks of this pentagon.

The wire that passes through the top stick of the green pentagon now gets a stick at each end. Connect a dangler to each of these sticks, to each dangler another stick, to each stick another dangler. The free ends of the wires from these danglers are now joined to the dangler at the bottom of the green pentagon. You now have two intersecting pentagons. Code the five sticks of the new one red.

The dangler to the right of the top stick on the green pentagon goes to the middle of a top stick on the red pentagon. Code it blue, and work around, completing a blue pentagon. You'll introduce three new sticks and incorporate another dangler near the bottom. This dangler is in the red pentagon, and goes to the middle of a stick on the green pentagon.

You should see the symmetry by now, and it's easier to be guided by that than by instructions. Just keep color-coding the pentagonal rings and refer to the pictures in the text. Each pentagonal ring runs straight around the system; if it changes direction suddenly you've made a mistake. When you're nearly done, the system will suddenly pull out into a spherical shape. When you're finished, go around the sphere tightening wires till every stick is very slightly bowed and the system is springy but firm.

Geodesic Dome

The least bother is to order Kit Model #102 from Dome East, 325 Duffy Ave., Hicksville, N.Y. 11801; precut sticks plus connectors and instructions. Or buy "D-Stix" rubber connectors from Edmund Scientific Co., Barrington, N.J. 08007. They cost about $3.50 for fifty. Order the six-sleeve type; forty will make a dome. You need ninety-two for a complete sphere. With these you use ⅛" dowel for struts. Cut with an X-acto knife as accurately as possible. Lengths are in centimeters, with connectors allowed for.

A	5.4 cm.	Make thirty.
B	6.4 cm.	Make thirty.
C	7.6 cm.	Make fifty.
D	8.3 cm.	Make ten.

The easiest way to keep track is to paint them four different colors.

(1) Pentagon subassembles. Five A's radiate from a connector, leaving a sleeve unoccupied. Join ends with B's. The pentagons will be slightly saucer-shaped. Make six, using up all the A's and B's.

(2) Star subassembles. Six C's radiate from a connector. Make five.

(3) Final assembly. Lay a pentagon on the table, and surround it with the five stars. Join two adjacent rays of each star to the pentagon, so they make a triangle with the pentagon side. Fill the empty sleeve at each pentagon corner with a D. The five remaining pentagons go on the ends of the D's, the D lined up with a pentagon spoke. Join the loose ends of the stars to the upper corners of these pentagons. The remaining D's close the bottoms of the stars, with the remaining C's for base ring and triangulated infill.

You now have a ⅓-sphere dome. A's and D's outline the icosahedral triangles, each edge divided into thirds (so this is called a three-frequency dome). Since it also sits flat, it's called a *truncatable*. Most geodesics won't sit flat except along the equator of the parent sphere. The calculations for this version were done by R. Ashworth and Tony Pugh of the Southern Illinois University Department of Design.

For more geodesic models see *Domebook 2*.

ACKNOWLEDGMENTS

Bucky Fuller talked to me just as freely after he knew this book was under way as he had before, and Naomi Wallace and Brendan O'Regan of his Carbondale office filled numerous requests for data and reprints. Bob Snyder showed me his film *Buckminster Fuller on Spaceship Earth*, lent me a soundtrack transcription to quote from and reminisced copiously. Mrs. Snyder (Allegra Fuller) lent me Bucky's sheaf of family reminiscences, *The Bear Island Story*. Barry Farrell gave me transcriptions from the many hours of tape on which he drew for his *Life* story and his *Playboy* interview with Fuller. Bob Easton of Domebuilders, Inc., and Lloyd Kahn of the *Domebook* have been generous with help and insight; Lloyd lent me tapes of Fuller's Big Sur discourses and a sheaf of student reports on design projects Fuller sponsored at colleges in the 1950's. These reports typify a large archive of mimeographed materials, duplicated for various limited circulations, of which I've seen only a fraction. The Architectural Library of the University of California, Berkeley, has more, three bound volumes' worth, mostly bulletins of the 1950's from the Fuller Research Foundation. The interlibrary loan staff at the University of California, Santa Barbara, deserves credit for extricating these from Berkeley's security arrangements. Peter Pearce of Los Angeles and Ed Applewhite of Washington have been generous in conversations, Professors John McHale, Edward T. Hall and H. S. M. Coxeter in correspondence. Fred Siegel interviewed Kenneth Snelson for me. Dr. Robert F. Roeming, Director of the Center for Twentieth Century Studies, University of Wisconsin (Milwaukee), sent me issues of the *Wisconsin Architect* serializing a wholly unedited talk of Fuller's. The Skeptic of Chapter 9 is an ideal composite; since some of the people who contributed to his remarks are known to me only by hearsay I'll mention no names. Marvin Mudrick, Provost of the College of Creative Studies, University of California, Santa Barbara, has supported this project since before it was really conceived. He sponsored most of the Fuller discourses I've been able to hear, saw to the availability of audio- and videotapes and made one brilliant suggestion which determined the organization of the book.

My wife, Mary Anne, and the personnel of the Montessori Center School of Santa Barbara helped with model-making and by telling me which expository tactics were and were not comprehensible. Anne Fuller, finally, by sharing her husband on what were officially days off, did no more than she's done for the world this past fifty-five years—something indispensable.

READING LIST

By no means all I used, but some I can especially recommend.

1. Books by Buckminster Fuller

The Time Lock, 1928, privately circulated. Reprinted 1970 by
Lama Foundation, Box 422, Corrales, New Mexico 87048.
There were several versions. The one reprinted by Lama
omits the patent drawings and specifications for the 4-D
House.
Nine Chains to the Moon, Philadelphia, J. B. Lippincott, 1938.
(Paperback reprint from the Southern Illinois University
Press, 1963, omits Predictions and Appendices.) The meta-
physical view from the Depression era.
Education Automation, Carbondale, Southern Illinois University Press, 1962. A freewheeling talk before a campus planning committee.
Untitled Epic Poem on the History of Industrialization, Mil-
lerton, New York, Jargon Books, 1962. Direct in language
and economically imaginative, it carries the story to the
date of writing, 1940. The promised sequel has never appeared.
Ideas and Integrities, Englewood Cliffs, New Jersey, Prentice-
Hall, 1963. Much of Fuller's most intimate writing, and
some of his most armored. Much of the book dates from
the 1940's.

No More Secondhand God and Other Writings, Carbondale, Southern Illinois University Press, 1963. Poems of the 1940's and 1950's, plus the stubbornly metaphysical prose epistemology, "Omnidirectional Halo."

Operating Manual for Spaceship Earth, Carbondale, Southern Illinois University Press, 1969. Tight, tidy, accessible.

Utopia or Oblivion, New York, Bantam Books, 1969. Mostly transcribed lectures, with much repetition that serves to illustrate the value of multiple pathways through the same node.

Intuition, New York, Doubleday, 1972. New poems, mostly about Brain and Mind.

2. FULLER PATENTS

From the Patent Office, which Kenneth Snelson calls "our civilization's King Tut's Tomb," the intrepid may obtain some of Fuller's fundamental expositions for fifty cents each. Address U. S. Dept. of Commerce, Patent Office, Washington, D.C. 20231, and order by number.

2,101,057, Dymaxion Car

2,393,676, Dymaxion Map

2,682,235, "Building Construction." The basic Geodesic Dome patent.

2,905,113, "Self-strutted Geodesic Plydome." Sheets of plywood, bored, bent and bolted.

2,986,241, "Synergetic Building Construction." The Octet Truss.

3,063,521, "Tensile-Integrity Structures." Tensegrity Spheres, with data on complicated ones.

3,203,144, "Laminar Geodesic Domes." How to make paper or plastic domes with no struts.

For further listings see *Domebook 2,* p. 122.

3. COMPILATIONS, ARTICLES, ETC.

Shelter magazine, vol. 2, nos. 4–5 (May and November, 1932). Edited and largely written by Fuller, his public diary from the fiscal deep-freeze.

Designing a New Industry, A Composite of a Series of Talks,

by R. Buckminster Fuller. Fuller Research Institute, 1946.
A big library may have this. The Wichita House and what
led up to it.

"Tensegrity," by Buckminster Fuller. Introduction by John
McHale. *Portfolio & Art News Annual,* No. 4 (1960), pp.
112–127, 148. The only systematic exposition of Tensegrity
principles.

The Governor's Conference with R. Buckminster Fuller, Governor's Office, Raleigh, North Carolina, 1963. A marathon
statement plus transcribed questions and answers.

World Design Science Decade Documents, Southern Illinois
University, 6 vols. 1963–67. Overviews and manifestos by
Fuller, data on planetary resources by John McHale.
Document #2 has a copiously illustrated hundred-page
talk by Fuller on his structures. Order from Design Science Institute, 3700 Massachusetts Ave., N.W., Washington, D.C. 20016, where they also sell the Dymaxion Map.

Planetary Planning, by R. Buckminster Fuller. The Jawaharlal
Nehru Memorial Lecture, New Delhi, India, 1969. In this
pamphlet the lecture is accompanied by an updated Energetic Geometry chart and an appendix outlining twelve
stages in human history.

*50 Years of the Design Science Revolution and the World
Game,* Carbondale, Southern Illinois University, 1969. Reprints papers, addresses and significant articles about Fuller spanning 1928–69.

Approaching the Benign Environment, by R. Buckminster
Fuller, Eric A. Walker & James R. Killian Jr., New York,
Collier Books, 1970. What three lecturers said at Auburn
University, 1968–69. Fuller's contribution is two-thirds of
the book and some of his most engaging exposition.

I Seem to be a Verb, Bantam Books, 1969. A shameless non-
book which coopts a few hundred words of Fuller's to
validate Editor Jerome Agel's McLuhanite trip.

4. ABOUT FULLER

"The Dymaxion American," *Time* magazine, January 10, 1964.
Anecdotal cover story (and remarkable Artzybasheff cover).

Barry Farrell, "The View from the Year 2000," *Life* magazine, February 26, 1971.

Robert W. Marks, *The Dymaxion World of Buckminster Fuller,* New York, Reinhold, 1960; since reissued by Southern Illinois University Press. Indispensable for its copious illustrations and succinct text, much of it edited from Fuller's words.

John McHale, *R. Buckminster Fuller,* New York, Braziller, 1962. (Out of print.) A good compact overview, written for a series on contemporary architects.

Playboy Interview, "R. Buckminster Fuller," *Playboy* magazine, February 1972.

Calvin Tompkins, "In the Outlaw Area," *New Yorker* magazine, January 8, 1966.

"The World of Buckminster Fuller," special section of the January–February 1972 *Architectural Forum*. Reminiscences and appreciations, and long expository article by William Marlin.

5. OTHER PERTINENT THINGS

Reyner Banham, *The Architecture of the Well-Tempered Environment,* Chicago, University of Chicago Press, 1969. Structure as environment valve; the approach highlights the shortcomings of Bauhaus designs.

H. S. M. Coxeter, *Regular Polytopes,* second edition, New York, Macmillan, 1962.

Keith Critchlow, *Order in Space,* New York, Viking, 1970. Beautiful drawings, intricate expositions, of how the polyhedra intertransform.

S. Giedion, *Architecture and the Phenomena of Transition,* Cambridge, Massachusetts, Harvard University Press, 1971. Roman and Renaissance domes.

S. Giedion, *The Eternal Present: The Beginnings of Architecture,* New York, Pantheon, 1964. Origins of our 90-degree fixation.

Lloyd Kahn, ed., *Domebook 2,* Bolinas, California, Pacific Domes, 1970 (distributed by Random House). Everything the model-builder or the Space-Age Crusoe needs to know about Geodesic Domes.

Arthur L. Loeb, "The Architecture of Crystals," in Gyorgy Kepes, ed., *Module, Proportion, Symmetry, Rhythm,* New York, Braziller, 1966, pp. 38–63. The uses of a coordinate system. Applying what is essentially Fuller's approach, a fiendishly intricate atomic array can be described by a few jottings.

Linus Pauling and Roger Hayward, *The Architecture of Molecules,* San Francisco, W. H. Freeman, 1964. Colored illustrations give an atom's-eye view of what it's like in there. For ambitious students, Pauling's *Nature of the Chemical Bond* is the standard text.

Edward Popko, *Geodesics,* Detroit, University of Detroit Press, 1968. Fuller structures superbly illustrated and diagrammed; miserable text.

D'Arcy W. Thompson, *On Growth and Form,* Cambridge, England, Cambridge University Press, 1944, 2 vols. The Bible of Nature's design principles.

Robert Williams, *Natural Structure,* Moorpark, Calif., Eudaemon Press, 1972. Polygons, polyhedra, natural forms.

Lancelot L. Whyte, ed., *Aspects of Form,* New York, Elsevier, 1968. The quest for modelability in the sciences.

INDEX

Agassiz, 74
"Aleph, The" (Borges), 29
American Institute of Architects, 15, 163, 171
Ananda Meditation Retreat, 244
Anderson, Quentin, 312
Andrews, Caroline Wolcott, 66–7
Antheil, George, 153
Apollo 16, 315–6
Archimedes, 1, 57, 82, 113, 239
Architectural Forum, 247–8, 251–2, 310
Architecture of Molecules (Pauling), 119
Architecture of the Well-Tempered Environment (Banham), 203
Aristotle, 93
Armour & Co., 18, 153–5
Augustus, Emperor, 301
automation, 294
Avogadro, Amadeo, 140

balloon frame, 210–11
Banham, Reyner, 203
Barlow, W., 116
Bauhaus, 203
Bear Island, 67–72, 77, 94, 166, 172, 217, 246, 261, 278

Bell, Alexander Graham, 56, 64–6, 285
Bergman, Carl, 61
Black Mountain College, 6, 121, 235, 237
Bleriot, Louis, 73
Bloom, Dr. Benjamin, 278
Boeing Company, 186, 262
Bohr, Niels, 9
Borelli, Giovanni A., 61
Borges, Jorge Luis, 29
Brancusi, Constantin, 153
Brand, Stewart, 261, 291
bubbles, 99, 127, 129, 132–6, 147, 315
Buck Rogers, 2
Buddha, 260
Bundy, McGeorge, 79
Burgess, Gelett, 56
Burgess, Starling, 215, 280
Byron, Lord, 36

Calder, Alexander, 238
California Time Machine, 48–51
Calthorpe, Peter, 259
Campbell, J., & Robinson, H. M., 4
Canterbury Tales (Chaucer), 6
Cantos (Pound), 6
Capone, Al, 51, 168

carbon molecules, 118–9, 150, 297
Cathay (Pound), 299
Catullus, G. V., 310
Champollion, J. F., 72
Chaplin, Charlie, 20, 267–8
Chapman, George, 251
Chaucer, 6
Chicago Institute of Design, 302
China, Mainland, 272, 304
Clinton, Joe, 246
college, uses of, 80–5
Columbus, Christopher, 194
compression, 70, 92, 100–1, 120, 121, 123, 144, 183, 201, 220, 234, 236–7, 315–6
Confucius, 260
Continuous Man, 194–5, 199
coordinate system, 10, 48, 109, 119, 121, 125–6, 133, 142–4, 150, 277, 312
Copernicus, 9
Coxeter, Prof. H. S. M., 2, 120
crank, American, 173–7, 276
Cronkite, Walter, 5
cube, 8, 43, 84, 108, 111, 113, 116, 119, 120, 126, 144, 170, 242–3, 258, 264, 276, 301, 316
cuboctahedron, 1–2, 82–3, 113, 117–8

Daniel, Arnaut, 83–4
Dante, 36, 83
Darwin, Charles, 75, 294, 299
De Forest, Lee, 101–2, 127
de Gourmont, Remy, 84
Delos, 180
de Monvel, Maurice Boutet, 202
Descartes, René, 161, 297
design, 43, 63, 154, 182–3
DNA, 52, 145
dodecahedron, 113, 243, 276
Domebook, 231, 232, 246, 259, 261, 262, 264, 312
Donne, John, 23, 267
Douglas, C. H., 191, 192, 193

Doxiadis, Constantine, 290
Drexler, Arthur, 239
Dryden, John, 301
Dumas, Alexandre, Jr., 58
Duryea, Charles, 56
"Dymaxion," 78, 113, 163
Dymaxion Bathroom, 212–3, 217, 265
Dymaxion Car, 3, 15, 51, 213–7, 281, 312
Dymaxion Chronofile, 166
Dymaxion House (includes 4-D House and Wichita House), 78, 201–9, 212, 224, 228, 233–4, 247, 253, 265, 268, 280, 302
Dymaxion Map, 1–2, 11, 111–3, 177, 178–9, 181, 224, 234–5, 251, 287, 289, 303

$E = mc^2$, 29, 111, 220, 222, 275
ecosystem, house as, 203–4
Eddington, Sir Arthur, 125
Eddy, Mary Baker, 268
Eiffel Tower, 55, 58–9, 77
Einstein, Albert, 9, 29, 126, 139, 220, 225, 251, 274–6, 296
Eliot, President, 80
Eliot, T. S., 4, 79, 84
Emerson, R. W., 73, 147–51, 158, 168, 169, 220
Empire State Building, 243
Energetic Geometry, 173, 177, 227, 276
ephemeralization, 18, 56, 59, 60
Euclid, 11, 37, 57, 177, 239, 241
Expo Dome, *see* Montreal Dome
extensions of man, 25

Fads and Fallacies in the Name of Science (Gardner), 174
Farrell, Barry, 278–9
Finnegans Wake (Joyce), 4, 144, 195, 301, 310, 311
Fitzgerald, F. Scott, 156

Flatiron Building, 56
Flatland, 39
Flaubert, Gustave, 272–3
Ford, Henry, Sr., 20, 26, 73, 161, 208, 220–1, 225, 229, 233, 254
Ford Dome, 53, 245–6, 247–9, 279
Ford Motor Company, 66, 245–7, 262
Fortune, 100, 177, 224–6, 296
4-D Control Syndicate, 167–8
4-D House, *see* Dymaxion House
Franklin, Ben, 217
frog ovum, 145–6
Fuller, Alexandra, 158–9
Fuller, Allegra, *see* Snyder, Allegra
Fuller, Anne (Mrs. B. F.), 17, 27, 47–9, 51, 156, 159, 168
Fuller, Caroline Andrews (B. F.'s mother), 66–8
Fuller, Hon. Timothy, 73, 75
Fuller, Margaret, 73, 147, 168, 233
Fuller, R. B., Sr. (B. F.'s father), 55, 67, 73, 74, 77
Fuller, Rev. Arthur Buckminster, 73, 74
Fuller, Rev. Timothy, 73, 75
Fuller, Waldo, 72
Fuller Research Foundation, 3

Galileo, 104
Gandhi, Mahatma, 313
Gardner, Martin, 174
genius, 21, 51, 64, 273
Geodesic Domes, 3, 5, 6, 7, 15, 40–1, 44, 62, 91, 116, 120–1, 133, 150, 173, 177, 229–62, 263–4, 270, 290, 301–2, 312–3
Giedion, Sigfried, 61, 210, 212, 265
Gilette, 174
Gnostics, 268
Gravitational Constant, 143
gravity, 96–7
Great Pyramid, 96, 121, 154

Hair, 310
Hall, Edward T., 256–7, 266
Hardie, Jim, 72, 79
Harvard, 30, 31, 73–80, 82, 84, 130, 151, 153, 275
Heisenberg, Werner, 161
Heraclitus, 8, 299
Hewlett, James Monroe, 156–8
Hexland, 140–3
Hidden Dimension (Hall), 256–7
Hippasos, 137
History of Aesthetics (Bosanquet), 153
Hogden, Lee, 87, 238
Holt, John, 308–9
Homer, 3, 8, 9, 20, 21, 80, 194, 251, 299
How Children Fail (Holt), 308
How Children Learn (Holt), 308

icosahedron, 78, 113, 117, 119, 120, 150, 239, 240–1, 243, 244–5, 276, 301
Ideas and Integrities (Fuller), 7, 130
industrial vs. craft tools, 10
infinity, 34–6, 76, 105, 132, 303, 309
Intuition (Fuller), 168
Inventory of Scientific Events, 222–3
irrational numbers, 137–9, 141

James, Henry, 66, 74, 254
Jeans, Sir James, 125
Jefferson, Thomas, 4, 246–7, 307
Jell-O, 29, 101, 239, 291
Johnson, Dr. Samuel, 151, 301
Joyce, James, 4, 8, 153, 285, 303, 311
Julius Caesar, 23

Kahn, Lloyd, 232, 260–2, 268
Kepler, Johannes, 147, 276–7
Khrushchev, Nikita, 18, 51
Kilpatrick, James J., 195
King, Andy, 71
King, Rockwell, 67

knots, 8, 22–4, 29, 30, 103, 111, 147, 198
Koestler, Arthur, 126–7, 277
Korzybski, Count, 94
Kriyananda, Swami, 259
Kuhn, Thomas S., 299

Lavoisier, 28
Lawson, A. W., 174–5
Le Corbusier, 203, 257
Lewis, Wyndham, 17
Life, 1, 278
life expectancy, 55
Lincoln, A., 10, 127, 130, 155
Lindbergh, Charles A., 161, 226
Longfellow, Henry W., Jr., 56, 71, 74
Luce, Henry R., 281
Lyell, Sir Charles, 299

Madison Square Garden, 243
Malthus, Thomas, 75–7, 130, 154, 224
Marconi, Guglielmo, 56, 59, 155
Marine Corps, 256
Marks, Robert W., 8
Marquand, J. P., 73, 264–5
Marx, Karl, 294
Mather, Cotton, 260
Maupassant, Guy de, 58
McCarthy, Sen. Eugene, 305
McLuhan, Marshall, 171
Mendelejeff, Dmitri, 298
Mercator, 2, 5, 11, 303
Michelangelo, 64
Michelson, A. A., 274
Miller, Henry, 260
Miller, Marilyn, 78
Milton, John, 171, 303
Milton Academy, 74, 77
Modern Times (Chaplin), 267–8
Moehlman, John, 238
Montessori, 38, 92, 271, 273

Montreal Dome, 133, 234, 253, 254, 264, 270, 302
Moore, Marianne, 220
Munson, Gorham, 192
Museum of Modern Art, 15, 57, 121
myth, 129–32, 295

NASA, 178, 184–5, 246, 313
National Geographic, 65
Nation's Business, 164
Nature of the Chemical Bond (Pauling), 119, 277
Nehru, 51
Newcomb, Prof. Simon, 60, 75, 165, 178
Newton, Sir Isaac, 29, 98, 130, 133, 147, 177, 274–5, 277, 298, 299
Nine Chains to the Moon (Fuller), 267, 269, 275, 280
No More Secondhand God (Fuller), 7, 226

octahedron, 49, 57, 108–9, 113, 114, 117, 119, 243, 276, 294
"Octa Spinner," 91
Octet Truss, 57–8, 66, 108–10, 117, 118, 143, 249, 285, 286, 297, 301
Odyssey, 20
Ogden, C. K., 94
O'Malley, Walter, 240, 263
Outlaw Area, 68–9, 168

Pantheon, 249–50
paper as paradigm, 301–3
Paradise Lost (Milton), 171
patent theory, 285
pattern, self-interfering, 22, 26
patterned integrity, 23, 98, 100
Pauling, Linus, 119, 277
phantom captain, 19–20, 23, 34, 54, 171, 267, 268
Phelps-Dodge Copper Co., 213, 217, 218, 222, 224

Phi Beta Kappa, 13, 80
pi, 10, 80, 99, 132-7, 146
Picasso, 20, 251
Pisa, Tower of, 77
Placer County Administrative Center, 259
Planck, Max, 59, 222
Planck's Constant, 143
Plato, 239, 276
Platonic Solids, 113, 117, 241-3, 276
Poe, E. A., 174, 175
politics, 18, 25, 26, 178, 303-5
pollution, 18, 36, 46, 164, 178, 197, 279
Pope, Ted, 238
Pound, Ezra, 4, 6, 8, 11, 38, 83-4, 152-3, 192, 299
precession, 99-100, 183, 225
Pythagoras, 11, 12, 48, 118, 140, 296, 297, 298, 299
Pythagoreans, 137-9, 146, 147, 150, 241, 251, 296

racism, 178-82, 287-8
Rauschenberg, Robert, 310
Reader's Digest, 3
regeneration, 102-3, 120, 128, 265
revolutions, 18, 227, 272
Richter, Don, 245
Rockefeller, Nelson, 182
Römer, Olaus, 275
Roentgen, W. K., 56
Roosevelt, F. D., 303
rope and knot, 22-4, 127
Rousseau, J. J., 271
"Rowing Device," 71
Russia, 272, 304

Sadao, Shoji, 262
St. Peter's, 249-50
Sala, Francesco della, 238
Salk, Dr. Jonas, 222

San Quentin Prison, 68
Santayana, George, 80
schools, 37-8, 79-80, 305-9
Shakespeare, 4, 5, 20, 84, 307
Shelter, 94
ship, car as, 215; man as, 19; universe as, 70
Skinner, B. F., 268
slaves, energy, 44-6, 188
sleep (Dymaxion), 3, 160
Sleepwalkers, The (Koestler), 126
Snelson, Kenneth, 121, 238, 285
Snow, George Washington, 210
Snow, Lord (C. P.), 5
Snyder, Allegra (Fuller), 159, 199, 205
Snyder, Robert, 306
Soddy, Frederick, 192
Somerset Club, 74, 77
"spending," 9, 99, 100, 184-98
sphere, 134-6
Stability and Change in Human Characteristics (Bloom), 278
Stanley, Ray, 77
Stein, Gertrude, 176
Stockade Building System, 155-8, 201
Stonehenge, 63, 250
Structure of Scientific Revolutions (Kuhn), 299
sunset, 14, 93-4
surfer, 98-100, 147
Symmes, 174
synergy, 31-4, 87, 90, 91, 138, 165, 173, 177-8, 192, 223, 234, 286, 313

Teed, 174
telephone, 56, 182-4, 201, 256-8
Tennyson, Alfred, Lord, 53
tensegrity, 63, 101, 173, 237-40, 292
tensegrity icosahedron, 238-40
Tensegrity Mast, 15, 121-3, 238, 285

Tensegrity Sphere, 86–93, 95–101, 103–7, 121–4, 263, 311

tensile strength, 32–3, 91

tension, 69–70, 71, 92–3, 95, 100–1, 120, 121, 122–4, 144, 183, 201, 220, 234, 236–7, 315–6

tetrahedron, 16, 49, 57, 64–5, 98, 105, 107–9, 113, 115, 116, 118, 119, 125, 145, 150, 173, 243, 276, 277, 297, 315

textile mill, 79, 151–2

Theobald, Robert, 193

Thompson, Sir D'Arcy W., 61–3

Thoreau, H. D., 73, 149, 189, 209–10, 217, 220, 232, 233, 297, 312, 313

Time, 3

Timelock (Fuller), 165–77, 279–80

Titian, 5

tree, 8, 69, 101, 144

triangles, 34–7, 39–41, 48–9, 64, 107, 136, 239

tuning, 24, 25, 30, 124–5, 128

TV camera, lunar, 184–7

Ulysses (Joyce), 131, 153

Untitled Epic Poem on the History of Industrialization (Fuller), 226–7

"up" and "down," 93–5, 124, 126

Utopia or Oblivion (Fuller), 130, 277, 278

Vector Equilibrium, 83, 107–18, 120, 126, 127, 129, 134, 142–4, 146, 294, 297, 298

vectors, 104–5, 118, 127, 133

Verne, Jules, 61

virus molecules, 120–1, 150

Walden (Thoreau), 209, 233, 313

Washington Monument, 57–8, 246

Watt, James, 130, 191

waves, 98–100

Whistler, J. A. M., 153

Whole Earth Catalog, 152, 178, 217, 232, 233, 261, 313

Wichita House, *see* Dymaxion House

Williams, William Carlos, 220

Wolcott, Alexander, 66

Wolcott, Roger, 66

Wombland, 28

Wordsworth, William, 133

World Game, 217, 224, 282–4, 288

World Resources Inventory, 217

Wright, Frank Lloyd, 142, 221–2, 264

Wright Brothers, 59–60, 63–4, 68–9, 222, 294

Yeats, W. B., 8, 52–3, 80

Zeno, 37

Zeppelin, Count, 59

Zulu, 44

paradigm = Pattern, example, model